Designing Highly Useable Software

Jeff Cogswell

SYBEX

San Francisco · London

Associate Publisher: Joel Fugazzotto
Acquisitions and Developmental Editor: Tom Cirtin
Production Editor: Susan Berge
Technical Editor: David Cronin
Copyeditor: Linda Recktenwald
Compositor/Graphic Illustrator: Jeffrey Wilson, Happenstance Type-O-Rama
Proofreaders: Laurie O'Connell, Nancy Riddiough
Indexer: Ted Laux
Cover Design: Ingalls + Associates
Cover Illustration: Rob Atkins, The Image Bank

Library of Congress Card Number: 2003115580

ISBN: 0-7821-4301-6

This book is dedicated to my students—past, present, and future—who aspire to create great software.

Acknowledgments

You've heard it before, and it's true: So many people contribute to the production of a book that the author is just one piece of the whole puzzle.

For this book, first I want to thank Joel Fugazzotto, Associate Publisher, whom I have known for several years now and with whom I am once again having the pleasure to work. And special thanks to Tom Cirtin, who wore many hats throughout the creation of this book, including Acquisitions Editor, Developmental Editor, and general Usability Idea Bouncer-Offer. (It's amazing how many hours we spent on the phone talking about our own usability encounters!) Thanks also to the friendly Senoria Brown, for handling the contracts, for the forgiveness of my losing an important CD-ROM, and for her amazing timeliness and concern. Thanks for the wonderful editorial work of Susan Berge and Linda Recktenwald and for their meticulous work and patience. A special thanks to the eagle eye of usability guru David Cronin, who helped track down problems in the book and make it all the better!

And thanks again to my wonderful friend Margot Maley Hutchison of Waterside Productions.

Thanks to all my friends who helped me make it through my busy schedule, including my sister Amy Page, Jen Lesh, Andrea Vaduva (who just got accepted into medical school!), Fonda Dawson, Gregg Dodd and Jason Skinner, Nikki Ward, Jessica Smith, Mitzie Chrisman, Angel Whaley, and of course Jen Mueller and Jennifer and Greg Wood. And finally, a very special thanks to Christie McAlpine.

Contents at a Glance

Contents

Introduction

Can you think of some software you use but don't like? Most people can. And just what about the software don't you like? If you're like me, chances are the software serves an important purpose to you but doesn't function in the way you would like it to. It might be too complicated for beginners to understand. Or it might have bugs. Or it might be cumbersome to use, no matter how skilled you are.

In other words, the software isn't very *useable*.

In this book, I show you how to create *highly useable software*. Highly useable software is software that is easy to use, does what you expect it to, and does it well. Such software might sound easy to build, but it's not.

Software is big and complex. So many things can go wrong. And that's why I'm here with this book. I want to show you what you need to do to ensure that your software will be highly useable.

Over the years, helping programmers understand how to create highly useable software has become somewhat of a mission of mine. I've become so frustrated with software, and I've seen my friends become so frustrated, that I feel as though I, as both a programmer and a writer, must actually do something about it. You are my peers, and I want to show you why people are not always happy with the products that you and I have created. But even better, I want to show you what you can actually do to improve the situation.

And the result is this book you are holding. If you're standing in the bookstore, I promise you that you will not be disappointed with this book. You will find at least something you had not thought of, some little piece of information that will make your software better. But if you read the whole book, you'll probably find lots of great advice. (And don't worry; I crack a lot of jokes. I can't help it. It's just me. You would too if you were me.)

And while I'm at it, I offer numerous little stories or anecdotes about my own frustrations with things other than computers. Often these frustrations are with cars. Or with paper towel holders. Or anything. I present these anecdotes in the form of little side stories that I think you'll enjoy reading. But the purpose isn't to just amuse you. (Okay, that's part of the purpose, but not the only one.) The purpose is to demonstrate to you that you are a user, too. And when you use these products in daily life, you will start to realize that you stand on the other side of the fence every day, dealing as users with the products that other people have created. And you probably get just as frustrated with these people as (dare we admit) our users get frustrated with *us*. Thus, these stories will help you step into the shoes of your own users.

Helping the world create better software has become one of my missions in life, to show the world that you and I—we—can make better software. No more will people be frustrated. No more will people encounter bugs. From now on, software will function the way people want it to, and they will actually enjoy using the software we create.

Is this possible? Can we really all get together and finally start creating highly useable software? Yes. And I am going to see to it that it happens.

But just making good software isn't the whole focus. Let's be honest: If we were all independently wealthy, we probably wouldn't be writing software. The truth is, most of us are in this to make money. And how do we make money? By selling software. But do we sell just any old software? No. We sell software that serves precisely the needs of the end users. Our software shouldn't bog them down with unnecessary steps (such as clicking eight extra times every time they need to perform a simple, common task). Our software shouldn't complain to the user (for example, screaming at them that the disk drive is out of memory and then offering no solutions). Our software shouldn't run in a manner that drives the processor usage to 100 percent, possibly burning up the computer (we're nicer people than that!).

Back in the early 1990s, I used to argue that software should be like a telephone: If you're at work and are talking on the phone to a client, the last thing you want to do is to have to discuss issues pertaining to the phone you're using. The phone is a tool and you shouldn't even have to be thinking about the phone while you're using it. You want to be thinking about the conversation.

Similarly, software is a tool. But I don't use this argument anymore, because it trivializes the matter. Software is far more complex than a single telephone. (Although the entire telephone *system* across the planet probably surpasses most software in complexity!) Software isn't as invisible as a telephone. When you're using software, you really are thinking about the software, meaning that the software can't really be invisible. Instead, software should be more like your trusty assistant, helping you along the way.

For example, if you are using a word processor and you accidentally type *yuo*, wouldn't a good human assistant proofing your document just fix the error, changing it to *you* for you? Why should the assistant come and ask you for permission? That's a feature that Microsoft identified as a highly useable feature, and they put it into Microsoft Word in the form of the AutoCorrect feature.

Software is more than a tool. It's an assistant, a helper. It's a tool with a brain more powerful than the computers that put men on the moon.

But unlike a human assistant, highly useable software shouldn't argue with you or blame you when things go wrong. Instead, software should be quick yet show unending patience. Software should be gentle and kind, offering suggestions when necessary and automatically fixing problems when possible.

In this book, I show you how to create such software. It really is possible. And often it takes a shift in perspective, a move toward a new way of looking at your own products.

Read this book and you'll see what I mean. And you'll find yourself creating the best software you've ever created.

About This Book

I've arranged this book into three main parts:

Part I: Keeping It Simple

This part consists of seven chapters that tackle the more obvious components of the software, focusing on the user interface. The first chapter covers the user interface, where I talk about general GUI issues centering on usability.

Then I move on to Chapter 2, which deals with modeling the real world. I talk about how to model devices and cover such topics as simulators and controllers.

Chapter 3 focuses on windows and dialog boxes. Too many people think this topic is the entire scope of usability. Usability extends far beyond this area, but it is still an important part of usability.

Chapter 4 covers an odd issue, that of managing time with your software. As a user, I get so frustrated by software that seems to freeze up my computer or take forever to perform a task. In this chapter I show you how you can avoid such problems.

Chapter 5 deals with creating software that can be easily *navigated*. To use most software, you need to click buttons, select menu items, and use hot keys, all of which get you to some part of the program that lets you perform a particular task. Why make the users jump through hoops to get to the parts of the program? Instead, make your software highly navigable.

Chapter 6 is all about reports and data. I'm amazed at how difficult phone bills are to read, even after all these years. Reports and data have their own usability issues much like software does. In this chapter I show you how to reduce the complexity of your reports so that the people reading them can easily understand them.

Chapter 7 is about adding a web interface to your program. This is the twenty-first century, after all, and we're all using the Internet every day. Most likely, you'll want your software to be able to access the Internet. But be careful! In this chapter I show you how to keep your software free of problems while it interfaces to the Web.

Part II: The Lonely Engineer

This part consists of four chapters specifically for engineers and programmers. I go underneath the hood and talk about programming issues that might not seem like they affect usability, but they *do*.

Chapter 8 is a collection of topics that you, as a programmer, must do right or the usability of your software will suffer. For example, I talk about dynamic memory allocation, pointer variables, how to avoid tight loops that burn up laptop computers, and other fun programmer-related issues.

Chapter 9 is all about your software starting up, shutting down, and possibly dying. When I was researching this chapter, I was amazed to see just how many usability issues deal with the starting and stopping of software!

Chapter 10 is all about libraries. Libraries can be incredibly annoying to the user. How many times have you had to install software that dumped who-knows-what into your system directory against your will? I talk about that and similar topics in this chapter.

Chapter 11 is an exciting chapter that's all about object-oriented programming, or OOP. Now that we're all familiar with OOP, we can stop talking about the things we already know (such as how to create classes and inherit from them) and move on to the usability issues in OOP. You might be surprised to see just how much usability works into OOP and how mistakes in OOP can adversely affect the usability of your software!

Part III: The Business of It All: It's "Dollars and Sense"

This part moves away from the programming aspects and talks about business-related issues and how they affect usability.

The first chapter in this section, Chapter 12, covers general business topics pertaining to the design of highly useable software. For example, I talk about how in the '90s everybody was looking for the "killer application," and yet today we're not using any of those software products. Why is that? Because the designers of the killer apps totally missed the whole usability factor, resulting in software nobody wanted.

Chapter 13 is all about testing. All software must go through thorough testing. And almost all software companies have well-staffed test groups. But how many of these groups are looking for usability issues? Not enough of them. In this chapter I show you how you can help your test group move up to the next level and watch for usability bugs.

Chapter 14 covers three related topics: software training, online help, and software installation. Installers are themselves software programs that require high usability standards. After all, what good is your software if the users can't even get it installed? Training and online help even have usability issues. You want your users to be able to learn how to use your software, and here I show you how to make your training and help as useable as possible.

Chapter 15, the final chapter, is a special chapter devoted to bosses and managers. I'm assuming that both programmers and bosses or managers will read this entire book, but for most of the book I'm talking to programmers. In this chapter I'm talking specifically to bosses and managers, going into some issues that you might be surprised to see in a book on usability. For example, I talk about the different personalities of programmers and how to deal with programmer problems. What does this have to do with usability? Everything. A programmer who doesn't understand his or her own shortcomings could easily put a major dent in the usability of your software, resulting in bad software and lost sales. If that worries you, then you will certainly want to read this chapter.

Finally, I wrap up the book with an appendix that covers standards, groups, and sources of more information, all focused on software usability.

PART I

Keeping It Simple

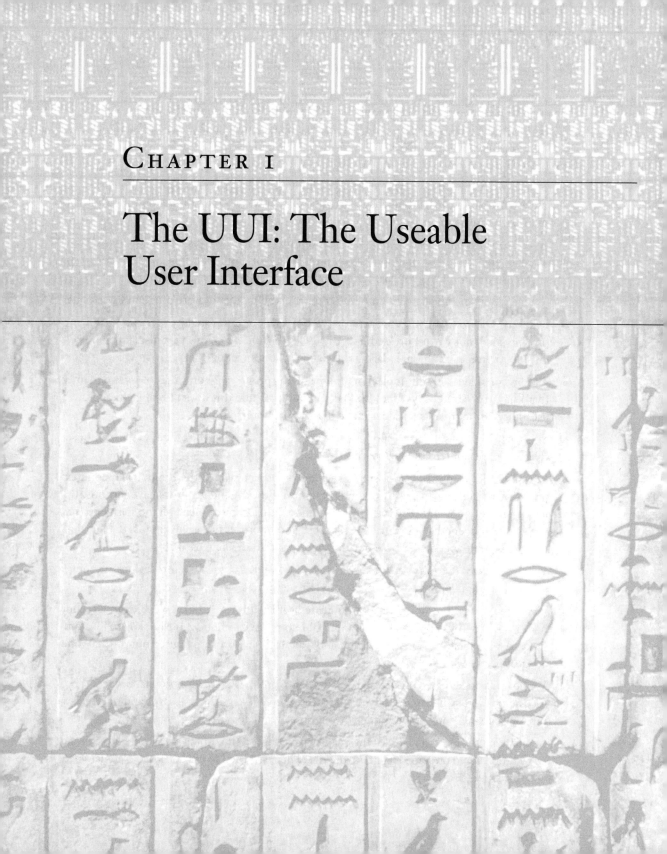

Chapter 1

The UUI: The Useable User Interface

And to think, the day had been going so well for me. I got up on time, I ate a healthy breakfast, the mail came early, the birds were singing, and the day was perfect. That is, it *was* perfect, until *it* happened.

What happened? The software that had long been my friend decided to try my patience one more time, and my head came very close to exploding. In desperation I looked to the sky and saw a few sprinklings of clouds as they started to turn gray, bragging of the looming thunderstorm they were about to bring.

You've probably had days like this. Think about the software you use on a daily basis. Can you think of anything that you don't like about it? Can you think of things that just go wrong when you use it? Or maybe you just have a list of annoyances about the software.

Without naming names, here's a list of my complaints about the software program I was using:

- I clicked the wrong menu item and a dialog box I wasn't interested in opened. That's fine (my mistake), but when I pressed Esc, the dialog box didn't go away. It just stayed there, grinning at me, taunting me, daring me to click the Cancel button.

- The buttons have a strange look about them and the program ignores the colors and themes that I have chosen for my Windows XP computer. While this doesn't really change the useability of the software, it does make it a tad bit more annoying.

- *Some* of the buttons do not respond to the keyboard. You must click them with the mouse. (Others do respond to the keyboard.)

- Various child windows (that is, smaller windows that are part of the program) open unexpectedly, without me manually opening them. And these child windows have buttons. If I happen to be typing into a different child window, and just by chance I hit the spacebar, that window that opened will receive the spacebar and interpret me as clicking its default button. (Wouldn't you know, these buttons *do* respond to the keyboard.)

- When I start up the software, I have to wait…and wait…and wait before it does anything. Worse, during this time, my whole computer seems to slow way down.

- This software has the ability to communicate over the Internet. I have a cable modem, but once I accidentally chose the modem option. I don't have a phone cable hooked to my computer. And so I had to wait…and wait…and wait until the software figured out the dial tone was not present.

- While using a dialog box, I pressed Tab to get to another control in the dialog box. The focus, however, switched not to the control I expected. Pressing Tab over and over, I saw the focus go in a very strange order throughout the dialog box.

- At one point the program let me type in a few paragraphs. After doing so, I wanted to edit the text a bit. I clicked on some text in the middle. Then, as I tried to use keyboard commands to select the text, I held down the Shift key and pressed the right-arrow key while holding down Ctrl to select some text word-by-word. (So far so good.) I went too far, so, while still holding down Ctrl, I pressed left-arrow. But instead of unselecting the rightmost word, the selection expanded to the left from where I began. This is not standard.

All this was just one program. Now here are some things I ran into with some other programs on that very same fateful day:

- I clicked the close button, and a small dialog box opened asking if I was sure I wanted to quit. I accidentally clicked back on the main window…and the small dialog box vanished. I could continue using the program as if I had not clicked the close button. But when I moved the main window, I could see that the dialog box was still there. It had just gone in back and was hiding.

- One program I use occasionally decides it has to do some figuring or calculating or something (I honestly don't know what it is doing), and it slows my whole computer to a crawl. It's not a good software neighbor. (It probably does what is called a *tight loop*, which is a topic I mention in Chapter 8, "Under the Hood."

- And then consider this example: A friend of mine was typing a long e-mail message using one of the free Internet e-mail servers. She clicked Send, and something went awry on the Internet and she got the infamous "Cannot find server" message. She clicked back. The message "Page has expired" came up. Her e-mail message? Gone forever. (I encouraged her to always press Ctrl+A and then Ctrl+C to select all the text and copy it to the clipboard… just in case.)

These are just a few items for you to think about. I'm sure you've created in your mind your own list of frustrations. You are, after all, a user of a computer as much as you are a programmer. In the sections that follow I talk about ways you can keep your software from being *frustrating*.

So first, let me present my Golden Rule of Software:

RULE Make it invisible. The user's mind can focus on either the work the user is trying to accomplish or the software itself. The moment the user focuses on the software itself is the moment she stops thinking about her work and starts to become *frustrated with your software*. Suppose you're expecting a phone call regarding a possible six-figure job. The phone rings, and you go answer it. Easy. But what if when you answer the phone, you are startled to hear a voice say, "This is your telephone speaking. I have encountered a software error. Please retype your password before accepting the incoming call." Can you say *blood pressure medicine*? I think you get the point. You want the phone to be invisible so you can just use it and focus on the real task of talking on the phone. *Same with your software*. The user has a job to perform and doesn't want to have to worry about your software because it functions poorly.

It's Intuitive! Trust Me!

Maybe I'll just quit using a computer. My life would be so much easier. But considering computers are supposed to simplify our lives, instead of quitting, I'm going to help you learn to create software that is not plagued with these problems so that we can all enjoy our computers (for hours on end, of course, unable to peel ourselves away). And to get the ball rolling, I want you to consider the following statement:

"Our software is intuitive."

This is not a direct quote by some marketing guy creating advertising copy for a circa-1985 computer magazine (although it might as well be). Instead, I made it up, but it's indicative of a mindset common among software developers, even to this day. We want to believe that our software is *intuitive*, whatever that means. Early in the days of personal computers, people bragged that their software was intuitive. People said the Macintosh was *intuitive*. The Amiga computer created by Commodore had a graphical user interface system that was named *Intuition*.

Various dictionaries give different definitions of intuition, but a common thread is that if you have to use your intuition, you are using a part of your brain where you don't need your cognitive and reasoning abilities. *Yee-ikes!* After reading that, I'd be terribly hesitant to suggest that my software is intuitive, because being intuitive would be a major thing to live up to. I'd hate to see my software put to the test: Send it off to a deserted island and hand it to Mr. Robinson, who has been stranded there since 1975, living, quite happily and healthily, off of the local flora, without any computers. Hand him a computer equipped with Microsoft Windows XP, and put him to work using my (ahem) *intuitive* software program, *without me giving him any instructions whatsoever.*

I can see it now. Assuming Mr. Robinson doesn't smash open the computer and tear out the parts and build a two-way radio (not intuitive, but definitely ingenious), I seriously doubt he would be able to figure out my program. In fact, I can see him getting frustrated and yelling at it the same way I did when I started my day. (While knowing how to use computers might not be hardwired into our brain, I strongly suspect *getting mad* at computers *is* hardwired.)

Okay, I think that pretty much drives home the point that we're deceiving ourselves to think we're building intuitive software. However, I would argue that we are constantly encountering things in our software experience that is *counterintuitive*, that is, stuff that simply doesn't make sense.

Consider the scrollbars, for example. Right now, as I type, I have a big Word document open, with several pages. I look over and I see a scrollbar. I am about to use that little work of wonder to scroll back to the previous page. Now in my mind, I can imagine what it will look like as I move the scrollbar's thumb *down:* The text will all move downward. The entire document will fall closer to the ground and soon the top of it will be at my eye level. And so I go over to the scrollbar and move the scrollbar down.

FIGURE 1.1
When the scrollbar's thumb is at the top, the document is at the top. When the thumb is in the middle, the middle of the document is in view.

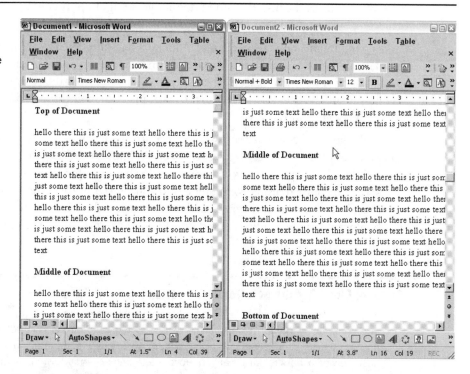

Right. In reality, if I move the scrollbar *down*, the text moves *up*—the text goes in the opposite direction. Does *that* make sense? Not particularly *at first*. But what does make sense is when you use a bit more cognition and logic and instead realize that the thumb of the scrollbar represents the *position in the document*. To go to the top of the document, I move the thumb to the top of the scrollbar. To go to the bottom of the document, I move the thumb to the bottom. At first my intuition might have told me one thing (or maybe not), and what really happened was quite different and required a bit of logic mixed with experience. Figure 1.1 shows the relative positions of the scrollbar within two identical documents.

And now when I press Enter at the end of a document, due to the current formatting selection, my insertion point automatically gets indented. That way, each paragraph has a nice half-inch indentation. Well that's fine and dandy, but what happens if I press the Up-arrow key? As I might expect, the insertion point goes pretty much straight up so it's sitting between two characters about a half inch into the last line of the previous paragraph.

But now I press the Home key so the insertion point goes to the left edge of the paragraph. And then I press the Down-arrow key, so I'm back where I originally started, indented in, ready to type a brand new paragraph. And *again* I press the Up-arrow key just as I did a few moments ago. But *this* time, the insertion point doesn't go straight up! It goes up to the next line up as expected, but instead moves all the way over to the left.

Again this might at first seem counterintuitive. Sometimes the Up-arrow moves the insertion point straight up, and sometimes it moves the insertion point up and to the leftmost edge of the paragraph. But logic and reasoning come in, and I realize that the reason is that Microsoft Word is smart and decides whether to move the insertion point straight up or up and to the left based on my *previous keystrokes*.

Clearly, intuitive computer software exists only in a fantasyland. But fortunately, you, as a software designer, can at least expect that certain idioms exist. In other words, you can be assured that the people using your program—for better or for worse—have certain expectations when it comes to using computers. And you, as a software designer, would have the happiest customers (and fewest angry e-mails) if you stick to these idioms. In the next section, I talk all about what exactly an idiom is and how, if you recognize idioms, you will have a software package that people will love.

Imagine Changing the Scrollbar's Direction

Want to really upset your users? Why bother trying to make your users happy when you could have some *fun* with them? Imagine the amused looks on their faces if you wrote a hack that reverses the functionality of all the scrollbars on a single computer. To scroll the text up, these new scrollbars require that you move the thumb up—not down as is the norm. To scroll the text down, move the thumb down. To get to the beginning of the document, move the scrollbar all the way to the bottom. And so on.

I'm sure the people you did this to would laugh and get a big kick out of it. They would want to meet you because you're so clever and they would invite you out to dinner and even pay for your meal!

Doubtful. We humans have a strange behavior when it comes to computers. The most relaxed, happy-go-lucky Homo sapiens will quickly turn into a *ragingus maniacus* given just the smallest computer problem. You don't want to be in the room when this happens, and you certainly don't want to be accused of writing the software that caused this extreme flow of adrenaline. Therefore, I suggest for your safety and for the mental well-being of your fellow humans that you stick to the norms when it comes to designing software. The psychiatrists of the world will thank you in the end.

Idioms and the Software Experience

Now that I've pretty much made the case that software cannot be intuitive, I want to show you what takes the place of intuition: the idioms. The term *idiom* is often used in reference to spoken languages. People learning foreign languages often study idioms before traveling to the countries using those languages. An idiom is a common phrase that, when taken for its pure word-for-word meaning, has nothing to do with the way people use it. I found a website that has a great list of common American idioms; you can visit it at `http://www.englishdaily626.com/idioms.html`. Here are some idioms this page mentions:

- Spill the beans

- Jump the gun

- Hang on

The first of these has nothing to do with spilling the beans. To "spill the beans" means that you are revealing something that you were not supposed to, like, "She spilled the beans that she's taking me to the mountains for a vacation."

The second, "jump the gun," has nothing to do with guns. It means somebody started something too early (although the root of this phrase has to do with races and a gun firing to signify the beginning of the race).

And finally, "hang on" has nothing to do with hanging on. You might use it like, "Hang on, I'm on the telephone," or "Hang on, I'll be with you in a minute." It means "wait." (Although I suppose it could be used as in, "Hang on, Dad! Grandpa is bringing the other ladder that's still in one piece! Don't let go!")

Software is filled with idioms, which are simply cues that are visual or otherwise that we know to mean something. One idiom is the Taskbar in Windows. I know what the Taskbar is, and so do you. It wouldn't take long to teach somebody what the Taskbar does. Now the Taskbar doesn't have much of a literal meaning: It's just a bunch of rectangles at the bottom of the screen, each containing an icon and some words. But we know that if you click one of the rectangles, the program by that name will come to the front. There's not much intuitive about the Taskbar, but it's simple and it works. Here's a sample Taskbar:

The notion of a window *coming to the front* is another idiom. Realistically, the screen isn't layered, and you don't have pixels behind the ones that you see containing the windows that are in back and obscured from view. But we do have an idiom: We all know that the windows have a layered look.

NOTE   However, Microsoft has made a bit of a mess, because in Windows XP, you can set up your Taskbar to group windows. This is a good thing, because instead of seeing 14 Internet Explorer rectangles all squeezed onto your Taskbar, you see only one, and clicking that one gives you a small menu of all the windows in the group. But the downside is that you have no way of knowing whether the window is minimized or not. If you accidentally click the icon for the window you're looking at, then the current window will minimize, showing what was behind it. That can be confusing.

Idioms also take the form of icons and symbols. We have all learned what the mouse arrow represents, what the hourglass symbol is, and what a folder icon is, even when it looks a little different between versions and operating systems.

These are by no means intuitive. Consider the blinking caret that sits in the middle of the text in a Word document. Does it represent some magical division line, where text to the left of the caret is important, while text to the right is unimportant? Or maybe it simply signifies the exact center of the document. Yes, I'm being silly, but you get the point: The blinking caret is an idiom, and now you and I both know what it does.

RULE   When you design your software, keep the idioms simple enough so that they don't get in the way of the real purpose of the program.

If I were to build a word processor, I might consider this idiom:

The speed at which the caret blinks denotes which characters you are allowed to type. If the caret blinks five times a second, you may type any character. If the caret blinks two times a second, you can type only vowels. If the caret blinks once a second, you may type only consonants. And if the caret blinks only once every four seconds, you may type only the letter *s*. Anything slower, and you may not type at all. Further, you can control the speed of the caret by moving the mouse....

You can see this is getting a bit out of hand. Yes, it's an idiom. No, it's not a good idiom. It's too complicated, and it doesn't provide a value to the user. What is the goal of the word processor? To type pages of text, not to mess around with some stupid idiom about the speed of the blinking caret. Soon you'd be more involved in trying to understand the blink speed rather than focusing on what you're trying to type. Remember the Golden Rule of Software: Software should be invisible. The moment the user's mind leaves the work that the software is serving and begins to focus on the software itself is the moment you're about to have a frustrated user. And to aid in this Golden Rule, keep your idioms few, and keep them simple.

How do you design good idioms?

RULE   Good idioms are the result of a combination of established idioms mixed with common sense and careful design.

That Stupid Desktop Metaphor

My desk is a mess. Now, if my mother, Pat, were sitting here beside me, she'd use the term she always used to describe my bedroom when I was a child: *It's a disaster*. (And trust me, she wasn't laughing at the time.)

Let me describe my desk for a moment. I have a monitor on it, surrounded by junk—a digital camera, several cards for the camera, two speakers for the computer that are turned off, numerous business cards, two empty glasses, a measuring tape for an item I recently sold on eBay, a digital thermometer from when I was recently sick, a dental appointment card, a pair of fingernail clippers, several pens (half of which don't work), a pile of papers with notes scribbled on them, a couple of books…and so on. It's a mess. Trust me; I'm not including a photo.

So why in the world would I want to base my computer organization on this thing that the gurus of the 1980s called *the Desktop Metaphor*? And tell me, where on my desk is an icon?

The desktop metaphor is a joke. But it was a good attempt. The idea was to give the people of the world something they could relate to: A desktop, nice and simple. And for the most part, it worked early on, because the computer trainer teaching the frightened secretary could say, "Think of this as your desktop."

Other metaphors have also worked their way into the computing world. The file cabinet is one. (And Microsoft even changed terminology back in 1995, when they deemed directories as *folders*. Apple, on the other hand, always had *folders*.)

Here's the basic problem with the folder metaphor: In my computer, I can put a folder in a folder in a folder in a folder. Try doing that with your real file cabinet, the one of the metallic persuasion. You probably could do it, but it would make for a bit of a mess. And where does the file cabinet itself fit in? Figure 1.2 is an example of a folder containing folders.

Now I admit, the folder metaphor has, for the most part, worked. People seem to understand the metaphor, *to a point*. However, when a user sits at the computer, and he opens a folder he has never seen before, why does he know what that is? Does he mentally make a connection to the metal file cabinet beside his desk? Of course not. Instead, the reason he understands it is that *yesterday* he knew what it was. And tomorrow he'll still remember what it is. In other words, his knowledge and understanding have nothing whatsoever to do with the metaphor of a file cabinet. His knowledge and understanding come from experience and from *recognizing the idioms*. That is, once he *learned* what a folder is, he could recognize folders in the future and continue using them. *The metaphor portion is gone.*

FIGURE 1.2
This window repre-
sents an open folder,
and you can see that it
contains other folders.

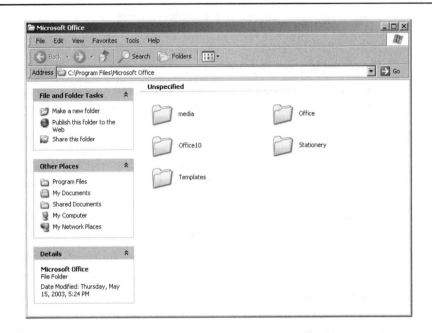

Metaphors are (sometimes) acceptable in training situations and have little use beyond that. Do not design your software with a metaphor in mind because, frankly, people will *no longer need the metaphor* once they understand how to use your software. Otherwise you'll be using a metaphor as a replacement for good idioms. Instead, focus on the idioms: few and simple.

When the newbie learned to use the folder, somebody probably said, "This is called a folder, and think of it like a folder in a file cabinet." But after that, the trainer had to explain how to double-click the folder and show him that a window would open, and that this window contains icons, and that he can drag them to another folder, and so on. And notice what's happening? The metaphor is gone! And is the newbie making a mental connection to the metaphor? Doubtful.

Even in training situations, metaphors can become a problem. If the student is too smart, she might try to relate every process to the metaphor, which will invariably cause confusion. Consider these metaphors: creating a folder in a folder (does that really make sense?), creating a shortcut to a program (I've never seen a shortcut in a folder inside a metal file cabinet). And instead of accepting everything at face value, the thinking student will start asking questions the trainer is unable to answer.

REAL WORLD SCENARIO

The Vintage Doorknob That Trapped Them Inside the Room

I had something scary happen. And I mean really *scary*. I noticed that the doorknob in one of the bedrooms of the old house I live in was loose. It had *play* on it. If I turned it just a bit, I would feel nothing happen, and only after I turned it just a little bit more would I feel it engage and begin to do its job. And so I decided to fix it. I didn't think a doorknob could be all that complicated, even though these are vintage doorknobs. I've replaced newer doorknobs before, and how different could this one be?

And so I fiddled a bit and figured out how to unscrew the outer mechanism, and soon I had the whole contraption sliding out of the door. The two knobs connected in the middle and had a little bolt attached to one that would tighten up into the other. All I had to do was tighten the bolt. And that's when it hit me: *If this thing ever so much as even thought about loosening up any more than it already had, the inside door handle would be rendered completely useless!*

I can see it now. I have my door closed in my office as I'm working hard doing all that computer stuff that we computer people do (like seeing how many web pages it's humanly possible to read in a single day), while the family is outside enjoying life. And finally at dinnertime I'm ready to emerge and return to the living. I walk up to the doorknob...closer...closer...and I finally grab it...I turn it...and nothing happens!

For years the neighbors would hear the screams of "Help!" emanating from that secret dark room. They would see my silhouette in the window as I peer out at them passing by, frightening them while I try to flag them down. Trapped. Unable to get out, for years upon years.

Now how is that for good design (or not)? Engineers can certainly make mistakes, and you, as a software engineer, can easily put yourself in the consumer's shoes when you experience objects and items outside the computer. Think about how they work, and if they frustrated you, think about how they could be designed differently. Become the consumer. And then you can relate to the consumers of *your* products.

Let's face it, the metaphor of the desktop and the file cabinet are pretty much here to stay, like it or not. But let's leave good enough alone and keep additional metaphors out of the business.

Besides, I don't keep my file cabinet on my desktop. I've heard horror stories of file cabinets tipping over and crushing innocent 19-year-old administrative assistants.

The Visual Basic Programmer Has Been Let Out of the Cage!

One of my biggest gripes about programming today is that it is unnecessarily difficult. For example, in one language I have to learn how to use standard templates if I want to create a list of strings. Another language has a type called TStringList. One is certainly easier to use than the other.

(However, please don't think that I dislike C++, which is obviously what I'm referring to here. C++ is one of my favorite languages. I'm just always looking for a simpler way to do things.)

And so I was very excited when Visual Basic came along. Visual Basic actually made programming *easy*. But some people might argue it made programming too easy. Alan Cooper (himself a guru in the useability world) created the original version of a development tool that soon became known as Visual Basic. What Cooper did in his proverbial garage was a breakthrough in the programming world. And today we see his original idea in everything from Borland C++Builder, Borland Delphi, Microsoft C#, various Java designers, and so on.

When Microsoft purchased Visual Basic and introduced version 1.0, they included an amazing feature that let people create their own *custom controls*. A custom control was basically a specialized control that could perform actions that the standard controls (buttons, listboxes, comboboxes, and so on) were not capable of.

Unfortunately, that's exactly the major flaw in this thinking. While some useful controls came out (such as various spreadsheet controls), the world was suddenly overcome with the most horrifying sight to the eyeballs. People made controls that were simply buttons but had the most unreadable 3D text that appeared to be carved out of gray rock. Other people made controls that used every single color that the graphics card at the time was capable of. These controls could spin, dance, whirl, sing, change your oil, and cook your dinner. And they were the ugliest things ever to grace a computer screen.

But to add horror to horrors, other programmers were actually *using* these things in their programs. Users would download these cool new programs and find out that they needed this file and that file to use the program. *This* file and *that* file were, of course, extra Visual Basic controls. And then when people would start up the programs, they would be treated to the crayon equivalent of an explosion in a spaghetti factory.

Come on now. This wasn't necessary, was it? Alan Cooper would be rolling in his grave, except he's still with us, thankfully.

A friend of mine summed it up well when he said, "There's nothing worse than a Visual Basic programmer let loose."

Fortunately, the days of outrageous custom controls have passed. People don't tolerate such abominations. However, creating user interfaces that look like such abominations is still possible, whether you use custom controls or not. Here, then, are some tips to help you avoid creating screens and dialog boxes that look like an expensive, original Matisse painting sent through a meat grinder:

- Use only the standard controls the operating system provides you. The built-in controls in Windows XP, for example, are rich with features and *are well-established idioms*. If you think you need a custom control, think again. Yes, it's true that occasionally people really do need a custom control. But these moments are *extremely* rare. Go about your work assuming you don't need one, and only if you get stuck while trying to program with the existing ones should you consider writing a new custom control. Following is a window containing the basic controls on all Windows systems; you can find these controls on other systems, too. Starting with Windows 95, you have at your disposal other controls, too, such as the ListView and the TreeView.

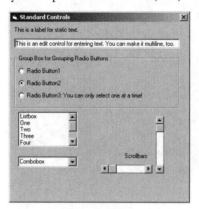

- Don't set *any* colors. I'm serious. First, simply call into the operating system, and let the operating system assign colors to elements such as buttons and listboxes. The operating system in turn chooses its color based on *user preferences*, which are set in the Advanced Appearance dialog box shown below (for Windows). But if you must assign colors for whatever reason, pick from the list of colors chosen by the operating system, since these colors come from the user preferences. These colors have names like ButtonFace (depending on the language you're using) and ActiveWindowColor, and they often match the names in the display preferences. (Of course, you can see the obvious exceptions: If you're writing a program for manipulating graphics, then you'll be setting the colors of the image. But I'm talking about the user interface: For the window title bar, the buttons, and so on, don't set the colors.)

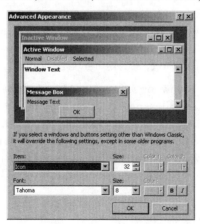

- Don't use 3D and all that other crazy stuff to "enhance" the look of your interface. (The one exception where this seems to be fine is with games. With games, people usually make their own entire user interface.) Okay, I admit, the following is pretty cool and I had fun making it. But I would never *dream* of releasing this in a software package!

- Avoid messing with text. There is a practical reason for this: If you obscure your text in any way whatsoever, you might make reading it difficult for visually impaired people. And a less practical reason is that it will annoy people, whether they are visually impaired or not.

Giving Users What They Want (Including Respect)

I'm going to make a bold statement here. Bear with me:

RULE   Don't assume your users understand the full inner workings of the computer (and don't hold that against them). But don't assume they're stupid, either.

Here's an example of where Microsoft messed up and assumed people are of a slightly lesser intelligence than they really are—and ultimately damaged many hard drives. The key sentence is "Hide extensions for known file types." Does this sentence ring a bell? Most likely, since you're a programmer, you *have* seen this sentence before.

When you first install Windows on a computer (any version these days), by default, the icons in the folders do not have their filename extension showing. So instead of `ThisIsCool.exe`, you will simply see `ThisIsCool`. The idea is that the icon itself should be a clue as to the type of program. If the file is `ThisIsCool.doc`, the icon will be that of Microsoft Word, since `.doc` files are normally associated with Microsoft Word. The users will then (supposedly) know what type of program the file goes with.

FIGURE 1.3
The users can choose whether to hide extensions for known file types.

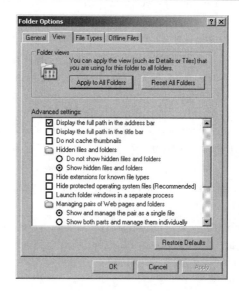

But the problem is icons are easy to fake. I could create a file called ThisIsCool.exe and embed a Microsoft Word icon inside it, making it look like a simple Word document, when in fact the file could be a virus. Very bad. Or, the icon might be meaningless to a user, and the user has no idea that he is opening an executable file. Not good at all.

And so we more experienced computer users always open the Folder Options dialog box on a new system (or on a friend's computer), click the View tab, and uncheck the Hide Extensions For Known File Types option, as shown in Figure 1.3. (It's checked by default!)

The idea was a noble one: Microsoft felt that users shouldn't have to worry about the file-name extensions, since that's more of an *internal* issue. Who cares what the file type is? What matters is what's inside the file! Right? Wrong. And now lots of users have been hit with viruses and inadvertently ran them without realizing they were executable files.

You can see that you have to find a balance: Don't assume your users are stupid and can't handle things, but don't require your users to possess a complete knowledge of the intricate workings of the computer. Microsoft felt it was unnecessary to make the users understand what a .dll or .exe extension is. A little knowledge is important, and knowing what a .dll or .exe file is *is* important.

Software Libraries and Required Knowledge

These assertions about assuming that your users aren't stupid but not making them understand the internals apply even if you're creating software for other programmers. Suppose you're creating a library of C++ classes. With this library you will ship a set of header files, possibly the source code, and likely a library file containing the linkable object code, either in the form of a static library with a `.lib` extension or a dynamic library with a `.dll` extension.

Now with such a library, don't force your users (the programmers) to learn completely how the library works *from the inside*. They need to know how to use the library. If the library uses Newton's Method to calculate a root of a polynomial, then definitely let the users know the algorithm used. That way they can decide whether it's right for them. But don't require them to understand that you used a stack structure and to know the names of the internal variables you used in your function. Do you see where the line is?

Of course, some users might *want* to know (or need to know!) such information. For those users, you can give them access to the source code of your Newton's Method function. (However, you might not want to; it's up to you.)

Just like with user-oriented software, keep your software libraries simple to use without requiring an advanced knowledge, but don't make the advanced users suffer by not giving them the access they need.

The Private versus Protected Debate in Software Libraries

When you design a class library in a language such as C++, you have the option of declaring members of your class private rather than protected. (Remember, the only difference is that derived classes can access protected members but not private members.) This has been a great source of debate over the years. If you are designing a library, always give a lot of thought to whether you really want your class members, especially member functions, to be private. The reason is that people using your library might want to derive their own newer, refined classes from your classes. By making some of the members private, you might prevent these new classes from calling some important functions. By making them protected, the functions are still secure from being called by outside routines; however, the derived classes can call them when necessary.

Asking Too Many Questions

One sure-fire way to annoy your users is to program your software to ask too many questions. Remember, your users are intelligent people, and you're safe making certain assumptions. And for those assumptions you're not sure about, choose some answers that seem safe, and place these answers in a user preferences section. Then the users can change the preferences if they're not happy with your answers.

In this section, I provide you with some questions that are annoying and you should avoid.

Are You Sure You Want to Quit?

Before you include a question such as "Are you sure you want to quit?" in your program, think about what would happen if you *don't* include such a question. Here's an example:

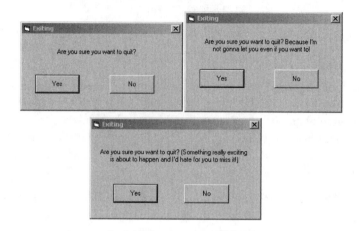

For fun I included two extra windows that answer my question, "Why is it such a big deal?"

Suppose Happy User is using your program, and then she decides to quit. She saves the file she was working on and chooses File ➢ Close. The program shuts down.

But then she realizes she forgot to do something before quitting. Would the "Are you sure…" question have helped here? Not really, if you look at it from a practical standpoint. What did she lose? Nothing. No data was lost. No problems ensued. All she has to do is restart the program and reload the previous document. No big deal. By having an "Are you sure you want to quit?" message, you are not giving any help to your users. If they mess up and really didn't want to quit, let them go back in. Better that than frustrate the users by always having to click the "Yes I'm Sure!" button.

One popular online messaging program opens a dialog when you quit, warning you that the program will no longer function if you quit. Not only is that annoying, it is, frankly, *insulting*. If you're going to choose to annoy your users, fine, but don't insult them on top of it all. Annoyed users don't like to be insulted. (And remember the *ragingus maniacus* hiding inside.)

Do You Want to Save Your Changes?

Although a question about whether you *really* want to quit is annoying, a question about whether to save the changes before quitting is important, *unless* you follow some important tips that I provide later on in this section. If a user has been working on a file and then quits the program and forgets to save, you want your program to warn the user and give him a chance to save the work.

However, a dialog box asking whether to save before exiting has the potential to be extremely confusing. Look at this:

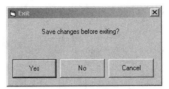

This dialog box has three buttons: Yes, No, Cancel. To us initiated folks, we know exactly what this means. But the reason I have a problem with it is that the beginner has to stop for a while and contemplate what this means. "Let's see..." he thinks. "Yes, I want to save changes." Or "No, I don't want to save them." But what happens if you click No? Does that mean the program will *not* save but *will* quit? To us, we know that's exactly what will happen. But to the beginner this isn't necessarily clear. And what about Cancel? What does that mean?

Now you might argue that this is just an idiom; deal with it, and move on. But it's not. Here's why. I've fallen victim to the following dialog:

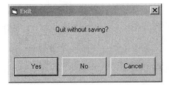

This dialog box is diametrically opposed to the previous example and, therefore, not just a little bit evil but 100 percent evil. If I click Yes, this means the program will not save my work, whereas in the previous example, the program *will* save my work. The programmer who created this program was doing his duty by ensuring that work will not be lost. But the person messed up by flipping the logic from what we're accustomed to.

Here's a better dialog box:

Unfortunately, this one is not standard. People who use Microsoft products all day long will have trouble with it, even though it's a perfectly good solution. Oh, what to do? Instead, try this:

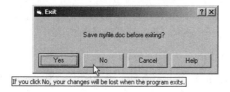

This is a slightly modified version from what Microsoft Word uses, for example. This one conforms to the Windows way of doing things but gives the beginner a bit more help. If the user is confused, she has three ways to proceed:

- She can click the Help button.
- She can hold the mouse over the different buttons and see a *tooltip*.
- She can click the little question-mark button and then click a button.

Now the tooltip and the question-mark button might seem a bit unintuitive to the beginning user. So these two choices are for the users who have explored Windows a bit and are familiar with these two conventions. The Help button, however, is a safe place for all users.

However, I personally feel this is not the best option. I think the previous option (with the radio buttons) was clearer. This is a case where you have to choose between clarity and conforming to the standard. What would I personally do? I'd prefer to take the Fifth on this, although I have a feeling I'd probably choose the radio button version.

But you have another option, as I alluded to at the beginning of this section. Instead, you can *automatically save the file* when the user quits the program. To a lot of programmers, this might seem like a shocking thing to suggest. But I would encourage you to explore it, because some programs already do it with success. Microsoft Outlook is one example. When you exit Outlook, you don't have to save your changes. Instead, all your e-mail is saved automatically, and when you exit, you just exit.

But in the case of a word processor, this option might seem a bit strange. Here's how you can make this work. First, remember that when the user is working on a document, most likely the work he's doing is intentional. (He doesn't just randomly hit a bunch of keys.) After the user works for about 10 minutes (or 30 seconds if the user presses Ctrl+S obsessively as I do!), you can assume that the work the user did was *intentional*, and if the user exits, you can simply save his work automatically for him, no questions asked.

But what about the .01 percent of the time where the user didn't want to save his work? You can provide two approaches for these users:

- Allow the users to open a *copy of a file*. Then, when the user exits your program, the program will save the changes to a new (possibly unnamed) file. (Of course, the very first time, you might want the user to type in the name of the file.)

- Save a backup file before saving the new file.

- Possibly include the undo list with the file itself. That way the user can undo any changes that were made prior to exiting the program. (I like this idea the best, because it really allows you to *continue working* the next time you come back to the document.)

Remember, your goal is to make the majority of the users happy. Occasionally a user might have a strange situation. She might have wanted to do all this work without saving it. In that case, include in your online help instructions for getting the old version back. But for the other thousands of times, the users really did want to save the work, and there was no reason for you to ask before doing so, each and every single time.

If you don't believe me, think about this: How often do you save your work just before exiting? And if you don't, how many times in your life have you seen the dialog box asking if you would like to save before exiting? And now think how much time you wasted by having to click that dialog box or by manually requesting a save just before exiting.

Questions That Yield an "I Don't Know!" Answer

A question that yields an "I don't know!" answer is typical during installation programs. Here's an example of a question that most of us, even a skilled programmer, might sit and stare at for several moments, wondering what to do:

Although I made this window myself, I based it on a dialog box that I actually saw the other day. First of all, the choice of "Yes" and "No" is rather arbitrary. Better buttons would be "Install New" and "Keep Old", because "Yes" and "No" could easily result in a mistake.

But worse is the question itself. How should I know if I should install a newer version? A typical end user would have no clue and would just randomly pick one option. And for me, a programmer, I know that some other program might need the version that's currently on the disk and won't be able to run with the newer version (but I don't know what program that is), and the program I'm installing might need the newer version and won't be able run with the older version!

And if I'm feeling particularly ornery, I might even ask, "Why are you installing files in my System32 directory? Keep out!"

Don't ask questions like this when you write an installation program. Put the files in your own directory, and the issue won't even come up. And if you're working with Windows and have to register an OLE component, either make your own version of the OLE component or know what the differences between versions are so you can be more specific in your questions.

Would You Like to Restart Windows Now...or Later?

After installing a software package, if the program tells me I need to restart the computer, I usually laugh and say "No" and run the program anyway *just to see what happens*. Maybe that's a bit too impish, but I've reached a point in my computer life where I'm a bit fearless. I mean really now, what could possibly go wrong? Will I see an image of a little beastie go across the screen eating up all the bits on my hard drive because I forgot to restart Windows? Will my monitor start leaking poisonous fumes? What could go wrong?

Yet time and again, I'm told I need to reboot Windows. Here's a typical dialog box:

In addition to the fact that the beginning user might wonder what the Cancel button does (does it undo the installation?), there's no reason for this dialog. Don't make your users reboot Windows. If you make changes to the Registry, those changes take effect automatically. If you register an OLE component, those changes take place immediately. Don't make them reboot. It's not nice. (I will concede that there might be some exceptions to this, and that's primarily when you're installing lower-level software such as device drivers. However, make sure you absolutely have to, because these days even device drivers can be loaded and unloaded without having to reboot Windows!)

Tip of the Day

Although this isn't a question, a Tip of the Day box is just as annoying as most unnecessary questions. Since the mid-1990s, the Tip of the Day dialog box has become popular. Here's an example of one:

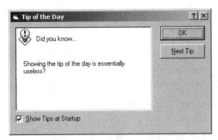

Don't use these. Period. Although in theory the idea is great (what better way to convey important information?), the reality is the Tip of the Day dialog box breaks every imaginable rule. First, very few people read them. They either always click OK or the first time the thing opens they click the Don't Show This Again box. The information in the box is wasted, as is the time and energy you (the programmer) spent creating the box.

But worse, just what are the chances that your Tip of the Day dialog box is going to give the users some information that actually pertains to what they are going to do today? If I'm using a word processor to write a letter to a client, why would I need to see a Tip of the Day that explains how to import clip art? The Tip of the Day is wasted time and wasted space. Don't bother with it.

Saving User Preferences

One way to minimize the use of annoying questions is by implementing a user preferences system, as I mentioned earlier. In the user preferences section, you can allow your users to customize your software through the use of a User Preferences dialog box.

But don't go overboard; a User Preferences dialog box with 20 tabs and a million controls is frustrating, too, if the user is searching for a particular preference. Keep your User Preferences dialog box simple and easy to use.

Here are the steps you use for User Preferences:

1. When the software opens, read the user preferences, either from a file or from the Registry, a database, or wherever you stored them.

2. If the preferences are not found, set some defaults.

3. When the user opens the User Preferences dialog box and clicks OK, save the preferences internally. (As for whether to save them to the file or the Registry at this point is up to you.)

4. When the user shuts down your program, save the preferences to the file or the Registry.

You have some choices in implementing this kind of a system. For one, you might save only those preferences that are not defaults. If you're writing software for the PalmOS, for example, where space is tight, this might be a good idea. Also, you have different ways in which you can allow access to the user preferences. Microsoft products typically have a Tools menu, with an Options dialog box underneath it. This is pretty much standard, although some other big software packages (most notably Netscape Navigator) use other means, such as putting Preferences under the Edit or File menu. Since Microsoft has created many of the standards we see on Windows, then if you're writing a Windows program, I recommend following the Microsoft approach.

> **TIP**
>
> If you are programming for Microsoft Windows, make use of the Registry. You can save your preferences in the HKEY_CURRENT_USER area. In this area you will find a key called `Software`. Under this key you can create a key for the name of your company, and under the company key you can create a key for your product name. Standard practice is to have version numbers under the product name key. Finally, under the version numbers you can place your user preferences.

Another issue that comes up is that of multiple people using your program. You have various ways to handle this, too. If you're storing your preferences to a file, you can save the file in an area specifically designated for the particular user. However, be careful with this approach. I don't like it when a program dumps a file in the C:\documents and settings\jeff directory on my Windows computer. (I have a bad habit of purposely deleting such files!) Instead, under this same directory is another directory called Application Data. Under that directory, you're free to create your own directory (again, don't put the file right in the Application Data directory), and inside your own directory, you can put your file. The advantage there is then you know what the file is if you go poking through these directories.

For example, right now I see this file on my computer: C:\Documents and Settings\jeff\ Application Data\dmqr.ini. I have no idea what this file is, but it's the only file in this directory. Everything else in this directory is a subdirectory with the name of a company or product. I think I'll go delete it (but if you put it there, please expect a support call from me when your program doesn't work; but don't worry, I'm friendly and don't bite).

TIP   Remember that multiple people may well use your program. Therefore, if you have a user preferences system, save the preferences on a per-user basis, not just on a system-wide basis. When programming for Microsoft Windows, you can save on a per-user basis by saving the preferences in the HKEY_CURRENT_USER area of the system Registry and *not* the HKEY_LOCAL_MACHINE area.

Remember the Keyboard?

A long time ago when Windows 3.1 was the great new thing, I wrote a memo to several coworkers explaining that the notion of a keyboard shortcut was stupid, and it's safe to assume at that day and age (roughly 1993) that every computer running Microsoft Windows had a mouse attached to it.

What was I thinking!

Hey, I had 10 years less experience than I do now, and I had a lot to learn about life. (Sounds like a song.) Needless to say, I no longer agree with the notion that keyboard shortcuts are not needed. In fact, I use them all the time. Lots of people do. Why? Because:

- They're faster if you're a fast typist (like me and all the piano players of the world).

- They're more convenient than reaching over to grab the mouse, moving it to where it needs to go, and clicking it.

- They're configurable; I can make Ctrl+Alt+S do what I want it to do, which is something you can't say about clicking with the mouse.

However, these points are true only when the software application includes a decent keyboard shortcut interface. What makes for a decent keyboard shortcut interface? Here I list what I personally expect out of one. (And trust me, I use keyboard shortcuts a *lot*, so for now, consider me your favorite user.)

NOTE   People used to use the term *hot key* for keyboard shortcut. Somewhere along the lines, Microsoft instilled the term *keyboard shortcut* into our vocabulary, and these days, that's what most people say. I still prefer hot key, because I like shorter words, and the word *shortcut* is overused in Microsoft products: A shortcut on a desktop is a symbolic link to another program; a shortcut in Internet Explorer is a hypertext link.

The Shortcut System Is Implemented.

You want to make sure you actually implemented the keyboard shortcut system. For starters, most better programs include shortcut keys on the menu items. The Mac often uses the Apple key for its shortcut keys. Windows often uses the Ctrl key. On both the Mac and Windows you can see the shortcut key for a menu item by clicking on the menu; the shortcut key is shown to the right of the menu item name.

Further, on Windows, you can add an additional shortcut key for the menu bar. Put an ampersand, &, inside the text for the menu, and the letter following the ampersand will show up underlined. For example, if you call your first menu &File, the menu will show up as <u>F</u>ile. Then, when the user holds down Alt and presses F, the File menu will open.

For menu items under the menu, you again use an ampersand to specify which letter is underlined. But for these shortcuts, the user first must open the menu (such as by pressing Alt+F) and then type the underlined letter (with or without the Alt key).

The Dialog Boxes Make Use of the Tab Ordering.

As a self-professed keyboard shortcut whiz, I find the lack of tab ordering always frustrating. Yet, it's amazing how many software designers and testers completely overlook this. Again and again I find software where the tab ordering is all messed up.

When a dialog box opens, typically you will want the focus to be on the control closest to the upper-left corner of the dialog box. For example, if that's an edit control, then the user doesn't have to first click that edit control to type text into it. The user simply starts typing and the text appears, because that's the control with the focus.

Then, if the user presses Tab, the focus should move to the next control to the right, if there is one, and down if there's not one to the right. The focus should move from right to left and top to bottom, just like the words in your code editor.

However, the Enter key is special, and so is the Esc key. When you design a dialog box, you can specify which button is the active one. The active button shows up with a dark border around it, like the OK button shown here:

Regardless of which control has focus, if the user presses Enter, the OK button should click. Pressing Esc should be the same as clicking the Cancel button. (Doing so is in line with the standard idioms that people expect of your software.)

Standard Keyboard Shortcuts Mean What They Usually Do.

Prior to version 2000 of Microsoft Outlook, many of us had a problem with sending e-mail midway through the composition of the e-mail. Why was that? Because Microsoft made a blunder. For quite some time, Microsoft has always used Ctrl+S as the keyboard shortcut for Save. And so those of us who had "Save Early Save Often" beat into our heads would press Ctrl+S almost obsessively. (I do to this day. In fact, I better go do it right now. There, I feel much better. Never know when a power outage might come and I'll lose the last three words.)

But not with Outlook 97. In Outlook 97, Ctrl+S was the shortcut for none other than *Send*. And so during the composition of an e-mail, many of us would out of sheer reflex, about halfway through the e-mail, press Ctrl+S. And much to our shock, the message window would disappear and we'd see the little words "Sending Message 1 of 1" appear at the bottom of our Outlook screen.

See, Microsoft violated a standard idiom. We all knew that Ctrl+S meant Save. And guess what? In Outlook 2000 and beyond, Ctrl+S now *saves* the e-mail into your Drafts folder. It doesn't send the message. *Whew!*

Remember that most people expect various keyboard shortcuts to mean something. Please don't rearrange these, because you'll frustrate users like me who operate out of 90 percent reflex. The big ones are:

Ctrl+S = Save

Ctrl+C = Copy

Ctrl+V = Paste

Ctrl+X = Cut

Ctrl+F = Find

Ctrl+R = Replace, although Microsoft these days usually insists on Ctrl+H. Should we listen to them or not? This one is your call.

And some people like to use Ctrl+Q to quit. That's fine, if you like that one. We all have slightly different opinions on these. Just don't make Ctrl+S send e-mail. Please?

Keyboard Shortcuts Should Be Configurable.

Even though I just listed the "big ones," some people still get frustrated at these. But that shouldn't be a problem, because you're about to make your keyboard shortcuts configurable. Include some sort of dialog box that allows me (the user) to choose what I want the keyboard shortcuts to do.

The common way to do this is by developing a set of *use cases* for your product, which are basically the elemental things that people can do with your product. Some people call these *commands*. If you start one of the Microsoft Office products, and right-click on a toolbar or menu and choose Customize, you'll see a dialog box listing all the commands. For example, in Microsoft Word, you'll find a command for pretty much everything you can do, such as Toggle Italic; Toggle Bold; Insert Column Break; and so on.

When you design your software, if you divide the functionality into use cases or commands and then break each of these into its own function (or member function if you put it in a class), then you can easily create a configurable system. All you have to do is list all the names of the commands in a dialog box and for each one let the user choose a keyboard sequence. The sequence can include the Ctrl key, the Alt key, or the Shift key, or any combination thereof. For example, you might want to assign Ctrl+Shift+I to the command Toggle Italic.

And how do you implement this? Through function pointers, of course. Use a common function prototype for each function, and it's a snap: Store the function pointers in a table of keyboard shortcuts (or some other list or array), and then when the user presses a key sequence such as Ctrl+Shift+I, look up the function that goes with that key (such as the address of `toggleItalic`) and call the function. Since all the functions have the same function prototype, you will know exactly what to pass to the function.

This is actually easier than it sounds. Although this part of the book doesn't focus so much on coding, here's a sample design pattern in C++ that does the trick using the C++ standard library's map class. I wrote the code from scratch and compiled it using the gnu gcc compiler:

```cpp
#include <iostream>
#include <map>
#include <string>

using namespace std;

typedef void (*command)();

// Here are the commands
void toggleItalic() {
    cout << "italic toggled" << endl;
}

void toggleBold() {
    cout << "bold toggled" << endl;
}

// Here's the class for the shortcuts
class Shortcuts {
protected:
  map<string, command> shortcuts;
public:
  void CallCommand(string sequence);
  void ReplaceCommand(string oldsequence,
    string newsequence, command cmd);
};

void Shortcuts::CallCommand(string sequence) {
  if (shortcuts[sequence] != NULL) {
    shortcuts[sequence]();
```

```
      }
    }

    void Shortcuts::ReplaceCommand(string oldsequence,
      string newsequence, command cmd) {
      if (oldsequence != "")
        shortcuts[oldsequence] = NULL;
      shortcuts[newsequence] = cmd;
    }
```

Then, using this code is easy. To assign the keystroke Ctrl+I to the function called `toggleItalic`, call `keys.ReplaceCommand("", "cI", &toggleItalic)` (where keys is the name of the object). Then when the user presses Ctrl+I, simply call `keys.CallCommand("cI")`. Here's a sample `main` demonstrating this:

```
    int main(int argc, char *argv[])
    {
      Shortcuts keys;
      keys.ReplaceCommand("", "cI", &toggleItalic);
      keys.ReplaceCommand("", "cB", &toggleBold);
      // Assume user pressed Ctrl+I. Then call this:
      keys.CallCommand("cI");
      // Assume user pressed Ctrl+B. Then call this:
      keys.CallCommand("cB");
      // Assume user pressed something unassigned:
      keys.CallCommand("aQ");
      // User reconfigures italic to be Alt+I:
      keys.ReplaceCommand("cI", "aI", &toggleItalic);
      // Now user presses Alt+I
      keys.CallCommand("aI");
      return 0;
    }
```

Once you implement a design pattern such as this, keyboard shortcuts (and menus and toolbar buttons) all become a snap. You can use the same interface for a menu; instead of mapping keyboard shortcut names such as "caI" to a function, you map menu item IDs to a function. And similarly with toolbars, you would map toolbar button IDs to a function.

Such a system is incredibly easy to implement, provided you know how to program various design patterns and that you fully understand your programming language.

The Real Risk of Repetitive Motion Injury

Let's face it and be up front here. Not only do you not want to annoy your users, you probably don't want to actually *injure* them, either. (If you've simply annoyed your users, you might know what it's like to receive e-mail from them, where they threaten injury.)

Now I know we're computer people and many of us are more likely to perform an exorcism than to actually *exercise*. But whether you work out daily or only during major holidays on every tenth year, you're probably familiar with that sore-muscle feeling the day after you work out.

The feeling of sore muscles is actually due to the muscles tearing at a microscopic level. When this happens, with the proper nutrition, your muscles heal themselves and become stronger. The key, however, in addition to proper nutrition, is in allowing time for recovery.

But the one exercise many of us do on a daily basis is type at the computer and use the mouse. While this might not seem like much, if you type and work the mouse for eight hours straight, you're likely to feel it a bit. My personal problem is that my elbow will often ache from reaching over to the mouse. I fixed this by getting a Logitech trackball instead, but I still have to reach over to the trackball. And sometimes my elbow still hurts, although the trackball has definitely helped a great deal. Other people feel pain in their fingers and hands from all the typing.

And, unfortunately, rarely do we give ourselves a few days off to recover from these aches and pains, which are, in fact, torn muscles, tendons, and ligaments. (Now isn't that a pleasant thought!)

NOTE   Right through the middle of your wrist runs a nerve called the *median nerve*. This nerve is especially susceptible to trauma from using a computer keyboard. Damage to this nerve is known as carpal tunnel syndrome (CTS), which most of us have heard of. CTS is an example of a repetitive motion injury (RMI) or repetitive stress injury (RSI).

What can you do to help prevent repetitive motion injury and carpal tunnel syndrome? Since it would be a serious bummer to think that your software was responsible for somebody's bodily injury, here are some things that you can do:

- Don't require overuse of the mouse. In other words, include keyboard shortcuts for everything that might otherwise require the mouse. This includes menu items, controls in a dialog box, buttons in a dialog box, the works. And if the mouse is required, don't make the user bounce back and forth between using the mouse and the keyboard. For example, if you're writing a graphics program whereby the user can use the mouse to do drawings, set up the software so that the user can work the keyboard with one hand and the mouse with the other. Make this configurable, and don't forget about the left-handed people, either, who prefer to put the mouse on the left side of the keyboard.

But also don't require that the user constantly click in the upper-right part of the screen, then the lower-left, then the upper-right, and so on. For that matter, a lot of very small mouse movements can be bad as well. Further:

- Allow the user to do most of the keyboard work without bouncing the right hand back and forth between the J-position and the cursor and page keys and numeric keypad.

- Create a macro system, whereby users can program repeated keystrokes and activate the keystrokes with a single keystroke or click of the mouse.

- Design your software such that users can take a break from the keyboard without loss of data. This might seem like a strange request, but there are situations where this could be a factor. (Games come to mind.)

TIP   A lot of people who suffer from RSIs find they're most comfortable with the Dvorak layout of the keyboard rather than the standard QWERTY style. However, if you're writing software that responds to the keyboard in any way (as most software does), don't build in Dvorak capabilities. Instead, Windows allows users to configure their own keyboards. This means that if your program receives the letter *j* as input, you can be assured the user typed *j*, regardless of where *j* is on the keyboard.

The common factor here is minimizing the movements of your users. Don't force them to go through jumps and dances just to get the task done.

Finally, if you want to learn more about the various repetitive motion and stress injuries, I have found a great place to start is by going to Yahoo! and searching on the phrase "repetitive stress injury."

Moving Forward

In this chapter I presented you with a set of introductory material on designing highly useable software. If you follow the principles I develop in this chapter, your software will already be more useable than that of the competition.

In the next chapter I move to the next step and look at the real problem of modeling the real world. Life can get touchy then; remember what happened with the "desktop metaphor." Ahh, that was an attempt to model the real world, wasn't it? Sure, it kind of worked, sort of, but let's leave good enough alone and skip the metaphors. Still, sometimes you have to model a business process. I take that up in the next chapter.

And finally, before you move on, here's one more quick story of a timely nature.

REAL WORLD SCENARIO

The Atomic Clock that Wouldn't

They called it an atomic clock. But really, it's a clock with some kind of radio-controlled device that picks up the exact time over the airwaves broadcast from some station in Colorado that has an atomic clock attached to it. My mother gave it to me as a gift a couple of years ago. She thought it was cool, and I had to admit, it was....

Until today (no kidding—the very day I was finishing writing this chapter). The clock has almost no user interface to speak of; you don't set it. Instead, you pick your time zone from a switch on the back and let it go. When you turn it on (by inserting a battery), you just wait. The second hand ticks a little sporadically, and then suddenly the second hand starts flying, going very fast, and the clock appears to be in fast motion. The minute hand moves at about the rate of a second hand. The clock spins like this for maybe 45 minutes or however long it takes until it gets to the current time. Then it slows instantly and ticks normally. After that you never have to set it.

The clock understands daylight saving time. At least it's supposed to. And it's always been correct until this evening when I looked at it and it was an hour *ahead*. Instead of saying 6:35 it said 7:35. I figured I bumped the time zone setting on the back when I moved the clock earlier today. So I flipped the clock over and looked. It's been about three years since I've had to do anything with the clock, and the instructions are long gone. But it should be straightforward. I saw that the user interface consisted of a little dial where you choose your time zone. (Only continental U.S. time zones are included, since those are the only ones within range of the electromagnetic waves shooting out of Colorado throughout our bodies). But here's the catch: The dial has a notch for every time zone, plus a *final* notch for daylight saving time. How can that be? Daylight saving time is not a time zone! But the selector lets you choose Eastern, Central, Mountain, Pacific, or Daylight Saving Time. That doesn't make sense.

Now I know the clock automatically adjusts itself in the fall and the spring, if you somehow tell it that you live in one of the areas that practices daylight saving time (that would be nearly everywhere in the U.S. except Arizona, Hawaii, and most of Indiana). And so somehow I'm supposed to tell it which time zone I live in *and* (not *or!*) whether or not I want it to automatically adjust for daylight saving time. But how can you do that when all you have is a single dial with separate notches for each time zone plus one for daylight saving time?

I don't know. I'm at a loss. I hope I don't have to throw out the clock because it got messed up and I can't figure out how to reconfigure it.

It's just another user interface gone bad, I guess.

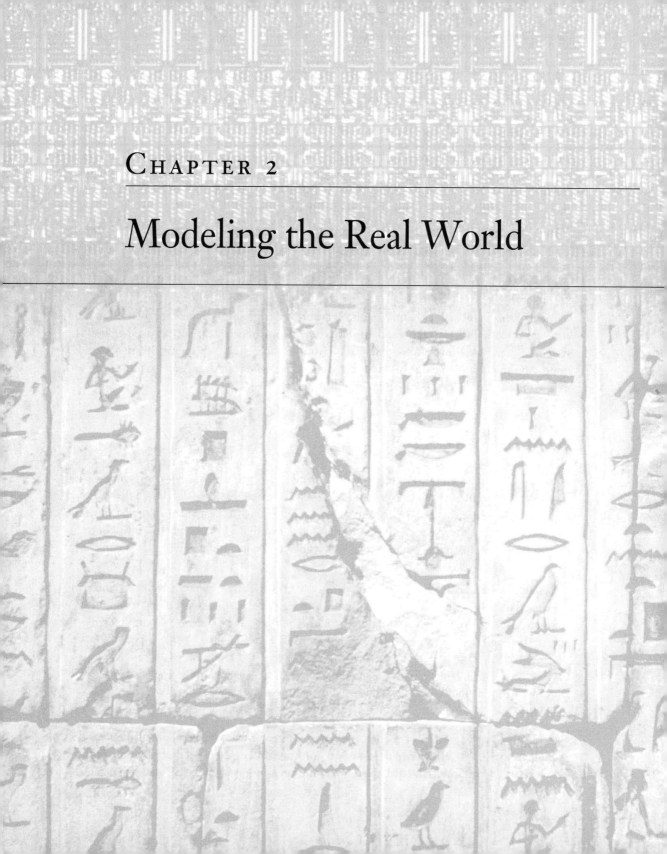

CHAPTER 2

Modeling the Real World

"I want to write a program. It's gonna be a good program. Big, too. Lots of good stuff. So here we go, start coding."

Let's hope that if you're reading this book, you've progressed beyond that mindset. A long time ago a friend of mine referred to how, when we're just learning to program, we usually decide at some point that we're going to write a "really big program." And we dive in coding, and eventually the thing just falls apart, probably sooner than later.

And yet, even though when many professional programmers who try to write a "big program" use all the correct engineering approaches, they still fail in other areas. These areas are:

- Usability design (what some of the gurus simply call *design*)
- Correct use of modeling

Much of this book in your hand focuses on usability design. But this chapter focuses on modeling. By *modeling*, I mean taking something in the real world (such as a paper-based accounting system or perhaps an airplane cockpit) and writing software that represents this real-world thing. And that's where people usually go wrong: When they build software to model the real world, they try to make it completely duplicate the real world.

Modeling That's Too Real

Here's the ultimate in modeling. (Wouldn't this be so cool!) I can envision a new kind of computer screen that lets you reach right into it. Instead of typing into a spreadsheet, you see what looks like a sheet of paper with rows and columns, and you have a special device that lets you actually *write* on the sheet of paper. And when it comes time to recalculate all the fields in the spreadsheet, off to the side sits a program that looks just like a calculator. And it has buttons that you push just like a real calculator. Once you do your calculation, you reach over and write the answer on the spreadsheet.

If computers ever reach the point that we can do this with them, I'm selling mine and buying a boat and getting the heck out of here. But do you see the absurdity here? This "program" I'm suggesting models the world so closely, it reaches the point of *Why bother?* Computers give us so many capabilities and we should be making use of them. Further:

> **RULE**   When you model the real world, recognize that because of a computer's storage space and speed of calculations and general power, you don't have to duplicate the way things used to be done.

In formal circles, this idea of changing the way things can be done is called business process reengineering (BPR). BPR doesn't just cover software processes; it covers the whole offline business, too. Consultants in BPR help companies revise their whole processes, and often this even impacts the customers. Here I'm not going to get heavily into BPR, because as computer folks most of us would be in over our heads. Besides, BPR requires not only an investment from a company but a *willingness to change*. If you're writing off-the-shelf software and your software will be used by thousands or millions of customers, how many of them would want to be told that to use your software they have to change their offline business processes, too? Not many, I imagine. And thus I have this rule of thumb:

RULE   The software you create should not require that your customers change their business processes just to use it. If it does, they'll buy somebody else's software that doesn't require a change!

REAL WORLD SCENARIO

"The Computer Can't Change, so *You* Will" (I Once Said and Nearly Got Fired).

Years ago, in the early-to-mid-1980s, when the IBM PC just came out, I was helping a small business get their computer going. The owner had bought himself a Commodore computer to have at home, and he liked it so much he decided it was time to computerize his office. He bought a PC, along with a really good accounting software package called ACCPAC. (Quick side note: This particular software package lives on in a modern form and is still quite successful!) The ACCPAC software in the early 1980s had something that was ahead of its time, a complete report-generation language. To create a report, you would write lines of code describing the report. The report generator had its own unique language and included constructs for accessing fields in the accounting database. (As you can imagine, I had lots of fun playing with it!) But we had a bit of a problem: We had this giant dual dot-matrix/daisy wheel printer that could take paper as wide as 18 inches. And I couldn't figure out how to get the font set from within the report for the smaller 8 1/2 x 11″ paper. So I set up my reports to print on the big paper and…(brace yourself)… *I told the boss he would have to use larger paper for all his reports*.

No, he didn't get angry. He simply looked me in the eyes and said, "No. I can't do that. I need smaller paper. I can't have these great big sheets of papers; they won't fit in my binders." I argued a bit. But to my amazement, he managed to solve the problem quickly and easily. His solution was this: "Go fix it. I don't care what it takes, but *go fix it*."

And I did. I spent a few more hours and eventually solved the problem. I was all proud of myself that I managed to figure out the font codes required by the printer and embed these font codes right in the report, switching the printer to small enough fonts for the smaller paper.

I learned an important lesson that day; the lesson, as you can see, some 20 years later as I write this, has lived with me: *Don't force people to change for the sake of the computer*. Why? Because they *won't*. (And worse, they'll either hire somebody else or buy somebody else's software.)

The two preceding points might seem a bit contradictory, but in fact, they provide for a fine line that you should walk on: Use the computer's power, but don't just create a completely virtual version of the real world. Build software that models the real world and does a good job at it, optimizing processes when possible. But at the same time, don't go overboard on the optimization. Keep what you model within reason, and make sure the software doesn't require your users to change the way they do things. And *that's* the topic of this chapter: how to build models that are both useable and reasonable.

The Case for Using Use Cases

The concept of a *use case* has created a bit of stir. Use cases were invented by one of the foremost experts in object-oriented design, Ivar Jacobson, who is now part of the team who created UML, the Unified Modeling Language. (And today, use cases are an important part of both UML and the Rational Unified Process™, which is one of the primary design methods that make use of UML.) Yet, in many ways, they are completely functional in nature, as opposed to object-oriented. But that's okay. They work. And you should use them.

What's a use case? A use case is a small description of one piece of functionality in your software. Right now I'm using Microsoft Word to type this chapter. Here are some of the use cases for this huge piece of software:

- Toggle italic
- Set a style
- Indent
- Run a particular macro

(I should mention, however, that some of the experts treat groups of functions as a single use case. Their idea is that a use case is a sequence of actions that together provide a result for the user. This is, in fact, the more formal definition of use cases. These people usually have a considerably smaller list of use cases when they design their software, but the use cases embody several features.)

NOTE   If you read Chapter 1, "The UUI: The Useable User Interface," you might be experiencing a bit of déjà vu: I talked about these features of the word processor, but in a different light. In that chapter, I talked about them as *commands*. They're the same thing. From the user's perspective, these are commands. From a design perspective, they are use cases.

When done properly, use case analysis helps you figure out the features of your software. Further, if you implement the command-driven approach I described in Chapter 1, then you can easily bring your use cases (and hence, your software functionality) to fruition.

Clearing Up Some UML Misconceptions

While on the topic of use cases, which are now an official part of UML, I'd like to clear up some misconceptions about UML. When asked what methodology people use, some people will say, "We use UML." That's not correct. If you're interviewing for a job, and they say that, it means they're not using any methodology, because if they were, they'd see the problem in that statement. UML, which stands for Unified Modeling Language, is *not* a methodology. UML is a *visual language* or *notation*. It is a set of diagrams along with a complete formal grammar describing how the diagrams interact with each other. Further, it is extensible; when necessary, you can add your own diagrams to the language. UML can be used in many areas of engineering, not just software. However, software is certainly where it is mostly used since, frankly, most people outside of the software world haven't heard of UML.

Many programmers, when first exploring UML, quickly become disenchanted because they get a bit confused. They read a book on UML, and they learn what all the symbols mean, but they're left with feeling lost in how to use UML to actually build a software system. That's because they studied only half the story. They're missing the second half, the *process*, which some people call a *methodology*.

The usual process people use with UML is the Rational Unified Process. (However, you can use other processes, too, with UML.) The Rational Unified Process, created by the same people who brought us UML (Grady Booch, Jim Rumbaugh, and our use-case pal Ivar Jacobson), is a formal set of steps that take you through the complete design and building of your software, all the way through testing and deployment. The process contains many of the usual steps you've come to expect out of a good methodology: requirements, analysis, design, implementation, and deployment.

If you want to learn more about *both* UML and the Unified Process, the best introductory text I have found is *UML and the Unified Process* by Jim Arlow and Ila Neustadt (Addison-Wesley, 2002).

Entire books have been written on use case modeling, and trying to cram it all into one section of one chapter would do the topic a serious disservice. So instead of teaching you use cases, I'm going to go up one step on the proverbial Ladder of Abstraction and explain how to make use cases work for your system.

Use case modeling takes place early on in the engineering process, long, long, long before you write any code. Use case modeling is part of the requirements phase. You write use cases in a human language such as English so that the managers can read them.

NOTE Really, use cases don't just describe the features of a system from a human perspective. If you're building, for example, a system that primarily interacts with other software (such as a web server), you will still design use cases. But for these use cases, the user is not a human; it is another software system.

People heavily into object design like to use the term *discover* to describe how you create your use cases (and other parts of a system, such as objects, for that matter). I'm not fond of this, because I like to think of us engineers as having a little more cognition in the software process beyond simply discovering something as if it came to us out of the ether and fell into our laps. However, the people who use the term don't really mean it like that, and so I'll accept the word and use it too.

After you have followed the procedure for discovering use cases (such as that outlined in the Unified Process), I want you to do two things:

1. Hand the use cases off to somebody in the business who is not technical and understands typical users.

2. Take a good hard look at your own use cases from a user perspective.

As for number 1, wear a thick skin and allow the coworker to be brutal. (Better now than later when you start getting e-mails from the *real* users!) Listen, take notes, and take the user's concerns seriously. Then go back and fix the problems. As for number 2, ask yourself: Are these use cases *reasonable*? Do they *make sense*? Are they *easy to use*? Are they *complete*?

But go beyond that. Here are some more questions:

- Can you combine some into a single use case?

- Is there any redundancy that will confuse the users?

- Are any of them too specific?

Here's an example. Suppose you were creating a word processor, and you came up with the following two use cases:

- Turn italics on

- Turn italics off

So far these seem reasonable: You, as the user, highlight some text that's not in italics, and you somehow initiate the Turn Italics On command (either through a keystroke, or a menu item, or a toolbar button). Then you realize the middle word shouldn't be italicized, so you highlight that one word and trigger the Turn Italics Off command. And what if you highlight text that's a mixture of italicized and non-italicized text? Then choosing Turn Italics On will make all the highlighted text italicized, while choosing Turn Italics Off will make all the highlighted text non-italicized.

But stop. Wait, time out! If you let this go all the way through the development process and into the final product, you're going to have some unhappy customers. Imagine if the word processor had two separate buttons on the toolbar, one called Turn Italics On, and one called Turn Italics Off. Is that really necessary? Instead, is it possible to combine these into a single use case called *Toggle italics*?

If you use Microsoft Word, you will see that you have a single use case called Toggle italics. It's not two separate ones, and it works fine: If you highlight non-italicized text and choose

Toggle Italics (Ctrl+I works), the text becomes italicized. If you highlight italicized text and choose Toggle Italics, the text becomes non-italicized. And if you highlight a mixture of italicized and non-italicized text, all the text becomes italicized. It works fine, and it's one less use case to worry about and one less angry customer who keeps clicking the wrong button. Oh yes, and one less confused customer who can only seem to turn italics on but just can't seem to turn them off because somehow he accidentally removed the Turn Italics Off button from his toolbar and doesn't understand how to bring it back by using the Customize dialog box in Microsoft Word. (Wouldn't you like to work tech support when he calls?)

Incidentally, this toggle approach has the added benefit that the toolbar button can now show state: When you highlight italicized text, the toolbar button appears depressed. To unitalicize the text, "unclick," or deselect, the toolbar button (that is, click it so it's no longer depressed). It works great.

Now here's another example of a Use Case Gone Bad. This is another one that might have ended up in our word processor program. This one fails in the question, "Are any of them too specific without enough configuration?" Here's the use case: *Indent every paragraph by a half inch*. This one is easy to fix: Make the "half inch" part configurable! Change it to this: *Indent every paragraph by a user-supplied amount*.

That's better, but still, a sophisticated word processor such as Microsoft Word wouldn't have much use for a use case like this, because Word has a powerful set of use cases that deal with setting *styles*. You can define a style to have a certain indentation and assign that style to any paragraph you want. Then if you change the style's indentation, every paragraph using that style will automatically change to the new indentation level.

So how did Microsoft come up with the notion of styles? I wasn't there, so I can't say exactly, but I suspect somebody had considered a use case such as the paragraph indentation one. I could imagine that somebody else might have then added a use case changing the font of every paragraph. And somebody else suggested that you somehow notate which paragraphs to change the font. This type of brainstorm is good, because if you go with it, you will get to the real solution, provided you don't stop. If they had stopped, then I might be having to go through and somehow manually select each paragraph in this text as I write it, choose the special style the publisher created for me, and then one by one set the font attributes and indentation attributes.

But instead, Microsoft combined redundant use cases into a single set of use cases that are, in the end, extremely powerful. I like styles in Microsoft Word, because they make my life much easier, whether I'm writing a book or a letter.

Let's continue with the brainstorm. Microsoft saw that these use cases were somehow related, and they saw the common thread: setting a feature in every paragraph. But thanks to the guy who suggested that you somehow notate which paragraphs to set, they decided to combine these: You can create a style (that's a good word) and assign it to a paragraph (that's a use case). Then you can set the indentation for that style (that's a use case, too). And you can set the font for that style (another use case).

Now this leads to another rule for dealing with use cases:

| RULE | Create logical groups for your use cases. |

REAL WORLD SCENARIO

The Electronic Music Synthesizer that Had It All

I'm a musician, and back in the 1980s I remember seeing an issue of *Keyboard Magazine* that had a feature covering all the music synthesizers that were made by small startups (akin to the dot-coms 10 years later) that just never quite made it. These synthesizers were actually quite amazing, even if there was only one of each, and it was a prototype. They featured multiple keyboards stacked like you find on a pipe organ and some pretty advanced technologies that were ahead of their time. They used some modern digital techniques for sound synthesis, mixed with older analog techniques. They were what was at the time known as *polyphonic* (meaning they could play more than one note at once—a feature, believe it or not, that was not present in every synthesizer back then). Some even had pedals on the floor like a pipe organ has. Some had buttons, some had drawbars called stops like the old organs had (that's where the phrase *pulling out all the stops* comes from), and some had dials and knobs like the newer keyboards. Some even had LED displays.

Are you starting to see the problem here? There was a common thread among all these keyboards that was the fundamental reason behind their failure in the sales department: *They had way too many features*.

When you start to discover the command approach to software present in such applications as Microsoft Office (as I described in Chapter 1), you start to realize how easy it is to add features to your software. But don't do it! Settle on a good solid set of use cases, and once you begin coding the software, don't add new features. Resist, resist, resist! Yes, you'll likely discover some important (but *minor*) use cases you forgot, and you can go ahead and add them. But don't keep adding more and more features. Otherwise you'll have two results: (1) You will release your software far, far later than you planned (if ever), and (2) People won't buy it because they'll find it overwhelming, just like these synthesizers that failed. (And maybe 20 years from now your software will be mentioned in a book as an archeological oddity, like I'm mentioning these synthesizers. That alone should be reason not to let *feature creep* take over.)

You don't want to just have a billion features in your product. Imagine if you had one menu, and that menu could scroll, and it would scroll endlessly, on and on, until you finally found that feature you wanted. Yuck. Or imagine if the software you used had only one toolbar and it had

350 buttons on it. Yikes! (I pity the graphic artist hired to come up with all 350 button images.) Instead, like the style use cases, your use cases should have logical groups. Then:

RULE   If you have a use case that doesn't seem to have a group, reconsider the use case.

You might have a good reason to keep a use case that's not part of the groups you created. It might be a powerful one, like *Quit the application*. However, most likely, either you're missing some use cases or you have a use case that you don't need. The use case about indenting every paragraph is an example of a use case without a group. By itself, it seemed a little bizarre and was probably the idea of somebody who has a fixation with indentations. But further analysis led to more use cases in a similar group, which ultimately led to my invention (oops, I mean Microsoft's invention) of paragraph styles.

Modeling Non-computer Gadgets with a Computer

Take a look Figure 2.1. This is an example of a gadget modeled on the computer. The idea behind this gadget is to control the device it represents.

FIGURE 2.1
What do you think
of this?

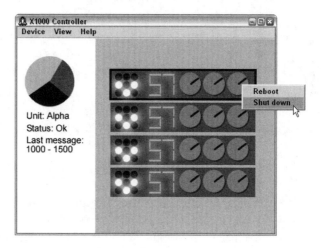

Not too bad, is it? Or is it bad?

The world of software has a huge division line right up the middle. On one side of the line is off-the-shelf software that targets masses of people. Off-the-shelf software has the one-size-fits-all mindset, where everybody can benefit from the same software. Most of the software people use, such as the Microsoft products, is off-the-shelf.

On the other side is software that is custom-built for a particular need. This is software used in-house by businesses, usually large corporations or manufacturing plants. Most of us rarely ever see the enormous volume of software out there that was custom-built. The fact that you're reading this book implies that you work in the software field, and if so, chances are high that you're working on such a project. Why? Because that's where most of the programming jobs are. Only a small percentage of the programmers work on off-the-shelf software.

I once worked on a software package that did real-time data acquisition for the wireless telecom industry. I also worked on a software package that helped salespeople look up current prices for long-distance phone service. (Most of my work has been in the telecom field, quite by accident.) Neither of these two software packages was ever for sale. They were both done in-house, one for use by employees at the same company and the other for use by only certain other companies. Other similar packages might be created for hire by a software shop, but they are still done in-house.

These custom-built software packages sometimes have a good amount of visual modeling in them, where the computer screens show a visual rendering of what looks like some gadget, either directly or as an abstraction. For example, I once worked for a company that created large circuit breakers for factories; we had a program that drew out schematic symbols representing the circuit breakers, all within a bird's-eye map of the factory right on the computer screen.

One example of this visual modeling that's not custom-built is the calculator program that ships with many operating systems. The one for Windows is rather ubiquitous. (Did you know that this particular calculator program on Windows has an option that transforms it from a basic calculator into a scientific calculator? Just choose View ➤ Scientific.)

So my question for you to ponder is this: How useable and how easy to learn is a program that essentially draws a device on the screen? Certainly you can't generalize and say all such programs are great, or all such programs stink, but I can at least draw out some guidelines for you to use when you're considering building such a software package. Among these guidelines will be some ideas whether to even attempt such a thing: Should you really draw out a gadget on the screen, or is there some better way to do this?

The fundamental issue at hand here is metaphor versus idiom. The calculator drawing on the screen is sort of like a metaphor, although really it's not a metaphor at all: It really *is* a calculator, not just a metaphor for one. (The file folder representing a directory on a hard drive is a metaphor.) Yet at the same time it does a wonderful job of drawing on some well-established idioms. Most beginners automatically know how to use the calculator program if they are familiar with the mouse and are familiar with using a real calculator device.

Therefore, when creating a program that draws a device on the screen, you want to make sure you don't lose the simplicity of your idioms. In the sections that follow I show you how you can do this, regardless of whether your model will draw a picture of the device or not. As a preview, here are the problems with the program I created for Figure 2.1. (I'll assume that this program is a virtual representation of four actual devices that the computer is hooked up to.)

- It's not immediately clear from the interface whether you can only reboot and monitor the devices or if you actually control the devices by attempting to turn the knob images.

- Are those LEDs or buttons on the left of the devices? I think they're LEDs but it's not totally clear.

- If you can turn the knobs, using a drawing of a knob as I did would be rather difficult with a mouse. (A slider control is better, or at least a control that looks like a knob but that you move left and right and is, in fact, a slider.)

Really now. Are we actually benefiting by seeing a *picture* of the device?

Now here are some good things about the program:

- Apparently when you click on a device, you immediately see information about the device to the left. You don't have to open a dialog box that stops the program just to see information.

- Although the program shows four devices, only one, which has a dark border around it, is displaying its properties to the left.

- The program has two levels of abstraction: One is for interacting with the program itself, and one is for interacting with the devices. I explain this in greater detail in the following sections.

My general feeling? Although there are three good points, my feeling is this program is *pretty bad*. Read on.

Defining the Scope of the Virtual Device

One of the problems people run into when they model a device is that they fail to lay out some of the purposes of the program they're building. Here are some questions to ask yourself:

- If you have the device, why model it on the computer? (This is a good question especially if the computer weighs more than the device!)

- Are the users of your model familiar with the actual device?

- Are you simulating the device for training and educational purposes, meaning that the virtual device isn't going to cause injury, damage, and death if used wrongly? (You may laugh, but I'm serious. Think of a flight simulator!)

- Does the actual device control something or does it perhaps read data from somewhere? If either of these is the case, then: Is the computer version going to simply *control* the device or will it behave *as* the device, alleviating the need for the actual device? (In most cases, the computer version controls the device, although in the case of the little calculator program the computer version actually acts as the device.)

Another way to look at these final two points is this: Is your software simply a management system?

A management system monitors the devices, making sure they are running and there aren't any problems. But the management system doesn't actually acquire any data that the devices use. For example, a telecommunications network would have several devices that handle the phone call routing. In the middle would be a management computer that monitors the devices and makes sure they are functioning. If any devices aren't functioning, the management computer might notify some other devices of the problem so the other devices can pick up the additional load. But the management computer doesn't receive any data about the phone calls and the work the devices are actually doing. Why? Because it doesn't care about that information.

My experience is that people creating software such as this all too often skip these fundamental questions. Answer these questions up front and you will be a step ahead of the crowd.

Here's another question: Will the computer be communicating directly with the devices or through various bridge devices?

Figure 2.2 shows an example of a setup where a central computer is controlling several devices. The computer sits in the middle *managing* the network of devices, and the devices all radiate outward from the central management computer.

Figure 2.3 shows an alternate approach. In this case the central computer is still managing the devices, but only through *bridges* that are themselves management devices. The central computer interacts only with the bridge devices, which provide filtered information back to the central computer. This is common in telecom and electrical power management systems.

When you model a real-world device, you want to make sure that both you and the people requiring and using the software are in agreement on what the function of the software will be and what the answers to these questions are. Putting it this simply might seem trivial, but believe me, your users might be expecting something different from what they described! You want to build something they can *use*. Remember, our goal here is to build highly useable software.

FIGURE 2.2
The central computer controls several devices.

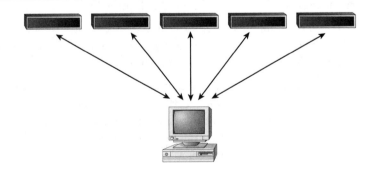

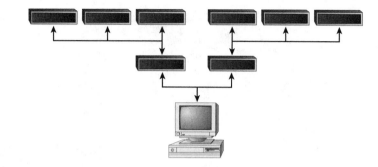

FIGURE 2.3
The central computer controls the devices through two bridges.

Building the Virtual Interface

The virtual device on the computer will ultimately have two levels of interaction: One is where the user interacts with the device on the computer screen. The other is the usual Windows ways of interacting with the software itself. I call these two levels of interaction the device level and the software level, respectively.

But if you're not sure what I mean by this, here's a good example. If you develop for the Palm operating system, you have probably seen the Palm Emulator. This is a piece of software that runs on a Windows computer that looks like a Palm device and runs Palm software. It's an emulator complete with an interpreter that reads and executes the Motorola assembly code in the Palm software. The idea is that when you're writing software for the Palm, you can run it on your PC and test it and debug it without having to keep transferring the software to the device itself. (I do some Palm software development, and this tool is a lifesaver.)

The Palm emulator is a pretty good example of how to draw the interface while remaining true to both the device itself and the idioms of the Windows operating system. Take a look at Figure 2.4. This figure shows the Palm Emulator running a Sony Device skin. The picture looks almost shockingly like the real device, right down to the correct color for the metal. And the emulator functions like the device, too: If you click the little image that looks like a house, the screen switches to the list of applications in icon form, just like the real device. And if you click an icon on the screen, just like in the real device, the program the icon represents will run.

But the program also follows the Windows standards. A device without a mouse (as is the case with this device) doesn't provide for a right-click (you just tap the screen with a stylus). That means the developers of the emulator were free to make use of this "leftover" user interaction, the right-click. When you right-click anywhere on the emulator, you see the pop-up menu shown in Figure 2.4.

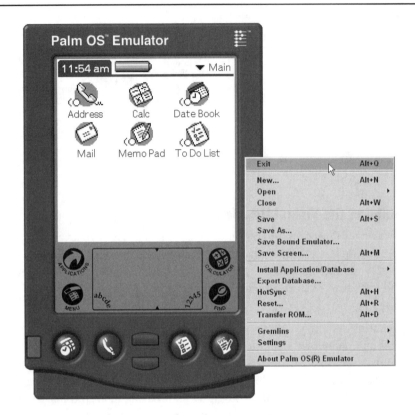

The device, as you can see, has the two levels of interaction I described:

- Interaction with the emulated device through an interface that mimics the device's interface. This is the device level of interaction. On this level you are *using* the virtual device.

- Configuration of the device through the Windows interface; in this case, in the form of a pop-up menu. This is the software level of interaction, where you're controlling the software representing the device.

Look at the pop-up menu and you can see some familiar Windows functions: New, Open, Close, Save, Save As, and About. You also have some interaction that's particular to this software: Save Bound Emulator, Save Screen, and so on. The Install Application Database is particularly interesting; the submenu shows a list of applications you've recently installed, along with an Other... item that lets you choose a program to install.

Now why would the installation be on the Windows level and not the device level of interaction? Don't you install software on the actual device by using the device? Yes, but not by clicking icons and interacting with the device in the way you interact with its programs. Instead, you run the Palm HotSync Manager software on the PC, which transfers software to the device. That's not part of the device's usual interface. Thus, the makers of the emulator needed a way to install software on the emulator, too. And so they simply included a menu item, which displays a simple File Open menu.

Yes, they could have been difficult and included a HotSync Emulator, which transfers software to the emulator in the same way the HotSync Manager transfers software to the actual device. But come on, that would have been a bit cumbersome. A simple File Open box was all that was needed.

RULE   Remember as you are modeling your devices to be aware of the two levels of interaction.

This will be the case even if you're not drawing the device on the screen as the Palm Emulator does. For example, later on when I talk about class design, I'm going to discuss a phone dialer program. This is a program that uses your modem to dial a telephone number for you, and then you pick up the actual phone and speak. The phone dialer program has two levels of interaction: On one level, you interact with the phone. You tell it to dial, even if you don't see a silly picture of a telephone. (And yes, if it is a picture, how much you want to bet it will be an antique phone?) But you can probably do things that are outside of the device; I would hope that you can save your phone number list. That's on the software level of interaction.

Take a look at the calculator program, as another example. This also has two levels: You can push the buttons (or just type the numbers) and do math calculations, thereby interacting with the calculator. Or you can click the View menu and toggle between standard and scientific view, where the calculator will transform from a circa-'70s piece of junk to a more modern scientific calculator. (I only wish the little junky calculator in the attic had a button that would transform it into a modern calculator!) This transformation is on the software level of interaction.

But what if the calculator program didn't have a transformation between types of calculators? Then you will probably have a minimal software level of interaction, but that's okay. You'll still probably want a Help menu, and certainly a File menu with an Exit item (or at least some way to exit the software).

RULE   When designing the two levels of interaction, if you have minimal features on the software level of interaction, try to think what might be missing. Adding to this level will greatly enhance the functionality of your product, making for a more sophisticated, professional product.

The phone dialer lets you actually save phone numbers; the Palm Emulator lets you save sessions. Without these features, the software would have considerably less *usability*.

In the next section I talk about the specific issue of sessions and how you will probably at least want this basic functionality in your software level of interaction. Then after that short discussion, I talk about another feature, that of Undo.

Saving and Loading Sessions

While I can't tell you exactly how the notion of a session would apply to your specific software product, I can give you examples of how to do it. Does your software need sessions? In other words, do your users need to be able to save the current state of the virtual device and reload it later? Most likely.

The calculator program doesn't allow for sessions, but I can think of a simple way that would make the program just a little bit more useable. While a Save/Save As mechanism would be a bit too much for the calculator program (and add a level of confusion), the program could benefit from simply saving its current state and restoring it when it starts back up.

From a programming perspective, this would be incredibly easy. You can save the current state either to a text file or, if you're on Windows, to the Registry. Here's some of the data that the program might save:

- The current value that's showing on the display
- Whether the calculator is presently in standard or scientific mode
- If in scientific mode, whether the calculator is presently in Hex, Dec, Oct, or Bin mode
- If in scientific mode, whether the calculator is presently in Degrees or Radians
- The value that's currently stored in memory

The calculator program also has some statistical features that I've never tried. I'm not kidding. But these might be worth saving as well!

RULE   Think about how you might save states in your software and how your users could benefit from such a state-saving mechanism.

SUGGESTION

Also, consider whether you want to simply save the state (as I described for the calculator program enhancement) or to include a full Save/Open mechanism. (The Palm Emulator has a Save/Open mechanism.)

Undoing the Work

Another feature you might include in your model is an undo capability. Now this might not always be practical; for example, the Palm Emulator wouldn't benefit much from an Undo feature (not to mention that it would be incredibly hard to implement). Or, if your program is used in a production plant and something gets soldered, welded, dismantled, or altogether modified, then, well, an undo just might not be feasible.

But an undo mechanism would certainly be nice for most systems. Consider, for example, a program that lets a sound engineer control an audio device on stage for a rock band. Imagine if the engineer made several changes to the various sound settings and said, "Oh wait! I liked it better before these changes!" There you go, this is a perfect opportunity for an undo.

Now please, if you're going to go through the trouble of including an undo system, please don't just make it one level of undo. If at all possible, please make a multilevel undo system, where the user can undo and undo and undo again, gradually stepping back in time. (And that means, of course, you'll also want a redo feature in case the user goes back too far in the undo.)

RULE   Including an undo system adds a nice touch to the software level of interaction, and the majority of software out there can benefit from an undo system.

An undo system is normally in the software level of interaction, unless the device itself supports an undo. (Most hardware devices don't.)

Since an undo mechanism applies to more than just a model of a device, I talk about how to implement an undo system in Chapter 8, "Under the Hood."

Deciding about the Virtual Interface

In the case of the calculator program, somebody sat down and drew up an interface that looks just like a calculator. That's fine, and it works pretty well: The user can type numbers on the keyboard or can click the mouse on the buttons. While clicking the mouse is a bit cumbersome, it works pretty well. Most beginners I've seen who are first introduced to the calculator program are able to immediately start using it by clicking the buttons with the mouse. Only later do they realize they can also type on the keyboard. (And why are the users able to quickly figure out how to use the software? Because it draws on the familiar idioms.)

But consider a more complex device. Suppose you are writing software that runs on a laptop that lets a sound engineer control all the electronic sound devices on the stage at a rock concert. One of these devices might be a sound wave generator that plugs into a keyboard, letting the keyboard player have additional sounds beyond what the keyboard first had. The sound engineer will use the software to do the following:

- Determine whether the device is functioning
- Choose the sound for the device

- Control the volume of the device

- Reboot the device

(That's good enough for our purposes. A real program one would probably do more.)

Since we already know what the software does, the next question is how to design the user interface: Do you simply draw a picture of the device on the screen or not? And from there what do you do? First off, let me say that if you draw a picture of the device on the screen, the users will be happy (at least initially). But if you do draw a picture, you must be very careful to make sure that that little picture interacts with the user the way the user expects!

REAL WORLD SCENARIO

The LCD Dash in the Car Died, and Now I Can't Drive It!

Talk about an experiment gone bad. During the early 1980s, my dad bought a car whose entire dashboard was one giant LED screen. The car had no speedometer, no fuel gauge, no temperature gauge…nothing. It had just one giant LED screen. When you booted (er, I mean started) the car, the LED would light up. Although it didn't show a big splash screen advertising the car manufacturer, it did have a speedometer, a fuel gauge, and so on, all rendered on the LED screen. The thing was a blast. Everybody would comment about it. (Oh and did I mention the car talked, too? I'm totally serious. "Your fuel is low." "A door is ajar.")

This whole LED screen thing was great until something happened: One day it died. Not the car, just the LED. No biggie, take it into the shop, right? Sure, but getting to the shop wasn't easy. My dad had *no* speedometer and *no* fuel gauge! The whole dash was black. He had no way to know how fast he was going and no way to know if he had enough gas to get there!

When he got back he wasn't so shaken as just plain irritated. But that was only half the problem. The other half was that it seemed the only real way to fix the LED was to install a new one, which required that my dad purchase a new one. The thing cost several hundred dollars.

I notice few cars these days have a dash like this. It was an experiment gone bad. Oh, and as for the talking aspect of the car? Let's just say that the words "Shut up!" became a common utterance among the passengers of the car, and that feature, too, is strangely absent from today's cars. However, I understand that some of the new global positioning systems have a similar problem. One editor said she was in a car where a GPS device was driving her nuts because it kept yelling, "You missed your turn. Please make a u-turn as soon as legally possible," over and over and over.

Now for some issues to help you decide whether to draw the device:

- Does the user of the software already know how to use the device itself?
- Does the user of the software *need* to know how to use the device itself to use your software?
- Most important, will the user benefit from seeing a drawing of the device?

In the case of sound engineers, most likely they will already know how to use the device itself. That takes care of that one. But in other cases, such as an operations center at a telecommunications center, while some of the operators may know how to use the device itself, others (such as hired temps) might not know how to use the device.

If you are sure the people know how to use the device, then you might consider drawing the device on the screen. But if people don't know how to use the device, then you have the chance to create a different user interface for the product that's possibly better than that on the device itself.

But if the user of the software is going to be managing the device (making sure it's functioning and that sort of thing) or reading data from the device, then will it even make sense to draw the device? If the device is just a box with no blinking lights and no buttons, then why draw it? Or if the device does have blinking lights and buttons but these things have nothing to do with the way the software will be interacting with the device, then again, why draw the blinking lights and buttons?

In the two subsections that follow, I tackle two approaches: drawing the device itself and not drawing the device itself.

Drawing the Device Itself

Drawing the device itself can be exciting and fun, but the truth is, usually you'll just be opening up a can of worms with a drawing. Remember, this drawing serves a purpose beyond simple artistic value. Your ultimate goal in drawing the device, then, is to create something *useable*. Don't just draw a picture of a device for artistic sake.

RULE   Just because your interface is a drawing of a device doesn't mean you need to skimp on the usability aspect of the user interface. Every rule about interface design applies here just as much, if not more.

Since you're starting out making a user interface that is different from what people expect on the computer screen, you're already at a bit of a disadvantage. Therefore, you have a double-edged job ahead of you: Be true to the device, while creating a user interface that still manages to adhere to the idioms people expect out of the computer (be it Windows, Mac OS, etc.).

How do you do this? By recognizing *and implementing* the two levels of interaction: that of the device and that of the software representing the device. Therefore, you need to figure out a way for your users to "escape" from the device and interact with the software. You have some choices here. You can:

- Use a pop-up menu that responds to a right mouse click, as the Palm Emulator does, since most likely the device's interface doesn't have a need for the right mouse click.

- Draw the device inside a regular window that itself contains a menu bar, and possibly toolbars and a status bar. The user would interact on the software level through these menus, toolbars, and status bar.

In addition, make sure that the software interaction level supports most of the usual functionality itself. This includes, when possible, the ability of the user to create a new session (a New File menu item), save a session (Save and Save As menu items), and open a session (Open menu item). Sometimes, of course, these menu choices might not be feasible, but such cases are rare. If you have a way of configuring the device, then you have a way of saving sessions.

But remember, if the device has a strange interface (unlike the Palm computer, which has a simple interface requiring simple taps with the stylus), then you will probably do more harm than good trying to draw the device. Drawing LED displays and big dials and actually making these things functional is complex and results in a difficult interface to use with the mouse; further, doing so totally violates the standard idioms we know and love. But, on the other hand, you might just be drawing these items for the "coolness" factor and they won't actually be functional. So my decision? Here it is:

RULE   Don't draw the interface unless doing so adds to the usability and the interface is easy to use. Yes, having a cool-looking device with knobs might be visually appealing at first, but I guarantee that if you have pictures of dials and buttons that aren't functional, the first thing people will do is try to click them.

Besides, over time, the users will no longer even notice the graphical appeal, and they will care only about the usability.

Look again back at Figure 2.1. Wouldn't you try turning those knobs? I did even though I wrote the program and know they don't actually do anything. (I just used a graphics program to draw out the thing and paste it into an image control in Borland Delphi to create the program!) I think deep inside a part of me really wanted to believe the dials would turn.

Given the choice between coolness and usability, opt for usability. Do the pictures of the devices in Figure 2.1 even serve any purpose? No. So get rid of them. Are there situations where such drawings do serve a purpose? Yes, but only if they actually provide some important visual feedback. In my sample they do nothing. Does the drawing of the Palm device serve a purpose? Yes. You can actually click the buttons and the screen in the Emulator.

The moral is, then, think twice before drawing the device. But if you do, make sure that the interface is useable.

Not Drawing the Device Itself

Suppose you've chosen not to draw a basic mock-up of the device. Instead, you're going to adhere to the standard of Windows or the Mac or X or whatever you use. Life is easier, right?

Maybe, but you still have to come up with a way to interact with the device; you *still* have the two levels of interaction. Consider the case of the audio box used by the rock band and the sound engineer. The sound engineer needs a software application that will let him quickly and easily control and interact with the device.

A good way to do this is to list the functionality of the device and then find user interface elements that are standard parts of the operating system (such as buttons, sliders, and what-not) that can serve to represent these aspects of the device.

For example, while the device itself might have knobs that you can turn, the software application might instead have sliders that are more within the standard of the operating system. While the device might have an LED output, the software version might use a static text control in the default font (rather than some ugly LED font) or use an edit control that the user can type into. The following graphic shows a slider control on Windows XP alongside an edit control. If this setup were in a program controlling an audio device, it would be much easier to use than a custom control showing a knob would be. You can quickly move the slider left and right, which changes the text to the right. Or you can just type the value into the edit control.

But remember as you design this kind of program to still make a distinction between the two levels of interface, the device and software levels—even if the user isn't going to be totally aware of these levels. In other words, if you're using the menu bar in the main window for the software level of interface, with such menu items as Open, Save, and so on, don't confuse the topic by mixing a menu item that says Set Volume Level in with the other menu items. Instead, divide up your menus and also allow the user to set the volume level using the slider control you previously decided on. That way, your software will still maintain the two levels. (In Chapter 5, "Highly Navigable Software," in the section "Constructing Sensible Menus," I give more details on menu design.)

Real-Time Interaction and Instant Updates

The virtual device you have on screen may or may not be connected in real time with the actual device. In other words, if you moved the computer and the device side-by-side, and you saw the image of the device on the screen, complete with its LEDs and blinking lights and buttons, would the image and the device look the same?

Or, if you're not drawing the image as is, but you still have some duplicate functionality (for instance, the numbers showing up on the LEDs on the actual device also show up in the status bar at the bottom of your software), then will the numbers you see on the device and on the software always match and change simultaneously?

In some cases, maybe not. If the software is management software, it may poll the device for data and update its user interface only when the polled information changes. If the device goes down and its LEDs all go blank, the device on the screen might not change for another 30 seconds or even two hours, depending on how often your system polls the device.

And when the user interacts with the virtual device, will changes to the virtual device immediately occur in the actual device? In most cases, you will write your software to have changes happen automatically. But again, maybe not; it depends on your situation.

RULE   If you're building software for hire, find out if the users require immediate updates or if polling is acceptable. And whatever your decision on the timing of the interactions, make sure the users of the device are fully aware of how the software will behave. If changes don't affect the device immediately, make sure the users know.

Further, whether you use polling or not, another important factor to consider is the communications protocol. In the telecom network management world, one common protocol is UDP. If you're familiar with TCP/IP and UPD, then this might surprise you. Why? Because a UDP packet of data sent from one computer to another is *not guaranteed to make it.*

Unfortunately, many devices in the network management world are set up to use only UDP, and so even if you want to switch to TCP for your protocol, you can't. You're stuck with UDP. But that's not always bad, because most network management devices send out data over and over (not constantly, but periodically) when there's a problem, and if a few packets get lost, no big deal.

RULE   When you design the software to interact with the device, make sure you are aware of whether the protocol you are using is guaranteed, and make sure your users are aware also.

Designing Classes that Model

Underneath the user interface, at the code level, you will probably consider building classes that model a real-world element. When done correctly, this is an ideal usage of object-oriented design. But classes such as these have their own set of problems, many of which are similar to the user interface problems.

Before I proceed with this lively and entertaining discussion, I need to clear up a definition: *proxy class*, or *proxy object*. A proxy object is an object that is instantiated locally on the computer that represents something that's not on the computer. In order to interact with the outside entity, the rest of the software interacts with the instance of the class without any concern for how the class in turn interacts with the outside entity. As far as the software is concerned, the instance of the class *is* the entity.

For example, suppose you have a device that has the amazing ability to connect over wires that are present in the house, send out a sequence of carefully generated tones that a remote system hears, decodes, and uses to connect to another similar device. (Most people call this device a telephone.)

Now suppose you are building some software that controls the phone. The software is a phone dialer. It's not for dialing into the Internet; rather, the software dials the phone line and you pick up the phone and hear the ringing, as another human answers the phone.

If you're using C++ (or Java or any other object language), you'll probably build a class that represents the phone. The class might have a member function called Dial, which takes a string that the phone will dial (such as "555-1212"). When the user of the program is ready to dial, she types in the number (or chooses the number from a list of saved numbers). She clicks the Dial button on the screen, which triggers some code. The code creates a new instance of the Phone class (or obtains an existing instance) and then calls the instance's Dial function, passing the string.

The Phone class in this case is a proxy class. It represents an object elsewhere, and to use the class in your code, the rest of the code doesn't even need to know how the class is ultimately controlling the telephone.

Another place people find proxy classes is in remote object systems (such as CORBA, or Common Object Request Broker Architecture). These are systems where you build a class library and put it on a remote computer. Then a local computer will use the remote library. The local computer will create an instance of a proxy class and call the methods in the proxy class, and everything seems local. However, the methods in the proxy class in turn send out data to the remote computer, causing the member functions of the class library to run on the remote computer. The local code feels like everything is local, even though the real code is running elsewhere. And then when the remote function is finished and returns a value, the value goes back over the wire to the proxy member function, which returns the value as if it had come up with the result on its own.

RULE   When you build classes that model devices, think in terms of proxy classes. Imagine that the classes are the device. To use the device, the other code uses the class, which represents the device.

As with most classes, the proxy concept has the advantage that if you remove the existing device and put in one with similar functionality, then you might have to change the class to accommodate the new device, but you won't have to change the code that uses the class. For example, you might have a new device that isn't really a phone; rather, it's a device that has the ability to listen for the dial tone and generate the correct tones for the phone call. (A modem can do this, for example.)

This means you wouldn't want to give your class a public member function such as this

```
void GenerateDualTone(int Frequency1, int Frequency2);
```

and require the users of the class to somehow know what frequencies to fill in to generate one of 10 digits plus a star or pound symbol. Further, you might not even want a function such as this

```
void DialDigit(char digit);
```

since the simplest function, `Dial`, should be all you need. After all, can you think of an example where code calling the class would just call `DialDigit` once and not again? Maybe if you're designing such software you might have a special need, but for a generic phone-dialing class, such a need is hard to imagine.

Now remember, however, I'm not saying *you shouldn't have these other functions*. Instead, I'm saying these functions shouldn't be part of the primary public interface, unless your class is to be used in special situations where you need such functionality.

| RULE | The public interface (that is, the set of functions deemed public) should be as simple and clean as possible, providing the primary way into the class. |

But what if you want to provide for specialized usage for the more advanced programmers using this class? Then you have a choice here. Before I present you with the choices, however, don't skip these and simply add these advanced functions to your public interface! You will confuse some of the other programmers. (Remember, there's a *reason* you're also an advanced programmer, right?)

Here are your choices. (And believe me, a lot of people have not considered these before.)

- Create another class derived from your class; this class adds additional, more advanced (and possibly specialized) functionality in the form of its own public interface; the advanced users can use this class instead.

- Put the advanced interface in the form of protected functions, and allow the advanced programmers to derive their own classes.

Now don't just pick one of these choices and roll with it. Instead, consider when to use each. If you anticipate lots of people requiring the advanced usage, then by all means, use the first solution, and write the derived class yourself and ship it along with the other class as a class library. But if you anticipate only a few brave souls venturing into the advanced realms, then I would recommend simply making the functions protected and letting the users derive the classes themselves. If they're advanced programmers like you are, they'll figure out what they're supposed to do.

Moving Forward

In the next chapter, I take you through the one issue that comes to mind first when many people think about usability: screen and window layout. There, I talk about what you need to think about when laying out controls on your windows, when creating dialogs, when making keyboard shortcuts relating to windows, and a lot of other great topics.

As you move forward, however, remember that usability extends far beyond just the obvious user interface. That's why in this book I devote only one chapter exclusively to organizing controls on your screen. See you there!

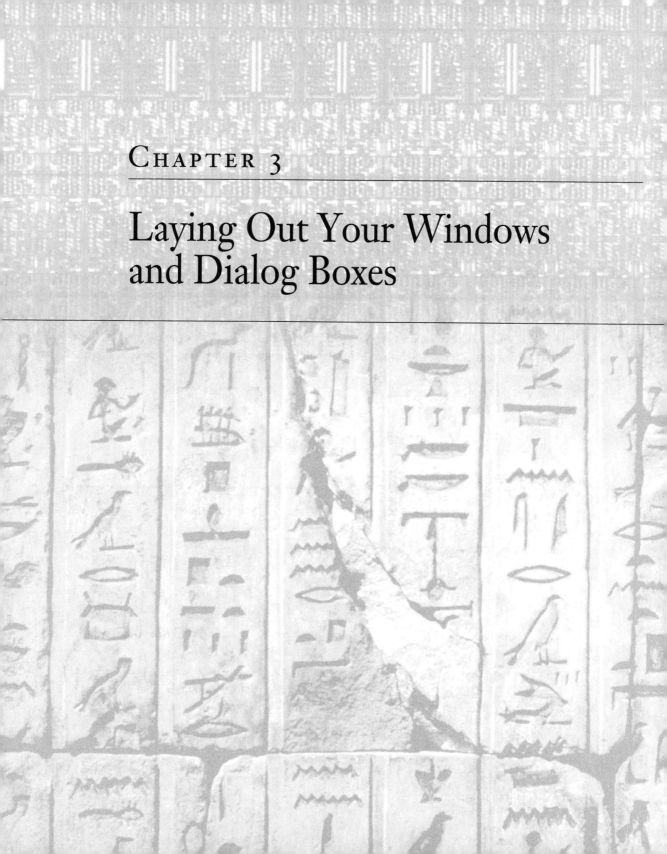

CHAPTER 3

Laying Out Your Windows and Dialog Boxes

I n this chapter you get to make a mess.

Or, if you follow the techniques I describe in this chapter, you can prevent a mess. In this chapter I show you several ways to make your windows cleaner. Having clean windows makes for useable software. What do I mean by clean windows other than all shiny and clear? A window is clean if:

- The controls on the window follow the standard idioms and are, therefore, easy to use.

- The layout of the window makes sense.

- The user doesn't have to jump through hoops to get to certain parts of the window.

- The window doesn't have extra information and extra controls.

- The window serves a clearly defined and easily identifiable purpose.

In this chapter, I show you some easy ways to lay out your windows so that these items are all covered. I also discuss several related issues that will come up when you're designing your windows.

NOTE Most of the tips in this chapter apply to both windows and dialog boxes. However, I make it clear in the text when a tip refers to only a window or only a dialog box.

Now for a thought-provoking tidbit to get your gears spinning…

REAL WORLD SCENARIO

"I Deleted the Icon, but the Program Is Still There!" (She Lamented).

In the earlier versions of Windows, users often ran into a bit of a problem when they decided they didn't want a program on their computer anymore. You can see where this is going: They would just delete the icon from the desktop. Of course, the software wasn't gone, but some software was so smart that it would replace the icon the next time the computer booted up. To the less-savvy users, this was like bringing an angry old neighbor back from the dead and was a frightening experience. (Remember, these people were afraid of computers!)

Why did this happen? Well, the obvious answer to us programmers is that the icon was a separate entity from the software. But why did it *really* happen?

The problem is in the mindset. Put yourself in the place of the beginning user for a moment: To such users, that icon *is* the program. They don't have much of a concept of the hard drive and the files on the hard drive, much less the software consisting of a set of files buried somewhere.

Continued on next page

Microsoft has tried to help solve this problem: When you delete an icon from your desktop that is a shortcut (or a link, really) to an executable, Windows XP will warn you that you're removing only the icon and that doing so *will not uninstall the software*. On the little message box that appears is also a suggestion to go to the Add Or Remove Programs section of the Control Panel. (We could probably debate whether this is really an effective solution; wouldn't it be easier to ask the question, "Would you also like to uninstall the software?")

When you are designing your software, put yourself in the shoes of the users. Remember that while you know that there's a whole lot of activity going on under the hood, and that the software may consist of numerous files, to the user, the user interface (along with, apparently, the icon) is the program. And that's true not for just beginning users; in addition to being a programmer, I'm quite an advanced user, and to me, this window I'm looking at that says Microsoft Word at the top *is* Microsoft Word. While I'm using it, I don't really care about the MSO9.DLL file that's down inside the directory somewhere, or what it does.

But let me take this a step further: Not only is the window the program, but if the controls in the window are complicated or hard to use, then that's going to make me dislike the program. I don't really care if the underlying code uses the latest technology and is highly optimized. None of that matters to me if the user interface *stinks*.

Organizing and Arranging the Windows

If your program has a main window (that is, a user interface!), then you've probably already got problems. Why? Because most programming tools these days make it so easy to create windows and organize controls that the tendency of most people is to simply throw together the user interface without giving it a lot of thought.

Here's a pretty good rule of thumb, however:

RULE   The amount of time you put into planning and designing the user interface for its usability is inversely proportional to the amount of time you (or the support staff) will spend on the phone fielding complaint calls and fixing all those problems the users complained about.

How does that sound? Personally, I like the idea of creating nice, solid, clean, useable software. In the sections that follow I show you how to do this.

The Usability Differences between Dialogs and Windows

You're a programmer, so of course you know what the difference between a dialog box and a window is. However, what I want to show you in this section is when to use a dialog box and when to use a window from a usability standpoint.

NOTE   If you've worked with the Microsoft Foundation Classes (MFC), you're well aware that you can use a dialog box as your main window. The Windows API even has a support function for doing this. When you use a dialog box for the main window, you end up with either a small utility that looks just like a dialog box (such as a Control Panel applet) or a window that has no resemblance to a dialog box. In the case of the latter, I would consider your GUI a window and not a dialog box; you simply used the dialog box features of Visual C++ to lay out the controls in your main window.

For my definition, I will consider a dialog box to be a modal dialog box. (*Modal*, of course, means that when the dialog box is open, the main window behind it is not functioning as it awaits a response from the user through the modal dialog box.)

What about modeless dialog boxes? They're a very, very, very bad idea. If you have a reason to open a second window while the user can still access the main window, then what you have is an *auxiliary* window, not a dialog box.

The purpose of a dialog box is to immediately receive input from a user. For example, when you connect to a website that uses HTTP authentication, a dialog box will open letting you type in a user name and password, as shown in Figure 3.1. The browser needs this information quickly, right here, right now, and thus used a dialog box.

Now imagine if the user name and password dialog box were modeless, allowing you to switch back to the browser window. Would that make sense? No, because once you were back at the browser you could surf to another page, and then what purpose would the user name and password dialog box serve? See, the problem is that when the user clicks the OK button, the user expects an action to occur and the dialog box to close. If the user clicks the Cancel button, the user expects her changes to the dialog box (what she typed and so on) to be forgotten and the box to close.

FIGURE 3.1
This dialog box
wouldn't make sense
if it were modeless.

Now think about a modeless dialog box. Suppose you have a Font dialog box that is modeless. When the user changes the font size, will the change happen automatically or only after pressing the OK button? Either way, once the changes are made, what happens if the user clicks the Cancel button? Will the changes be undone? It isn't perfectly clear.

Therefore, here's a rule to follow:

RULE   A dialog box is a modal window that allows the user to quickly enter information. Further, a dialog box has an OK button that the user uses to approve the input and a Cancel button that the user clicks to give up the changes she made inside the box. Finally, the dialog box might have a Help button.

If you think you have a need to allow for a dialog box to be non-modal, then rethink the interface. Do you want a secondary, auxiliary window? Maybe. Or do you want a pane? That sounds like a good idea, too. Or maybe a floating toolbar? Excellent. But please, not a non-modal dialog box.

So all this is great for the usability of a dialog box, but what about the main window? The main window does not have an OK or Cancel button. The main window has a menu that includes a File menu with an Exit item. The main window also has a close button in the upper-right corner. The main window doesn't stay on top of any other windows like a dialog box does.

TIP   Some usability experts say not to use a dialog box for the main window. I agree, with one exception. I'm fine if a simple little utility program uses a dialog box, provided an OK and Cancel button make sense for the utility program: The OK button should make the changes, and the Cancel button should actually prevent any changes from being made. A good example is the Display Properties program in Windows.

The Great Debate: MDI, Tabs, Separate Windows, and Panes

This section applies primarily to Microsoft Windows. One of the great innovations of the late twentieth century was…the Multiple Document Interface! (Or you can just call it MDI for short, but you pronounce it *em-dee-eye*, since MIDI (Musical Instrument Device Interface) gets the honors of being pronounced *middy*.)

To be honest, however, the MDI approach actually wasn't such a great invention, and it never quite took hold. The idea was that you would have one main window, and inside that main window you would have all your *document* windows. Each document window would hold a separate (you guessed it) document. What's a document? A document is a single file or distinct set of information that the user works on. An Excel spreadsheet is a document, a word processing file is a document, and so on.

FIGURE 3.2

Cascade arranges the windows nice and neat (to a point).

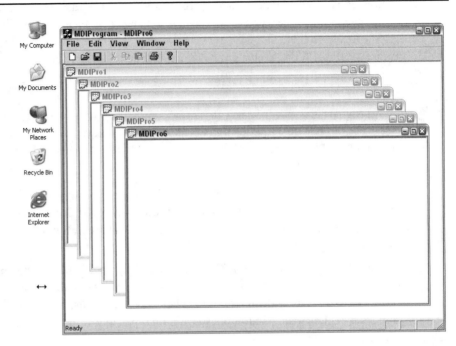

You could maximize your document windows within the single main window, or you could minimize them, again all within the single main window. You could arrange the document windows however you wanted, and you could even use the Cascade and Tile menu items that would move the windows around.

Let's talk briefly about these Cascade and Tile menu items and why they don't really work all that well. The Cascade item arranges your windows in a nice and neat fashion, letting you see the title bars of all your documents, as shown in Figure 3.2.

NOTE   Remember, my goal here isn't just to nitpick all the software out there while you sit back and say "Bummer," since you're unable to change what Microsoft or some other vendor does. Rather, the point here is to help you decide whether you want to use the MDI approach in your own software, after you recognize the drawbacks.

Many people would use the Cascade feature a few times because everything looks nice and neat. But it has a basic fundamental flaw: Take a look at Figure 3.2, which shows several MDI windows cascaded. Click on the upper-rightmost document window (which is also the one in back), and now you can't see any of the other windows. Or, if you click on one in the middle, half the windows will be obscured, making an even bigger mess. Or if you have lots of windows for a simple cascade, the windows will start getting doubled up, as shown in Figure 3.3. In this figure, if you count the lower-left corners you realize you can see only seven windows. But there are, in fact, nine. Window number 8 is aligned exactly the same as window number 1, and window number 9 is aligned exactly the same as number 2. What a mess.

The Tile menu item is nearly useless. Since it makes sense only with more than one window, if you tile two windows, your whole main window will get divided in half, and each of the windows will be either very narrow and tall or very short and wide, depending one which Tile method the program uses. For most applications, this isn't very useful. Add a third or fourth window, and you'll have no room to speak of for each document window. Nobody uses Tile (at least nobody I know), because it makes the windows too small to be useful. Figure 3.4 shows six windows tiled. Each one is really little and not particularly useful. (And imagine if each child window had several controls, or maybe a toolbar at the top.)

FIGURE 3.3
Cascade starts to become too confusing when you have lots of windows.

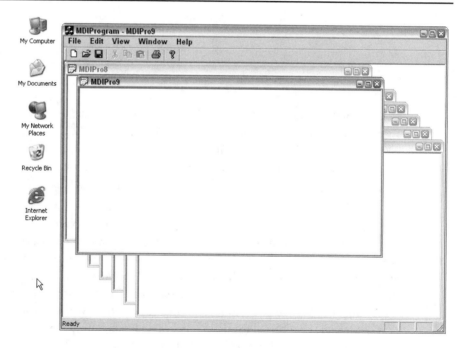

FIGURE 3.4
Tile isn't very useful with more than a couple of windows.

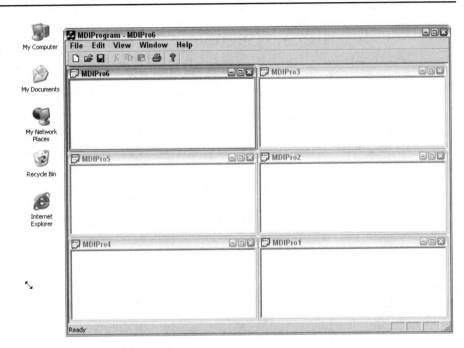

Nevertheless, you can still create MDI programs. Microsoft's development tools let you specify MDI applications quite easily. For example, the MFC Application Wizard lets you specify Multiple Document Interface. Borland's Delphi, as another example, has an MDI project type available when you create a new application.

Another problem with MDI is it's too easy for users to lose track of the document windows, with windows hidden behind others. But worse, the document windows don't appear in the main taskbar. The main taskbar shows the programs. Once you open the window, you see an icon. But what is an icon? In earlier versions of Windows, it was just that: an icon just like you would see on the screen. But in newer versions of Windows, these supposed icons aren't icons at all. They're little horizontal bars with the name of the window and a little icon imprinted on it. Nevertheless, the windows are minimized to an iconized version. *This is an outdated model.* Think about it: Where in Windows XP do you see windows that are minimized to icons? You don't. They get minimized to their appropriate button on the taskbar. The notion of being minimized to an icon hasn't been around since Windows 3.1!

But now that I've trashed the whole notion of MDI, when should you use MDI? While I don't recommend using it at all, most of the experts agree that MDI is acceptable if you're building an application with a single document window type. For example, if you're creating a spreadsheet program, and each document window is a spreadsheet, then fine.

However, I would like to suggest some alternatives to MDI. First, take a look at the way Microsoft Word handles its windows. It's one application, yet the separate document windows appear as separate buttons on the taskbar. Further, *each document window has the feel of being an entire instance of Microsoft Word*. In fact, you can't really coerce Word into running multiple instances. Instead, you'll just get another document window within the same instance of Word. (You can verify this by looking at the Task Manager; you'll see only one instance of WINWORD.EXE. Yup, it's still an 8.3 filename.)

If you plan to have multiple document windows, I recommend making your windows separate so that the individual windows appear in the taskbar, as Microsoft Word does.

SUGGESTION

> Having multiple separate document windows has the advantage that the user can easily navigate to the individual windows strictly through the taskbar, without having to first navigate to the program and then through a bunch of document windows.

But what if you really do see a need to have everything in a single window? I still don't recommend MDI. Instead, I recommend the following two options:

Tabs   Use the tab control to show a series of tabs at the top of the window, with each tab representing a document.

Panes   Divide your window into panes using sliders.

In the following two sections I discuss these two alternatives.

Designing Tabbed Windows

Figure 3.5 shows an example of tabs. This is a program called SciTE, which is a free editor that I personally use a great deal. (You can find it at http://www.scintilla.org if you're interested.) This program can hold multiple source code files (which are documents in this case), and it includes an option for displaying each file as a separate tab.

Typically when you create a tabbed window, you don't create a separate window for each document. Instead, you have one window maximized inside the main window. The tab bar across the top is itself a single control showing multiple tabs.

You would, however, have each document loaded in memory. (Some people prefer to use memory-mapped files right on the document file. I wouldn't attempt this on anything but your own proprietary file format, though, because Windows sometimes pads memory-mapped files with extra bytes at the end.)

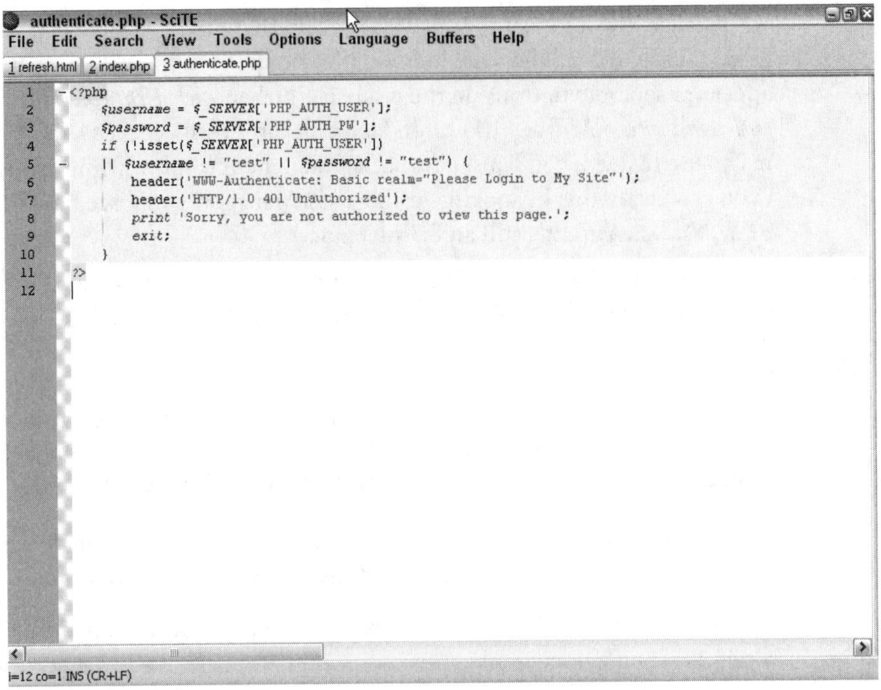

FIGURE 3.5
The SciTE editor has
a nice tab bar across
the top.

Next, you would have code that responds to the user clicks of the tabs. Check which tab the user clicked, and then display that particular document in the main window. The easiest way to do this is to have a C++ class (or whatever language you choose) for the documents. Create a separate instance of this document class for each document, like so:

```cpp
class Document {
protected:
    // member data about the document,
    // such as filename, etc.
};
```

Then, have a singleton class containing global information about the program, including the active document, like so:

```cpp
class GlobalInfo {
protected:
    Document *ActiveDocument;
    void Update();
public:
    void SetActiveDocument(Document *);
};
```

FIGURE 3.6

This is an example of two panes separated by a splitter. (Just don't use some silly animated dog, like they did here, please.)

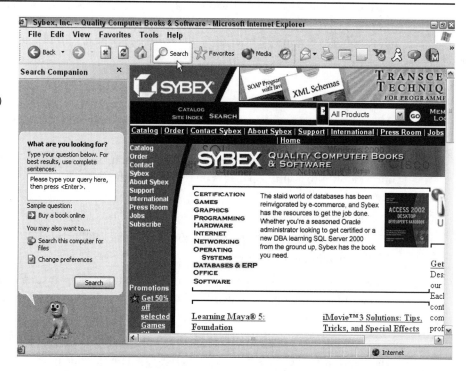

This active document would simply be a pointer to the document class. Then when the user switches to a different document, you simply change the value in the active document pointer. (Depending on your GUI library, either you would associate an instance of the Document class with each tab right in the tab class or you would maintain a separate association, perhaps through an instance of the standard map template class, mapping either the tab name or tab ID to the Document instance.) Next, have some kind of an Update function that re-renders everything, call it, and you're rolling.

Designing Split-Paned Windows without the Pain

First I want to apologize for the pun in the title. I couldn't resist. Anyway, the idea of a window divided up into panes is a relatively new idea compared to the bizarre MDI approach. One place you see panes is in both of the two big browsers, Internet Explorer and Netscape Navigator. Figure 3.6 shows an example of Internet Explorer divided into two panes.

When you click the Search button, for example, in IE 6.0, you see the window divide into two parts, as shown in Figure 3.6. Notice that the left pane contains a search window, and the right pane contains the usual browser window. But the cool part is what's in between the two panes: a moveable *splitter* control. If you hover your mouse over the line between the two panes, the mouse pointer turns into a horizontal line with an arrow on either end, like so:

When you hold down the mouse, you can adjust the sizes of the two panes by sliding the splitter left or right.

I call this approach to design the split-pane approach, because you are using splitters to divide your window into multiple panes. You then place different content or controls in the different panes.

But don't be fooled. Although programming a splitter is easy (especially in both MFC and Borland C++Builder, for example), designing a well-thought-out split-pane layout is not easy.

Notice two things about Figure 3.6:

- Each pane has a totally separate purpose. The left pane is an auxiliary pane to assist in working with the other pane, which I call the main pane (not to be confused with mane pain, which is when a horse has a bad hair day).

- The user doesn't have to stop using the main pane in order to do a search.

In other words, the left, smaller pane serves as a helper, while most of the primary work takes place in the larger pane. Imagine, however, if both panes were equally important. How would the less-savvy user react? Most likely he would look at it, wondering which pane he's supposed to use. In other words, he would be confused.

RULE   When dividing your window into panes, have one main pane, with the other panes serving as auxiliary or helper panes.

Microsoft has explored the use of panes in some of its products, Outlook, for example. Figure 3.7 shows several panes at work in Microsoft Outlook.

One important feature in Outlook is the way the user can choose to close various panes. (This is also true of the search window in Internet Explorer.) For example, I don't use the pane to the left (the one with the icons) very often, so I usually close that. This brings up another important rule:

RULE   If a user doesn't want to use a certain pane, let the user close the pane. But don't forget to include a way for the user to bring the pane back!

FIGURE 3.7
Outlook has several panes, and you can choose which panes you want to show.

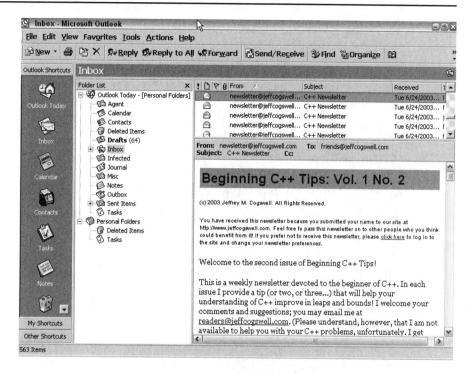

Windows Explorer (not Internet Explorer, but the file folder utility) also uses panes in an interesting way; the pane to the left shows property information about the currently selected item in the main pane. This is actually part of an important topic that I talk about later in this chapter, in "Avoiding Modal Dialog Boxes When You Can."

Let Them Be Free! Custom Layout

If you are writing a program that has multiple child windows in it, and the user is free to move the windows around, please be a good neighbor and include within your program the capability of saving the layout. If the user moves a window, please have the program remember where that window was the next time it starts up.

Now some people even take this a step further and let you give a name to the layout. If you've used some of the Borland development tools, you've seen how this works. Borland Delphi, for example, lets you name the current arrangement and layout of windows. Then you can move them around and create another name. After that you can type either name into a little text box, and the windows will all move into place for that particular name.

My feeling, however, is that this is overkill. In the case of Borland products, it's acceptable, because sophisticated users (programmers, actually) are using the products, and they can handle (and even require) somewhat more complex possibilities. But for the typical end user, providing a way to save different layouts is a bit much.

Keep it simple. If you're not creating a development too, then just save the layout when the program ends and read it back in when the program starts back up.

Remember, however, to do this on a per-user basis. As I've mentioned before elsewhere in this book, if you're using Windows, for example, you can save your information in the HKEY_ CURRENT_USER portion of the Registry.

Avoiding Modal Dialog Boxes When You Can

Earlier in this chapter, I spent a great deal of time talking about modal dialog boxes. Later in this chapter, I have more to say about them in terms of how to create the controls on them in a sensible manner.

But now I'd like to pause for a moment and suggest a different approach. Think about what happens when a modal dialog box opens: The entire application comes to a halt. If the dialog box is requesting information, and the only way the application can possibly continue is if it gets this information, then that's fine. But what about an information-only dialog box?

Consider Internet Explorer, for example. Suppose the web page I'm looking at has an image on it, and I right-click the image and choose Properties. Here's the dialog box that I will see:

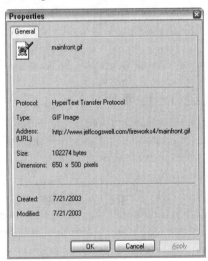

First off, why does this dialog box have three buttons, one of which is grayed out? Is there a difference between OK and Cancel? Considering that the dialog box is requesting no input from me, no, there is no difference that I can see. But besides that, does this information really have to be in a dialog box? What if I want to find out the URLs of two graphics and compare them? As it happens, you can actually highlight that little URL on the dialog box, right-click, and choose Copy. (I honestly didn't know this until about a year ago somebody did it in front of me and I was quite shocked.) Look at this:

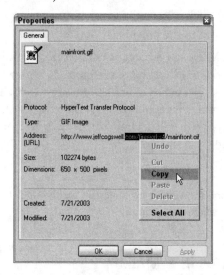

I'm sorry, but this is just a little bit too bizarre for me. If I want to compare this URL, I can open Notepad, paste the URL into Notepad, then return to IE, close the dialog box, open the properties for another image, copy its URL, paste it into Notepad underneath the previous URL, and finally compare them. And worse, what if the image whose URL I want to compare the previous URL to is on a different web page that I need to surf over to?

Yuck. Wouldn't it be easier if IE just gave you this information somewhere either in a floating auxiliary window, or maybe in another pane, or perhaps on a toolbar or status bar, and you could configure whether you wanted to see this information? Why should it be in a dialog box? (And oddly, the Windows Explorer application—the one for looking at folders—does show its properties in a pane off to the left.

RULE If you create a dialog box that is strictly for information purposes, providing no place for user input, then stop! Don't make it a dialog box. Instead find someplace else to put the information, such as in a pane or in an auxiliary window.

Keyboard Shortcuts and Windows Navigation

I've talked a great deal about keyboard shortcuts in this book so far, and I have more to say about them. The reason is I consider keyboard shortcuts *highly* important. And the keyboard shortcuts for navigating between windows are no exception.

If your program has multiple child windows, please accept the default window manipulation keystrokes. Here are those two keystrokes:

- Ctrl+Tab moves to the next window.
- Ctrl+Shift+Tab moves to the previous window.

Now unfortunately, Microsoft doesn't use these rules anymore. They use Ctrl+F6 to switch to the next window and Ctrl+Shift+F6 to switch back. Unless you have hands the size of a gorilla's, you need to use two hands to press these keystrokes. That's not good, especially considering there will certainly be people who try to do the keystroke acrobatics with one hand. Then with their other hand they'll get hold of a good lawyer, and you've got a problem on *your* hands. Again, not good.

SUGGESTION

> If you have a command for window switching, allow the user to customize which keyboard shortcuts move from window to window.

Laying Out Controls in a Window

If you're not careful, you can make a real mess with your controls. In the sections that follow, I describe the different things to watch out for so you don't end up with your own *dirty windows!*

The Purpose of the Controls

I'm not about to try to insult your intelligence. You know what a check box is and what a radio button is. So instead, in this section I want to briefly go through some design issues particular to some of the controls.

Buttons

Don't put bizarre images on your buttons. The purpose of an image or icon is to convey basic information so the user's eyes can quickly spot the correct item. When you're looking for the Recycle Bin or Trash on a desktop where the user completely rearranged the icons, you'll probably look for the icon and won't start in the upper-left and read the captions of each and every icon until you find the correct one. Even if you're visually impaired and need to hold your eyes close to the monitor, you'll probably still look at the icons rather than read the captions.

Now consider a button. Suppose you have an OK button and a Cancel button with images such as these:

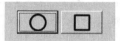

Which is which? It isn't clear.

NOTE   I feel compelled to comment about Borland development products, in particular Delphi and C++Builder. I love these two products; I've written books about Delphi, and I teach courses about C++Builder. They're great. But one thing that I will never understand is why they still have nonstandard graphics on their buttons. The two products have a class called TBitBtn, which stands for Bitmap Button (all the Borland class names start with a T). You can always spot a Delphi or C++Builder program because the OK button has a check mark on it, the Cancel button has an X on it, and the Close button has some strange figure that I still can't figure out what it is. I'm not going to say not to use these buttons, because I use them on occasion. But I do struggle with this, and my urge is to set the Glyph property (which lets you choose the image) to None.

Check Boxes

All I really want to say is this: Remember that check boxes are not mutually exclusive. The user can select one or more check boxes. If you are presenting the user with a choice where they must choose only one option, don't use check boxes. Use radio buttons instead.

Radio Buttons

Unlike check boxes, radio buttons (sometimes called *option buttons*) are mutually exclusive. The user can select only one. But what if you want the user to make multiple selections? Group the radio buttons either by using a group box or by simply keeping them close together. The following image shows three radio buttons grouped together:

If you prefer, you can group your radio buttons together; however, please make sure the items are closer to one another than to items outside the group. Here's a good example:

Finally, are two quick rules about radio buttons:

RULE Never have a radio button by itself. If you want a single selection, make it a check box. Besides, once you select a radio button, you cannot deselect it without clicking a different radio button. How would you do that with only one radio button? You can't.

And:

RULE When you have radio buttons in a dialog box, pick a radio button to be the default (or, if the dialog box reflects settings, then pick which one applies to the current setting), and make the dialog box open with the default chosen. Don't start the dialog box with no radio buttons chosen, because after the user clicks one, he cannot revert back to the "none chosen" setting!

Regarding the preceding rule, what if you want to give the user the option to select only one *or none* of the radio buttons? Some people have experimented with including a check box before the radio buttons. While the check box is checked, the radio buttons are active. While the check box is not checked, the radio buttons are inactive, meaning the user wants "none of the above."

This works, but another solution is to include a final radio button labeled None Of The Above. That's even better!

Labels

People usually use labels to give a title or name to each control. I recommend that you do this, but please position them carefully such that:

- It's obvious which control the label is referring to.
- You are consistent.

Some GUI designers prefer to give you more explicit rules than this, such as, "Please right-align your text." I do personally prefer right-aligning the text as in the following:

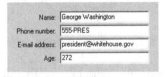

However, I question just how much of a negative impact *left*-aligning the labels would have on *usability*. In fact, while some people insist on a rule that says the labels should be right-aligned, the reality is that the usability studies have shown that left-aligned labels are easier for users. But this just shows how much subjectivity there really is in the usability world.

Be careful, however, when putting labels on your form, because the check box controls and radio button controls usually have the actual button to the left of the labels, while most people prefer to put the labels to the left of the control. (Indeed, if you use the built-in check boxes and radio buttons in Windows—which you should—then you don't even create a separate label; the text automatically appears to the right of the button.) If you're not careful in how you line things up, it can look pretty messy.

Arranging Your Dialog Box Controls

For English-speaking people, the natural pattern is that the eyes first look at the middle of the window and then move to the upper left and down to the lower right. If you're designing a dialog box, you can therefore assume that your user will start at the top of the dialog box, read from left to right, and work his way down through the dialog box until he gets to the OK and Cancel buttons at the bottom.

Remember, the purpose of the dialog box is to allow your program to receive immediate input from the user. If the user is going to be changing current settings, then please follow this rule:

RULE   Populate the controls with the current values. For example, if you are opening a Font dialog box, set the face (or name) and size with the current face and size.

The reason is that the user might make only one change. With a Font dialog box, the user might want to change only the size of the selected text but not the face. If you don't populate the Font dialog box with the name of the font and instead default to something such as MS San Serif, then when the user clicks OK, he will be quite unhappy to see the text he selected changed not only in size but in face as well.

How do you implement this in code? Normally, you would have a class for your dialog, and that class would include a constructor and a Show function. The Show function returns a Boolean value, true if the user clicks OK and false if the user clicks Cancel.

The calling function would create an instance of the dialog class and then populate the dialog instance with the current values. (You might consider having the dialog class populate itself by calling into code outside the class. Please don't do this, because doing so tightly couples your dialog class to the main code, making it impossible to reuse the dialog class elsewhere.)

How does the calling function populate the dialog instance? You can take your pick:

- Passes the current settings in as individual members to the constructor
- Fills a structure and passes the single structure (probably as a pointer or reference) to the constructor
- Fills a structure and passes the single structure (again, as a pointer or reference) to a separate function

I'm not too fond of the third item in this list. Other people may disagree (and we can agree to disagree), but I don't like forcing the caller to go through a whole bunch of rigmarole to use the class. And each extra function you require the caller to call is one extra piece of rigmarole. (Yes, rigmarole is made up of pieces.) Why force the user to do this

```
MyDialog dialog;
dialog.Initialize(&stuff);
dialog.Show();
```

when this is shorter and easier to remember:

```
MyDialog dialog(&stuff);
dialog.Show();
```

But other people have superstitions about passing data into a constructor, so the choice is yours.

At the bottom of your dialog box, put an OK button and a Cancel button. The Macintosh puts the OK button in the lower right, with the Cancel button to the left of the OK button, like so:

Windows puts the Cancel button in the lower right, with the OK button to the left of the Cancel button, like so:

Now remember, your code shouldn't change anything until after the user clicks OK. You can if you want, however, allow a slight exception to this rule in the form of a *preview*. In your dialog box you would include a check box (not a radio button, please!) with the label Show Preview or Preview Changes. Then the user can see the changes as she tries them out. You find this kind of thing often in graphics programs, such as in a filter or a color settings dialog box. But remember, when the user clicks Cancel, the changes better not stick!

From a programming perspective, a dialog box with a Preview option is kind of a pain to program. The reason is that you normally want your dialog box to live inside a simple class, and that class includes a Show function. If Show returns a true, meaning the user clicked OK, the calling code can then inspect the member variables of Show to retrieve the data the user entered and then make the appropriate changes.

The problem with a Preview (again, from a programming perspective, not from a usability perspective) is that the class now needs to know how to make appropriate changes. But please, since Preview is a good feature, don't be the mean, nasty programmer who says, "It's not possible," and forgoes the Preview feature. It is possible, and that's one of the themes of this entire book. (And besides, I'm a programmer, too, so you can't fool me.)

There are different ways you could make the Preview feature work, but please try to stick to good object-oriented practices. If you have code in your dialog box class that calls back into the main code, you are *tightly coupling* your code, meaning that the dialog box class isn't useful anywhere else, wiping out the whole notion of reusability.

Instead, provide a callback function. One way to do this might be like so:

```cpp
#include <iostream>
#include <stdlib.h>

using namespace std;

class MyDialog {
    typedef void (*PreviewCallback)(MyDialog *);
protected:
    PreviewCallback callback;
    int Height;
public:
    MyDialog(PreviewCallback acallback = NULL);
    int getHeight() { return Height; }
    bool Show();
};

MyDialog::MyDialog(PreviewCallback acallback) {
    callback = acallback;
    Height = 10;
}

bool MyDialog::Show() {
    // Suppose the user made a change
    // by setting Height to 20.
    // Call the preview function:
    Height = 20;
    if (callback != NULL) {
        callback(this);
    }
    return true;
}

void MyPreviewCallback(MyDialog *dialog) {
    cout << dialog->getHeight() << endl;
}

int main(int argc, char *argv[])
{
    MyDialog dialog(MyPreviewCallback);
    dialog.Show();
    return 0;
}
```

This is just a pattern along with some test code, and by itself it is not particularly useful. Notice how I'm passing a callback function to the MyDialog constructor, although I can optionally pass no callback. The Show function would open up the dialog box, set the default values for the controls, and include a Preview check box (all of which I'm skipping here). Then if the user clicks the Preview check box, or if the Preview check box is already selected and the user makes a change, the code would call the callback. (I'm just showing the call right inside the Show function, demonstrating where the user set something to 20.)

The callback would then make the appropriate changes for the preview and update the screen accordingly. Here, for demonstration purposes, I'm just printing out the value of the Height member.

This pattern is useful because now you can take the class elsewhere, and it doesn't have a callback hard-coded into it. I removed the tight coupling between the dialog class and the main code.

The one thing that I intentionally left out, however, is code that demonstrates how to undo the preview in the event the user clicks Cancel. There are several ways you might want to implement this. You might decide to call your Undo code to undo the changes if the Show() function returns false. But I don't like that. Why? Because then the Show() function has made changes even though the user clicked Cancel, and you, as the programmer creating the MyDialog class, are expecting the user to fix anything left around by the dialog box, even though the user clicked Cancel! That's bad.

Or, you could provide another callback that would undo the changes, and the dialog box code would call this callback from the code for the Cancel button. But now you're faced with a trade-off. I might be inclined to send in another callback for the Undo. While I don't like to have a million callbacks (each one adds more coupling), I do think this is a better alternative than the dialog box that was canceled, leaving a mess for the caller to deal with. (In Chapter 8, "Under the Hood," in the section "Implementing an Undo System," I talk about the specific issues of how your Undo system can be preview-safe.)

Now, moving beyond the preview issues, what about the following two buttons?

- Close
- Apply

Please avoid using these two buttons. If you correctly design a dialog box, you will have no need for the Close button. The Close button makes more sense in a modeless context, but as you saw earlier I single-handedly brought a complete end to modeless dialog boxes (or at least tried!). The reason is that no changes should take place (except for a possible preview, which is temporary) until the user clicks OK. If the user doesn't want the changes, he should click Cancel. Where does Close fit in here? *It doesn't*. The only way you would need a Close button is if your dialog box makes changes while it is open, which is bad.

But what about a short utility program where I said a dialog box is okay for the main window? If you find you're using a Close button, then please rethink the design and use a regular window, not a dialog box.

Now what about this Apply thing? Microsoft introduced the Apply button sometime during the '90s, and, if I might be so blunt, they made a big mistake with it. Please don't follow in their footsteps with it.

On the surface, it seems like a good idea: Make a few changes, click Apply and they stick. Make a few more changes, click Apply again, and they stick, too. Now click Cancel. What happens now? Do the changes get undone? In Microsoft products, the answer is "No, Jeff, they don't get undone." So much for the purpose of the Cancel button: When you click Apply, your changes are a done deal.

The problem with the Apply button is it's just too darn confusing. Don't use it. And don't use the Close button either. Stick to OK and Cancel.

But wait, there's more! Here are some others:

- Abort
- Retry
- Ignore
- Yes
- No

As for Abort, Retry, and Ignore, all I'm going to say is this: *Don't you dare*. Please, speak a *human* language. As for Yes and No buttons, they have (almost) no place in a dialog box. A dialog box is for entering information and choosing settings. There is no question involved and so no reason for the words *Yes* and *No*, which are answers to a question.

However, your program may have the need to occasionally ask the user a question. (But please, make sure this is only *occasionally* or *never*.) Since you're not allowed to ask, "Are you sure you want to quit?" because that's an insult to the user, you'll find that questions are rare. Still, you will occasionally have a need, in which case your combination of buttons can be:

- Yes, No
- Yes, No, Cancel

And you might want a Help button as well.

Don't Forget the Tab Order and Shortcuts!

One of my personal biggest frustrations is when I'm working with a dialog box, I'm in the very first control in the upper-left corner of a dialog box, I press Tab, and the wrong control gets the focus. Why did this happen? Because the programmer didn't bother to set the tab order, and what you end up with is probably the order in which she created the controls. Setting the tab order is easy (although how you do it depends on the programming tools you're using), and you should *always* do it. I don't use the mouse very often when working with dialog boxes, and I rely a great deal on the Tab key.

In addition to the tab order, remember that the OK button should be a default button that responds to the Enter key, and the Cancel button should respond to the Esc key.

Also, some people prefer to use keyboard shortcuts to navigate about a dialog box. Take a look at Figure 3.8, which is the Page Setup dialog box from Microsoft Word. Each control in the dialog box has a label next to it, which includes an underlined letter. The underlined letter is the shortcut key. For example, while this dialog box is showing, if you press Alt+G the edit control labeled Gutter will receive the focus.

But notice a slight disjoint issue here: The label control for the Gutter setting has the underlined G. But when you press Alt+G, the label isn't what receives the focus; rather, the edit control beside the label receives the focus. This is a simple programming matter. For example, in Windows, to specify an underline in the label, you put an ampersand, &, before the letter you want underlined. But doing so doesn't make the shortcut; it just underlines the letter. You separately specify a shortcut with the edit control using whatever method is present in the programming tool you're using.

FIGURE 3.8
This dialog box from Microsoft Word lets you use keyboard shortcuts to navigate about the window.

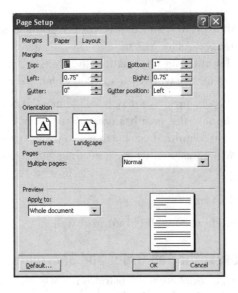

My Trip to the Grocery Store, or Adventures with a Self-Scan Machine

It looked intriguing. Day after day (okay, so I run to the grocery store every day...so sue me) I would see several machines at the grocery store that were purported to be self-scanning machines. The idea is that you scan your own groceries, running them over the laser that says "Beep," and the computer tallies the total. You then slide your credit card or debit card through a reader, or even feed cash into the machine, and pay for your groceries.

But I was scared. Maybe it was a premonition of bad things to come. But why should I be afraid? I'm a computer programmer for goodness sake! So finally I got up the nerve to use the thing. I had only three items, and I figured this would be a good day to introduce myself to the next Wonder of the Modern World.

In preparation, I stood off to the side, spying on the people who were using the machines. Looked easy enough. So I got in line and waited. Finally it was my turn.

The computer screen told me to scan. So I did. One by one I scanned my items, and the total appeared on the screen. Then just like when I'm only a customer in the traditional lines, and not a cashier too, I swiped my debit card through the little card reader. And the card reader said, "Waiting for cashier." So I stood and waited, not even realizing that *I* was the cashier in this case. I'm serious; it was waiting for an action from *me*. But I didn't realize that. As it turns out, the store staffs one single cashier (a paid one, not a volunteer one like my proud self) to oversee the machines. I figured *that* was the cashier the card reader was waiting for. So I called the friendly gentleman over. And he says, "Did you follow the steps?" I said, "Yes." He said, "What does the computer screen say?" (A slight argument ensued that involved me accusing him of talking to me like I'm stupid, but that's not relevant to our story, so I'll skip that part.)

And so I looked at the screen and everything seemed fine. There was a to-do list on the right, and I was going down through the items one by one. Each item in the to-do list was inside a rectangle. The first one said "Scan," which I completed. But it was just waiting. I didn't know what to do next.

The cashier finally lost his patience trying to help me discover the answers for myself, and he reached over and touched the screen, *pushing* the rectangle. Then the screen asked how I would like to pay. "Oh!" I yelped. I thanked him for his time and continued on my merry way as he walked off to help the next customer, presumably showing her exactly what he had just shown me.

What was the problem? The buttons bore *no resemblance to any buttons I had ever seen*. They gave no indication that they could be *pushed*. They just looked like rectangles to me, and that meant they were just colored, static text. Imagine how much stress the store could save on its own employees if the screens used more familiar idioms.

Hint Windows and Balloon Help

You've seen the ScreenTip on Microsoft Windows or the Balloon Help on the Macintosh. It's a great thing, provided you use it correctly. Here's an example of a ScreenTip in Microsoft Windows:

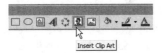

The idea behind the ScreenTip is to provide the users with a quick description of a toolbar button or control. The ScreenTip isn't intended to provide extended help; rather, it's just a short description. The ScreenTip appears when the mouse stops over a control or toolbar button and stays there for a couple of seconds. The ScreenTip opens, remains for a few seconds, and then disappears.

But please, if you're going to use ScreenTips, use them wisely. Here's a ScreenTip that's a bit ridiculous:

The Macintosh has Balloon Help instead of ScreenTips. Balloon Help tends to be a bit more long-winded and wordy. Personally, I'm not fond of Balloon Help because the balloons are a bit too flashy and they take up too much space in my opinion.

Programming a ScreenTip is easy. *Please don't write your own pop-up windows and fill them with text to create a ScreenTip!* The operating system has ScreenTip capabilities built in, and most programming tools include easy support for ScreenTips. For example, Microsoft Foundation Classes (MFC) includes a CToolTipCtrl class. Borland Delphi includes a Hint property for a control, which works provided you set the form's ShowHints property to True.

Layers of Tabs in a Dialog, and Piles of Dialogs

If you need to step the users through several tasks in a row, and an order is required, please don't use a dialog with tabs at the top. I've seen this done too many times. The problem is that the user can freely flip from tab to tab, and the user might not even realize she is supposed to go through all the tabs.

Instead, use a wizard, which is very similar in concept, but the tabs are not present. Instead, the users can move forward or backward through the wizard by clicking the Next and Back buttons, and the wizard will clearly show what steps they've completed and where they are in the process. However, please give the users the option to skip the wizard and go on to "expert mode." (Win-Zip, the popular zip and unzip utility, includes an optional wizard, which I can't describe because I've never used it. I prefer the expert mode, and that makes me perfectly happy.)

Or, better yet, rather than creating a wizard, keep your questions to a minimum, and fit them all in a single dialog box.

But if you're not walking the users through a series of steps, and instead simply have several categories of options, then you are probably okay using tabs at the top of your dialog box. However, keep the tabs to a minimum. Don't give the users more than one row of tabs. The reason is that strange things happen when you click a tab that's on the back row: All the back row tabs move down and in front, and all the front row tabs move up and back. The whole thing flips, and I personally find myself getting lost in situations like this. My fight-or-flight instinct kicks in, and I often find that this is a good time to go visit the candy machine. Forget the software. (And what if that's *your* software I'm using?)

A common place where people like to use tabs is in Options dialog boxes. This is fine, but too often people get a bit carried away. Figure 3.9 is an example from Microsoft Outlook 2000, where Microsoft kept the tabs nice and neat:

Unfortunately, this dialog box suffers from its own set of problems. For one, it isn't always clear to me where I should find an option. The Preferences tab shown in Figure 3.9 has some options that seem somehow a bit too interrelated to options on the Options tab, as shown in Figure 3.10.

FIGURE 3.9
Only a few tabs are present.

Further, the Options dialog suffers from the cascading dialog problem, where you can click a button and another dialog box opens, and then when you click another button, yet another dialog box opens! Figure 3.11 shows an example:

Do you know what the biggest problem with cascading dialog boxes is? The user's eyes don't always see a distinction between the dialog boxes. I personally have many times clicked the buttons of the dialog box that's in back of the current dialog box, because they looked like the right buttons to click. Ugh. Don't do this.

FIGURE 3.10
Some options are in strange places.

FIGURE 3.11
Where am I? What do I press? This is an example of cascading dialogs.

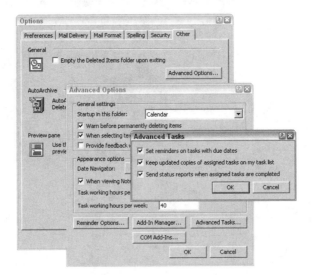

RULE   If you have many, many options in your program, go ahead and use tabs, but keep them neat and orderly. Or, divide the dialog box into multiple dialog boxes, but don't make them cascade. Give the user a separate command for reaching each dialog box.

And finally:

RULE   If you do include tabs on a dialog box, when the user changes something on a tab page and then clicks another tab page, makes some changes, and finally clicks OK, remember to record the changes for both tab pages the user worked on, not just the most recent.

More Window Design Issues

In this final short section, I provide you with some basic, miscellaneous tips about window design. For each tip that you follow here, you will have 100 fewer angry customers, and 10 fewer angry customer phone calls. Sounds like a deal to me! (That's obviously not a guarantee, so please don't sue me.)

Big Fonts, Little Fonts

Make sure you test your program using the Large Fonts setting on Windows. So many programmers forget this, and then they start getting calls from users explaining that they can't see all the controls on the dialog box! Very scary.

You can turn on Large Fonts (and even Extra Large Fonts, these days) from within the Display Properties in Windows. On Windows XP, this is in the Appearance tab, shown here:

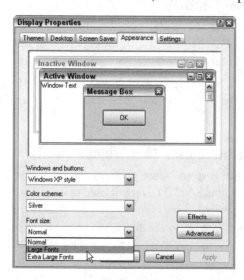

FIGURE 3.12
The status bar in IE shows you the URL of the link the mouse is hovering over.

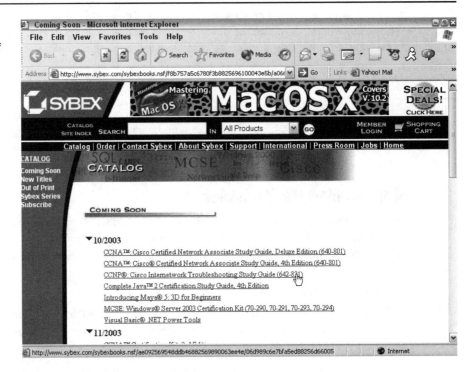

Adding a Status Bar Control

A status bar is an ideal place to display information about your program without stopping the program with a dialog box. Most of the development tools these days have easy support for adding a status bar to your program.

You can see the status bar in Figure 3.12. This figure shows Internet Explorer, and the status bar is at the very bottom of the window. The status bar shows the URL of the hyperlink the mouse is floating over.

Custom Mouse Pointers over Your Window (No!)

You can create your own custom mouse pointers that the user sees only when pointing to items in your program. Cool, huh? *No!* If I ever get hold of one of your programs and I see a custom pointer, I will never speak to you again, my friend. It's annoying and useless, and it adds no value to your program. The reason is that when I'm moving happily along and suddenly the mouse pointer changes, it throws everything out of kilter. The changing mouse pointer is akin to a misspelled word in a book: You're reading along just fine and when you suddenly hit something that's not quite right, your reading stops dead in its tracks. Similarly, a bizarre mouse pointer causes sudden (albeit slight) confusion, making your program harder to use. Just don't do it, okay?

(PS: Microsoft decided to add a custom pointer in early versions of Internet Explorer, and this pointer is now officially part of Windows. This is the little hand with a friendly finger pointing up. This is the one time we can allow it. But no more. No more custom pointers, please.)

Moving Forward

Well that's about it on laying out your windows and dialog boxes. People have written entire books on the topic, but I feel a better approach is to give you the general ideas, rather than fill a whole book with rule after rule. I do take up a bit more about windows in Chapter 5, "Highly Navigable Software," which covers the navigation of software. But meanwhile, I take a detour in the following chapter, "Managing Your Software's Time," where I talk about such little issues as raising your user's blood pressure to a dangerous level. Sound like fun? Not really, as I wouldn't want to be on the receiving end of *that* support call. See you there.

CHAPTER 4

Managing Your Software's Time

I consider myself a very patient person when dealing with coworkers and students. I understand that different people have different ways of thinking and understanding things, and so I'm okay if somebody doesn't quite get it at first. I can wait.

But this is *not* the case when I have to deal with computer software. When I click that button, I better get a response *now*. *Pronto!* In fact, if I find that something is misconfigured in my computer, causing me to have to wait an extra three seconds every time I open a certain file, I'm not above spending three hours to diagnose and track down the problem so that I can do things more quickly. (It's true! If you don't believe me, see the sidebar "My Own Hourglass Problem Solved" in this chapter.)

In the early 1990s during the days of Windows 3.1, I decided that most people have an hourglass threshold of about 30 seconds. But that was 10 years ago before we had been introduced to computers that are approaching 3GHz or higher. Today, I believe 30 seconds is way too long to wait. What if I have to wait that long for your software? I don't believe in breaking the computer (it's not his fault, after all; he's just a computer). But I do believe in deleting your software and using the competition's. Hee, hee, hee.

But what about custom software that large corporations contract to have written? Those people can't just delete it and go with the competition, first, because the users aren't the ones who make the purchase decisions, and second, because a competing product simply doesn't exist. And now imagine if you're the one who wrote the software, and you work at the company. You don't have a support staff, and you're the one who will get all the abuse of the angry, impatient people coming in to complain to you. (And you can't fix the software after they push you out the door and hire somebody else.)

Next, think about how much time is spent across the planet as people wait for the hourglass. If one million people in New York City alone lose one minute a day on the hourglass, that translates to about 695 *days*, which is nearly *two years* of time wasted per day in New York City alone! Think of the impact that has on the economy of New York City. Now think about the whole planet and the impact that has.

So how do you keep your users happy? Don't make them wait. In this chapter I talk about ways you can keep your software moving along, which will keep your users both happy *and healthy*. And that will keep your checkbook fat!

World, Meet Hourglass. Hourglass, World.

Ahh, I can see the ubiquitous hourglass. The hourglass has been around for some time (figuratively speaking, *I hope*). The original Macintosh had a little clock thing, and Microsoft used the hourglass. Before Windows NT came along, Windows was plagued with the hourglass, due to the single-threaded nature of Windows. Yes, it's true: Up to and including version 3.1, Windows did not have multithreaded capabilities. And so when that hourglass turned on, you were stuck.

When Windows NT came along, Microsoft added multithreaded and multiprocess support. And with that came a new icon: the pointer/hourglass combination. Here's this new icon from Windows XP (since I no longer have an old NT box to do a screen capture from):

This unusual form of the hourglass appears primarily when the operating system is working in the background, performing a task, such as starting a program. (In fact, the name of the hourglass in the header files is IDC_APPSTARTING.) If the program has to load a lot of DLLs, the startup can take a good amount of time. The pointer-hourglass icon, then, serves an important purpose: It tells the users, even though it seems like nothing is happening, trust me, that the program is loading. It's just taking a while. And meanwhile, you users can still do other work.

If the pointer remained a regular pointer with no hourglass, the users would think nothing is happening, especially considering that they can continue working, clicking icons or even trying again to start the program. But if the hourglass were to switch to the standard hourglass, then the slightly more savvy users hoping to continue working might not realize that no, the computer isn't frozen, and they can do other work.

In addition to the hourglass-pointer combo, Microsoft now supports a per-window hourglass as well. In this case, if your program is doing something that takes a while, and you turn on the hourglass, the hourglass will appear only when the user floats the pointer over your window.

This is a good thing:

RULE   If you're going to turn on the hourglass, don't turn it on for the whole system. Only your program is working. If the users move the mouse away from your program, since the system is multitasking, they shouldn't have to continue seeing the hourglass.

If you're calling into the API, just use the standard SetCursor function. This function will set the cursor for your windows and no others. And your users will be much happier.

Alternatives to Showing the Hourglass

Even though the hourglass works well, by and large, it is particularly rude, because it seems to be telling the user, "Leave me alone! I'm busy!" We all know what it's like to walk into a coworker's office only to be told that she is too busy to speak to us; now the last thing we need is for the computer to tell us this too! Life is difficult enough. Add computers to the picture and it can turn horrendous, right?

So before throwing up the hourglass (or, before choosing to omit the hourglass but nevertheless have your program work while unable to receive user input), consider whether your program really *can't* receive user input. That is, after all, the purpose of the hourglass: to inform the users that the program is busy and can't hear them.

Here are two important questions to consider:

- Can your program perform the operation in the background, allowing the user to continue working (and does it make sense to do so)?

- Should the user be able to cancel the operation your software is performing?

In some cases, either of these might not make sense. For example, if you're saving a file to the disk, a cancel operation might not be a good idea, because you might end up with a corrupted file on the disk. But for the first item, regarding doing the work in the background, to be honest, I'm having trouble thinking of an example where you wouldn't want this. For example, while saving a document, you might not want to allow the user to edit the document. But doing the save in the background isn't out of the question: You could copy the entire document's state to a new object and write that object to the file, allowing the user to continue modifying the main object. Then after you've finished writing the file, you could delete the copy of the object. This shows, then, that even if you think the task has no reason to be performed in the background, think it through carefully before deciding for sure.

Implementing a Cancel Button

Prior to Windows 2000, the print system in Windows has a strange quirk: If you started a printout and realized the printer was disconnected, and then you canceled the printout (by opening the printer window, right-clicking the document, and choosing Cancel), the document wouldn't immediately disappear from the printer window! Instead, you would wait, and eventually the document would disappear. Since I haven't seen the code for the print spooler portion of Windows, I can't know for sure why this delayed canceling was the case. But I suspect it had to do with waiting for the printer (which, remember, wasn't hooked up) to respond, and such. Or it might have had to do with the printer window attempting some interprocess communication with the print spooler, and the print spooler polled only occasionally for messages from the printer window. We can only guess.

But what I can say is that Microsoft fixed this, and Windows XP doesn't have the problem. When you cancel the printout, it disappears immediately from the window.

What Microsoft was faced with was the issue of implementing a cancel feature. Suppose your program is inside a great big while loop, grinding and churning, doing some particular job. In addition, you would like to offer your users an opportunity to stop the job. For this you create a window and a Cancel button. You follow the rules by adding code for the Cancel button. You're ready to start writing the code for the Cancel button when suddenly you get stuck.

What code do you write? Your while loop is running elsewhere. How can the code for the Cancel button stop the while loop? And speaking of "running elsewhere," does that mean you need to create a separate thread for the while loop? And then what? Do you just kill the thread?

Or do you perform some complex interthread communication? Yikes! This is sounding like a mess. And this is exactly what a lot of people are up against. In fact, this is such a bizarre situation that Microsoft gave us a cancel system for one type of process, printing. When your program starts a printing process, your program can also register a dialog box that allows the user to cancel the printout. But this is specific only to printing.

Since I don't want to show system-specific code, I'm not going to show you exact C++ code for implementing a Cancel button. Instead, I'll offer some suggestions. First, if you're using Windows, in which you create a callback function for each window, then these steps will work:

1. Inside the loop performing the work, *yield* to the operating system every few iterations. This allows the operating system to receive more user input for your process. (In the Windows API you can use the `PeekMessage` function.)

2. Have a window procedure for the Cancel button's window that awaits the Cancel button. If your work loop yields to the system, this window procedure will get called when the user clicks the button. Then you can set a boolean variable that indicates that the Cancel button has been pressed.

3. Back in your work loop, each time you yield to the operating system, you will then test the value of the boolean variable to see whether the Cancel button has been pressed.

If you're using a different operating system (such as the Palm OS) where you don't have a callback function, then you have to take a slightly different approach. Here's one way that I've used in my Palm programming:

1. Inside the loop performing the work, check for another event message in the queue.

2. Check to see whether the Cancel button has been pressed. If so, end the loop.

In the Palm system, without a callback procedure, life is a little easier, as you can see. However, the problem here is that your work loop now has to be fundamentally aware of how to check for messages and process a Cancel button request. (And further, you're also obligated to process other requests such as the Applications button so users can exit your program.) To many of us, that's coupling two separate items too much, resulting in code that's difficult to port and maintain.

Therefore, what I prefer to do is write a special function that checks the event queue for messages and then processes the events accordingly. In this function I can also check for other events such as the Applications button. But the really good thing is that now I can reuse this function in other situations. (And with Palm programming you want to do as much code reuse as possible, since you're working with a limited amount of memory.)

REAL WORLD SCENARIO

The Cell Phone: Love It, Can't Stand It

I love my cell phone, just like most people do. And, like most people, I have a lot of problems with it. One part I use a lot is the web browser, because I can use it to check my e-mail. But the browser has a very strange way of browsing: Each web page is a menu, and you can move up or down the menu. Yet at the same time the browser has a menu across the bottom that you can choose from. The leftmost item on the bottom menu is usually the word OK. If I push the left or right arrow, I can move the highlight on the bottom menu to the left or right. If I push the up or down arrow, I can move the web page's menu selection up or down.

But here's the annoying part: In order to select one of the menu items on the web page, the bottom menu must have the word OK highlighted. If, for example, I'm checking my e-mail and I accidentally press the right-hand button and move to the word Folders, and I click the green button on the keypad, then I will end up in the Folders list and won't select the item I intended to.

But that's just the browser. Some cell phones have strange organizations for the rest of the settings. For example, one of the editors of this book pointed out that he was trying to silence his cell phone and he had a terrible time finding the silent setting. It wasn't where he expected it to be, and he had to scroll through menu after menu until he found it. (Imagine if somebody were in a job interview, and the possible new boss was waiting on him to silence the cell phone.)

And how many times have you accidentally clicked Ignore when you meant to answer the phone? My phone has a separate OK button from the Call button. When the phone rings, if I accidentally click the OK button, I instantly ignore the call. Yet for all the other operations, I use the OK button. (The simple solution here is to make the OK button default to answer and allow me to scroll a small menu to the right, highlighting the Ignore word, and then click OK. This is better for me, since I'm more likely to answer the call than to ignore the call.)

When using the text messaging in my phone, one feature is really nice: The phone has a pretty good–sized dictionary and you can turn on a rapid entry whereby you can type just the key with the letter and then type the next key with the next letter, and the phone will start to make guesses on the word. For example, if you press the 4 key (which represents the letters *g*, *h*, and *i*), then the 6 key twice (which represents the letters *m*, *n*, and *o*), and then the 3 key (for *d*, *e*, and *f*), then the phone will first guess the word *good*. If that's not the right word, you press the 0 key (which has the word *Next* printed on it), and then the word *good* will turn into *home*. Press Next again, and you'll see *gone*, then *hood*, then *hoof*, and so on through several possible words. Often, the first word that comes up is the word you want, and this greatly speeds up the typing. It's a feature I love, and although it's a bit awkward as first, I find that I can type rather quickly.

Continued on next page

Unfortunately, my friends who don't like the feature have a great disadvantage: If they want to type an exclamation point, they have to press the down arrow, then the right arrow, then the OK button, then the down arrow three times (I'm not making this up!), then the OK button, and then the 8 key. That's seven keystrokes for a rather common key for text messages among friends.

As a consumer, think about how you use products that you didn't build. If you don't work in the telecom field and were not involved in any of the cell phone software, then you are likely a consumer of the cell phone. Think about how you use the cell phone and how easy it is. Then apply your discoveries to your own designs.

Don't Freeze Up the Whole Computer (or the Software).

If you have a task that you need to do that might take a while, please don't freeze up the whole computer. That's not being a good neighbor. Some programs that deal with communication have a tendency to do this; if the software encounters a problem, the software waits for a timeout, meanwhile freezing everything up. Don't do this. It's bad.

If you follow the standard procedures for the operating system, then you shouldn't have any problems. It's when you go out of your way to hack into the system that you get into a mess. One example of this is when you bypass the operating system and directly access the hardware. I've heard lots of engineers complain about this, saying, "But I *need* direct access to the hardware." That's fine if they're writing software for just them to use. But they can be sure that if such software ends up on my computer, it will be promptly deleted, and if it ends up on the computers of thousands of home users, it will result in a *lot* of support calls.

But along these lines is the issue of the software freezing itself. Some communications software, while friendly to the whole system, freezes up for awhile if it can't find a dial tone while trying to use the modem.

Here's a typical scenario: I start up the communications software, and I intend to tell it to use the local network rather than the modem. But I just returned from a business trip where I was using the modem, and I forget to switch the settings to the local network. The software tries to dial out on the modem, but I do not have a phone line hooked up. And I wait, and I wait, and I wait…until the software finally figures out that there's no dial tone.

This has a simple solution: *a Cancel command.* I should be able to press Esc or choose a menu item to immediately abort and not have to wait for a timeout from the modem.

My Own Hourglass Problem Solved

This is a *completely* true story (except for the obvious embellishments—but it really did happen). I have both a laptop computer and a desktop computer, and like so many other people, I was faced with the same old problem (grrrr) of how to transfer my files back and forth between the two without accidentally overwriting an older version. True, I could just use version-control software. But when I'm flying out the door with my laptop, I don't want to have to stop and remember to go back and check in the files on the desktop before I can use them on the laptop. (Remember, when it comes to computers I'm impatient, and proud of it.)

So instead I keep my files on a CompactFlash card, the same kind of card that goes with my digital camera. I have a reader on each computer, and I just use the 64MB card just like a disk. And it works great, except for one highly annoying problem: When I would open a Microsoft Word document that's on the card and then switch to another program and then switch back to Word, I would see the hourglass for anywhere from five to as much as 45 seconds! I would wait…and wait…and wait.

At first I told myself everything would be okay. I decided to just start typing and hope that the text would buffer (which it would). But little by little, my blood pressure began to rise until it reached dangerous levels.

To make a long story short, after spending hours upon hours hacking into my system, I figured out what was up: Microsoft Word maintains a working directory, and the software does some file and directory manipulation in a way that the card reader, for some reason, doesn't allow. And when Word gets stuck on a problem, it tries again and again and again before finally giving up.

What I discovered was an incredibly simple solution: I had to make sure Word's working directory is on the C: drive, not the CompactFlash card, which was the E: drive. I could do this by opening up a DOS window, making sure I was on the C: drive, and typing e:myfile.doc to launch a file on the E: drive.

I was incredibly proud of myself to have come up with this solution. Except, the fact is *I shouldn't have had to go through all this*. Some programmers, whether it was the driver developers or the Word developers, caused this to happen. It is reminiscent of the old days of floppy drives when certain situations would cause the old DOS to first always look on the floppy drive whenever a program performed a file operation, even though a hard drive was present. The computer slowed down and was difficult to use.

Microsoft Word should know whether the working directory is a removable disk or not and, if so, not use it for some of its behind-the-scenes work. I, as the user, shouldn't have to tell Word to always use the C: drive. But because Word has this usability problem, I was forced to stare at the hourglass much longer than I cared to.

Another reason for this is that when a program is waiting on a device, the operating system may actually think the program has frozen up. Windows XP is particularly interesting with this sort of situation because (believe it or not) XP creates a temporary "ghost" window that has a white interior, the same title as your program's window, and draws this ghost window. The user can drag this ghost window and click the close button. If the user clicks the close button, the operating system will respond with a familiar dialog box stating that the program is not responding. Then the OS may kill your program right then and there.

> **RULE** Don't write your code in a way that causes the whole computer to freeze up. Instead, yield to the operating system and allow users to cancel a command.

And while on the topic of freezing up, another similar "feature" that wastes time is that of grabbing the focus from another window. The most common example I see of this little problem is the pop-up reminders in Microsoft Outlook. I use the Calendar feature in Outlook extensively, and I appreciate the little pop-up windows reminding me of my appointments. But what I don't appreciate is that when they appear, they come all the way to the front and grab the focus. So if I'm typing this paragraph and suddenly a pop-up opens reminding me that I have to go to the dentist (ouch), and I just happen to press the Enter key, then the reminder will receive the Enter key as input and open the appointment window, taking me far away from what I was doing.

The Yahoo! Messenger program handles the pop-up situation much better: When you are talking to somebody, and you minimize the chat window, when you receive another line of text the chat window does not come to the front. However, Windows XP knows that the window changed and blinks the window's rectangle in the start bar, effectively notifying you, all without stealing the focus.

> **RULE** Don't interrupt other software by stealing the focus!

Shortcuts to Success: Bookmarks

In helping your users get the most out of their time, you can make your program faster to use by helping the users quickly get to what they need. One way to do this is through a bookmark feature.

Not all software, of course, can benefit from bookmarks, but a lot of software can. But to see this, you might need to expand your definition of a bookmark. Here are some sample bookmarks:

- A recently used file list in the File menu, if your software opens and closes files
- An easily reachable list of locations within a document if your software supports documents
- A list of currently open documents under the Window menu

- A most recently used item in a tool menu, such as a recent filter showing up at the top of a filter menu in a graphics program
- The most recently used fonts in a font list showing up at the top of the list (Microsoft Word does this.)
- A set of commonly performed queries in a database application, such as all products with a low inventory or all customers with outstanding payments (not to be confused with an outstanding payment history!)
- And, of course, the configurable list of favorite websites on the Internet

Of course, you don't need to limit yourself to just one item in this list; further, you can probably come up with some additional places where the bookmark concept fits in. (And yes, technically we might argue that the bookmark concept is a metaphor, but really now, how many times do we actually think of the little plastic thing with pictures on it used for marking pages in a book?)

When you include your bookmark, however, please include these features:

- The bookmark clearly identifies the item it refers to, such as which website or which document.
- The bookmarks are configurable and editable.
- The bookmarks can be sorted.
- The user can categorize the bookmarks and create user-defined categories (if there are many bookmarks).
- The bookmarks save when the program exits and reload when the program starts. (However, please don't make the user manually load and save the bookmarks!)

In addition, if you are providing your users with a means for a lot of bookmarks, you might want to include these features:

- Export the bookmarks to a file.
- Import the bookmarks from a file.

Typically you will want to export the bookmarks as a simple text file. But if you really want to get fancy, you can use XML or HTML. Note that I say "HTML" as one option since that's what Internet Explorer and Netscape use for exporting their bookmarks. Normally you would use HTML only if you expect the data to be read in a web browser. However, don't immediately assume that's crazy. Being able to list your files in a web browser is sometimes handy!

In Internet Explorer, if I bookmark the Yahoo! site, then I will probably want the text that appears on the menu to be "Yahoo!" But the data underneath the menu will be http://

www.yahoo.com. If you follow this approach, then that means your users can do the following:

- Choose the bookmark based on the current document.
- Pick the bookmark text.
- Edit the bookmark data.
- Delete the bookmark.

Internet Explorer's Favorites menu lets you do each of these for a single bookmark. While at the Yahoo! website, you can bookmark the site by choosing File ➢ Add To Favorites. This opens a dialog box where you can modify the information that will be stored. This dialog box lets you type in the text to appear on the menu item. You can also choose a category for the favorite (or create a new one). Ultimately these categories will just be submenus on the Favorites menu.

However, I find that this dialog box doesn't offer enough configuration. For example, some sites have a link-sharing system, and when I click a link and end up at a site, instead of ending up at http://www.somedomain.com, I might instead end up at http://www.somedomain.com/associateID=someone. If I bookmark the site, the extra associateID=someone ends up in the URL. If I want to remove the extra part and store just http://www.somedomain.com in the bookmark, I have to finish adding the bookmark and then go back in and edit it. That takes extra time, and remember, this chapter is all about wasting time. (Oh wait—you know what I mean!)

Therefore, in your Add Bookmark dialog box, if reasonable, please allow the user to specify the following:

- Text for the menu item
- Data (start with the current data and allow the user to customize it)
- Category (and allow the user to create a new category)

To implement a bookmark system, you will probably want to include a command system that takes parameters. Then, when the user selects a bookmark, you would call a command, passing the information for the bookmark.

Since bookmarks usually live as menus, you will want to store the information for the bookmark in a Bookmark object separate from the text that appears for the bookmark. For example, the data behind a bookmark in Internet Explorer is a URL. If you're writing a bookmark system for a code editor, then the data might be a named location within the code file. Or the data might be a filename.

You have several options for associating the data with a menu item. One possibility is that if your GUI library includes an extra data value with each menu item, you can store a reference or pointer to a Bookmark object. Or if you're just storing ASCII data for the data, you can put that data right in the menu.

I'm Embarrassed to Admit That I Couldn't Open the Door.

This is a topic I almost left off, because so many other usability books have mentioned it. But wouldn't you know, two days ago this actually happened to me. So this is a real-life experience that I'm about to share with you. But it's embarrassing, so please don't share this with my close friends and loved ones. (They laugh at me enough as it is.)

What happened is that I was on the road and I stopped in a hotel lobby to get a room for the night. It was pretty late (around 11:00 P.M. local time), and after a certain time they close the counter and then you have to use the little security window like you find at some banks and gas stations. But the lobby was still open, so I wandered inside.

After getting my room, I walked over to the door and I did the famous thing: I pushed the door and it didn't open. I pushed again, and it didn't open. I turned around and said, "Did you already lock...and then out the corner of my eyes (you can see this coming) I saw that infamous word:

PULL

Yup. I did it. I really did. I said, "Oh!" and pulled the door.

Now I'm not one to always blame my problems on other people (okay, not really, but this time I think it's justified). Usability experts (especially Donald Norman) have talked a great deal about the problems with doors. All too often, doors have a very strange bar on them that is flat and clearly looks like something you push.

Of course, this bar had nothing that instinctively told me that I needed to push it. Take an alien from Mars who has never seen the door, and it (they don't have hes and shes there) would have no idea whether you push the door, pull it, or just smash right through it. But we do have certain idioms that help us become familiar with unfamiliar mechanisms. The door had a flat panel that clearly looked like something I should push. But the panel stuck out a bit and I could get my fingers behind it and pull.

That's a bad design. If the door instead had a bar that fit my brain's usual idea of a "pull" mechanism, then I would have been fine. Instead I embarrassed myself in front of the nice young woman behind the counter.

A slightly more sophisticated approach is to store your bookmarks in a template container class that mimics the hierarchical structure of the menu. Such a data structure would be reuseable later on in other software. You would still want to link each menu item with an associated object in the container, however. (The real difference between this approach and just associating an object with each menu item is in whether you rely on the menu system to organize your data or your own container structure.) The problem with this approach is that if you give the user the ability to sort and organize the bookmarks, then you have to sort the container and the menus separately. To do that, you would probably sort the container and then completely rebuild the menu from scratch. Nevertheless, some people prefer this approach because it separates the GUI from the data. The choice is yours.

TIP   Take a look at Internet Explorer and see how you can also have the favorites appear in a pane to the left of the main browser window. This is a handy place for users to access the favorites and a feature you might consider copying in your software.

Finally, one very handy feature you might consider is the ability of your users to search the bookmarks. I'm one of those people who bookmarks several sites a day, meaning that as of today I have thousands of bookmarks crammed into my copy of Internet Explorer. One feature I would like to see is a search box where I can type, for example, *PHP*, and see all the bookmarks that have the word PHP in their title or description. Wouldn't that be nice? You might consider a similar feature in your software.

How Better Software Could Make People More Efficient

In this day and age, companies are always looking for ways to make people more efficient. Although we programmers tend to get obsessed with our work and don't think twice about staying at the office until 8:00 P.M. to finish up, people in other fields are out the door the moment the clock strikes 5:00 P.M. Therefore, the bosses want to get as much work out of these people in as little time as possible.

But also in this day and age, one of the biggest time wasters besides that little place known as the "bathroom" (or the "washroom" if you prefer) is the software we use. Software is filled with situations that cause users to sit and wait and wait.

Some time back Borland did something interesting. I believe it was their version 4.5 compiler, or perhaps 5.0, where they put the compilation in the background, supposedly allowing you to continue working. When I first heard about that, I thought it was kind of silly, because if I'm waiting for a compile, then it's not likely that I'm going to want to be typing in more code. That is, I felt that way until I actually tried it. Turns out that was an amazing feature. I could start a compile and then continue working on another code file. Bingo, the software no longer froze up the computer, and I was suddenly more productive. The boss loved me. People started saying "Good morning" to me. (Okay, that part's not true, but the boss liked me.)

I'm sure you can think of times when you use other people's software where you have to wait and wait unnecessarily. Now think of your own software. Does your own software freeze up at all or force the users to pause for a moment?

Maybe your program opens a dialog box showing information, when you could simply display the information in the status bar. If this is a common feature that your users use over and over, imagine what would happen if moving the information to the status bar could save each user 10 minutes per day. If a single company has 100 people, then if they each save 10 minutes a day, then that's almost 17 hours of productivity! Yes, this adds up *quickly*. Every bit of productivity counts.

In this final section, I close with some extra factors for you to consider regarding how better software can make people more productive.

Don't Reinvent the Wheel!

Today was quite a day for me. I wasted a lot of time. I was visiting my sister, and she has a DSL connection. I, on the other hand, have a cable modem. Once at her place, I wanted to hook my laptop up to her external DSL modem. She doesn't have a router, and I didn't want to go buy one, and so I just disconnected the Ethernet cord from her computer and plugged it into my computer.

But that wasn't all I had to do, oh no. Next I had to install the software that the DSL provider sent her. And that's where the fun began. (I use the term *fun* extremely loosely here.) The installer first made me watch a video (using Macromedia Flash) about how to hook the modem up to the wall, blah, blah, blah. Then once through that, I had to sit for half an hour while the installer put tons of software on my computer, including some kind of connection program that's *supposed* to make my life easier. In addition, the installer put some crazy new custom version of Internet Explorer that I had to later remove.

Once the software was installed, the connection software went through its business of trying, and trying, and trying to make a connection. Each time there was a problem I had to run a utility that would supposedly fix the network settings for me, and each time I had to reboot the computer! Being a somewhat slow laptop with Windows XP and a ton of auto-loading software such as a firewall, the computer takes a long time to reboot.

I had to reboot three times, and each time the connection software couldn't make a connection. And each time it gave me a rather obscure error message to the likes of "Incorrect parameters." That's it. It said the parameters were incorrect. The options were to Try Again or Cancel. *Cancel?* Excuse me? *Cancel?* Of course I don't want to cancel! I want to get online! And so I clicked Try Again, and the computer paused for awhile (I assume it was doing something, but I can't be sure) and then the same Incorrect Parameters dialog box opened, with the same options.

Since I'm a software engineer, I'm a bit more savvy than your typical user, and so I opened the network control panel and discovered that I now had a Broadband setting. I double-clicked it. It tried to connect and told me that the user name and password were wrong. And so I right-clicked the Broadband icon and chose Properties. In the Properties dialog box I saw an option for requesting a user name and password that was unchecked. I checked the option and closed Properties. I double-clicked the icon again, and this time I was asked for a user name and password. I typed the user name and password and was again told that the user name and password were wrong.

I went to my sister's computer, opened the network connections control panel, and found the same Broadband icon. I right-clicked it and set the same property that requests a user name and password. Then when I double-clicked the Broadband icon, the user name and password dialog box opened. But they were already filled in with my sister's information, showing me that lo and behold, I did have the user name wrong: I was supposed to follow it with an @ symbol and then the domain name.

I returned to my laptop, double-clicked the Broadband icon, typed in the username@domain version of the user name and then the password, clicked Enter, waited a moment, and suddenly I was online!

And so I finally got the DSL up and running. But let's backtrack just a moment, shall we, since although I was finally online, my blood pressure was still a bit elevated. What happened here? To ultimately get online, I skipped the software the DSL provider gave me that was *supposed to make my life easier*, and I went right to the network settings and did it myself. And you know what? Doing it myself was easier! (In fact, I showed my sister how to turn off the connection software and instead use the network settings. She now double-clicks that icon when she needs to connect and also skips the software that's supposed to make her life easier.) The error message the connection software had given me was wrong and incomprehensible, and the software wanted to reboot unnecessarily.

This has been a general complaint of mine for ages. Why do so many of my colleagues in the programming field get it into their heads that they need to write some software that will serve as a layer over existing software and that this layer is supposed to somehow be *easier* than the real thing? In this case, we have a layer of software that encapsulates the network settings. But the original network settings software is easier to use!

And that's the basic problem. As much as people like to bash Microsoft, the truth of the matter is that Microsoft has an entire usability group that helps oversee the usability of their software. And although the network settings section of Windows is by no means the most user-friendly software on the planet, the fact is, in these newer versions *it's not bad.*

Now during the hour I spent fussing with the connection software, I could have been up and running and writing this book. I lost an hour, thanks to two problems:

- I had to fuss with a software layer that was unnecessary.

- The software gave me incomprehensible error messages that offered me no real help, and then the software wanted to reboot unnecessarily.

> **RULE** Don't write software that serves simply as a simplification layer to another piece of software without doing a full usability study on the existing software. Otherwise, the software you write will likely be just as complex and cumbersome as (or even more than) the existing software.

What's particularly troubling, however, about this particular example is that the support people at the DSL service are probably getting inundated with phone calls for help on using the connection software, and if the connection software were not present, the calls would probably go down by 90 percent! And the managers and VPs at the DSL service probably don't even realize that the root cause of this high volume of support calls is due to the presence of the connection software itself, not due to just simple *problems* in the connection software that can be fixed. And so what do they do? Instead of scrapping the whole connection software, they try to make it better and better with each version, piling it on higher and deeper. And each time they introduce parameters that are simply going to result in *more tech support calls*.

But what's even more troubling about this is an issue I cover in detail in Chapter 15, "Book in a Book: A Guide for Programming Bosses." Why did this connection software even come into existence? First, and most likely, the DSL service was probably having some problems because earlier versions of Windows didn't exactly make it easy to configure network settings. But what followed is the extremely dangerous part: Somewhere in the company lived a programmer who said, "I can build you a program that will make it easier." And what did the bosses do? They said, "Go for it." And here we are today.

This is a rather touchy issue, because a lot of bosses and managers don't have a system of checks and balances in place to find out if the young programmer really *can* build such a thing and if doing so is even feasible. Further, the bosses might not know the whole software engineering process and how to do a full test of the new software. For more on this, see Chapter 15. For now, however, consider this point:

> **RULE** Know your own limits as a programmer and don't try to reinvent the wheel! Software is always more complex than it seems at first.

For example, if you need an audio playing capability on your website, don't simply assume you can quickly and easily write your own sophisticated audio player. As simple as software such as Windows Media Player may seem, the reality is that many programmers spent a lot of time working on it, and the programmers encountered many things along the way that they couldn't anticipate, and *so will you*. In the end, you will end up with software that has not gone through the extensive testing that the product of the bigger software company has, and you will end up with:

- Bugs
- Crashes

- Frustrated users
- More support phone calls

Know your limits, and don't reinvent the wheel.

REAL WORLD SCENARIO

Update!

Since I wrote this chapter, I visited my sister again, and we had another computer to hook up to her network. Remembering what I went through last time, I took a different approach: Let's forget the installation CD altogether and see what Windows XP can do for me. And guess what? I used the New Connection Wizard that's built right into XP, answered all the questions, put in the DSL user name and password, and within about *three minutes*, I was completely up and running without even using the special software. And even better, I don't have the DSL provider's extra junk (sorry, I mean *software*) sitting on the new computer. So again, don't reinvent the wheel!

Make Information Accessible

In Chapter 6, "Data, Reports and Printouts," I spend a good amount of time showing you how to present your data to the users. Here, however, I want to present some of this information in the light of time management.

Suppose you have an online e-mail account at one of the free web-based e-mail systems. Now imagine if every time you wanted to check your e-mail, you had to start the web browser, type in the URL (or choose it from a bookmark), wait for the web page to download (which might take a moment if you're behind one of the less-efficient firewalls), type in your user name and password, click the Submit button, get to a main page listing how many e-mails you have, click the folder name, wait for a new page to load, and finally see your e-mail. Of course, now you're seeing only the subjects; you have to select each subject to see the actual message.

Imagine that. Well, really, you don't have to imagine it, because that's exactly what you have to do for most of the web-based e-mail systems. That's not exactly the most efficient way to get to your e-mail. Of course, the trade-off here is that you can check your e-mail from anywhere, and for that reason I personally use a couple different free e-mail services a great deal. (In fact, for one of them I went ahead and sent in my $25 so I could get more storage.) And these web-based e-mail systems work really well, even if they are a bit slow to access.

But what if you had to jump through such hoops to get at all the local data on your own computer? Back to my famous patience (or lack thereof), I can't imagine I'd last long in a high-tech world. (See, computers have spoiled me!)

RULE When you're designing your software, make the data as easily accessible as possible.

As you read on, think about what your users have to do to get to the data. Do they have to make extra clicks that add a bit more time accessing the data? Is there a way you can add a short-cut to the data?

Moving Forward

In conclusion, remember to think about the patience level of your users. Since you built the software, you know very well what the software is doing when it stops and freezes up momentarily with that hourglass showing, and therefore you know that the program isn't dead. And you might even be running some debugging tools, monitoring its progress. But the users, on the other hand, don't know that. All they know is that they clicked the button and now nothing is happening.

But don't just focus on the hourglass. Think of other ways you can help your users maximize their productivity. Can you add bookmarks to give them single-click access to their favorite documents or commands? Can you think of other ways to speed up your software and make your users more efficient? Surely there's something you can do to speed up the software.

In the following chapter, "Highly Navigable Software," I talk about ways to optimize your menus and make your software more navigable. I show you how you can make it very easy for your users to get to the information they need. Then in Chapter 6, "Data, Reports, and Print-outs," I show you how you can present the information. As you read these two chapters, think about time management and how you can keep your users as happy as possible by making your software operate quickly and efficiently.

Chapter 5

Highly Navigable Software

I f there's any one thing you get out of this chapter, and nothing more, it should be this point: *Don't make your users jump through hoops to get what they need!*

By and large, people these days are in a hurry. And if you read Chapter 4, "Managing Your Software's Time," you're aware that many of us are impatient. We, as users, don't want to go through a bunch of rigmarole just to get what we need. For example, if I'm on the phone with my editor and he needs my agent's phone number and I don't have it handy, I want to be able to open my contacts database and instantly get the answers, all with mouse clicks, since I can use the mouse with one hand while holding the phone in the other hand, but I can't type well with one hand.

We're all familiar with the term navigate when it comes to browsing the web (especially since Netscape's web browser is called Navigator). But what does the term mean in reference to software in general? When I say navigate, I'm referring to how you get to where you need to be, or the order of tasks you use to accomplish what you need to do. For example, if you need to look up a phone number in your contacts program, do you need to open a menu, then open a second cascading menu, then watch a dialog box open, then click a bunch of choices in the dialog box, then click OK, and then…? Well, you get the idea. Instead, a better choice is that you click a toolbar button and instantly you see the list of contacts. Scroll down and you can find the one you need. Or, if the contact database is too huge, you should be able to easily type in the first couple of letters of the last name, for example, and quickly get to the item you need. The difference between the former and the latter is whether or not the software is highly navigable.

For this chapter, then, I would like to define highly navigable software as *software that allows you to get to your information using a minimal number of mouse clicks and key presses without having to jump through hoops.* (By jumping through hoops, I mean you don't have to traverse several menus, for example, even though doing so requires only a few mouse clicks.) In this chapter, I show you how to make your software highly navigable. As you read this chapter, remember these words of wisdom: The shortest distance between two points is a straight line.

While being literally true in geometry, this axiom is also true in using programs. Don't make your users jump through hoops and navigate a gazillion menus to get to where they need to be. Let them go right there; let them follow a straight line.

Avoiding Hoop-Jumping

Every time the user needs to click something or type something to reach a final goal, that user is, quite likely, performing one extra, unnecessary step. Usability guru Alan Cooper calls all these extra mouse clicks and key presses *excise tasks*. The term excise is a good one because it's normally used in reference to taxes. Anything you make your user do that's unnecessary is taxing the user in many ways, including the user's patience. If you read Chapter 4, you saw a story

REAL WORLD SCENARIO

The Case of the Misshapen Ice Cubes

This one will never cease to amaze me. A lot of refrigerators come with a built-in icemaker inside the freezer. The icemaker makes ice cubes and dumps them into a plastic bin; you've certainly seen this kind of contraption. It's a great idea; you never need to fill ice trays with water.

But what I just don't understand is why the ice "cubes" are actually a half-moon shape! Invariably, when I put ice in a glass, one of the ice moons will go right up to the top of the glass when I tip the glass, right where my mouth touches the glass. And the ice moon will rest perfectly along the edge of the glass, with its curved side along the curve of the glass, resulting in a perfectly neat little dam, blocking the water from flowing into my mouth.

Now come on. How many refrigerators will it take before they realize that this is a problem? (Or maybe I'm crazy and nobody else has this problem?) But the real issue is this: As a user of this product, I have to wonder whether there isn't a better way to shape the ice cubes. Is it simply not possible to shape them any other way? I seriously doubt that it's impossible to create them in a different shape. Now think how many times users are told, "It's just the way the computer has to do it and there's no other way." Nonsense. There's *always* a better way. Don't release software with bugs, and if people find bugs, fix them and make it better.

about cell phones and how you need to press a million keys just to enter an exclamation point when typing a text message. That's definitely excise.

I like the term *hoop-jumping* because for me that's more what's happening. I think of when I grew up in Michigan and in the middle of winter in college what it was like having to go out to the mailboxes to check the mail. I couldn't just run out; I had to put on my heavy boots and my heavy coat and get all "bundled up" (as we Northerners would say), *just to go check the mail.*

How do you recognize hoop-jumping? By remembering that your software is nothing but a tool. For years, I've been preaching this point to my students and clients: A software package is a tool like the telephone. When you are sitting at your desk talking on the phone, you don't want to have to be aware of the phone. Your goal at the time is to have a conversation, and, most likely, you're thinking about the person you're talking to and the topic of discussion. The moment something goes wrong (static on the line, strange noises, the phone falling on the floor, the cord falling out of the wall, and so on) is the moment that you are suddenly aware of the tool.

Software should be the same way. Right now as I'm typing this sentence, my brain is thinking about software usability. If I also had to think about where the mouse pointer is and if I also had to constantly click a bunch of menus and buttons, then my brain would not be able to focus on the task at hand, which is writing about usability. And that would be the moment the software becomes less of a tool and more of an annoyance.

In order to minimize (and all-out *eradicate!*) hoop-jumping, the first thing you want to do is recognize the three levels of users:

- Beginners and "newbies"
- Intermediates
- Power users

Also, I would probably consider a fourth level, programmers, if you're developing a product for other programmers. However, if you're developing a package for programmers (such as an IDE), you're still going to have the three levels of users in this list:

- Beginner programmers who are fumbling their way through your product
- Some people comfortable with the product
- Power users who are developing macros, add-ins, and other tools for your product to get the most out of it

Now this might come as a surprise to you, but most usability experts have figured something out: Menus are for beginners and also for intermediates and power users when they use a feature they haven't used before. Part of the reason for this is that menus provide a nice textual list that the users can easily read and scan with their eyes. While that's not true in all cases (I still use the File ➤ Exit menu and the File➤ Print menu), it is true in many cases. In general, here is what people use:

- Beginners use menus.
- Intermediates use toolbar buttons.
- Power users use shortcut keys and macros.

I will personally attest to the shortcut keys and macros. I did one project whereby I had to put a strikethrough through certain words in the document. But I wasn't just doing it for individual words; there were other cases as well. And so I wrote a macro and assigned a hotkey to the macro. Then when necessary I would press Ctrl+Shift+S and the strikethrough would automatically appear where necessary.

In Chapter 1, "The UUI: The Useable User Interface," I raved about a command approach to programming. This approach lends itself perfectly to removing hoop-jumping. I can only imagine how much more time my project would have taken if I had to reach over, grab the mouse, highlight the text to be "struck through," then click Format ➤ Font, then click the Strikethrough check box, and then click OK…over and over and over. Those are definite hoop-jumpings. Without going into a bunch of heavy theory, then, here's what I recommend you do:

- Implement a command-based system, as I've talked about many times. Make *everything* a command: the printing feature, the page setup feature, the options dialog, everything.

- Include menu and toolbar access to all of the commands.

- Make the menus and toolbars configurable (Microsoft Office is a good demonstration of this).

- Include configurable shortcut keys.

Then, for example, a user can configure Ctrl+P to open the Print dialog box. After that, said user doesn't even have to worry about the File ➢ Print menu item. He can just press Ctrl+P to print. (And, for most users, pressing Ctrl+P *is* faster than reaching over, grabbing the mouse, and choosing File ➢ Print.)

In addition, you might want to consider some kind of macro system where your users can write their own macro programs. One interesting (albeit rather advanced) way to do this in Microsoft Windows is by *exposing* your software commands as functions in a set of COM objects. Provide a root COM object whereby a COM client can access your program. Then, believe it or not, people can automate tasks using the Windows Scripting Host (WSH). I've done this, and it provides almost instant macro capabilities to your program, and further, the users can use whatever language they want that's compatible with the WSH engine. (By default VBScript and JavaScript are available; you can also obtain Python, Perl, PHP, and a whole bunch of other languages.)

> **NOTE** I should probably point out, however, that in all truth, such a macro system isn't a requirement and is more an extra perk for the really advanced people. Usability studies and book sales have shown that very few people actually write macros, and those who do are usually themselves programmers. So consider a macro system only if your schedule has time. Instead, focus on other aspects.

The only additional step is that you'll need to implement your own shortcut keys. But that's not hard either; the shortcut keys can simply launch the WSH engine. How do you do that? If the file association mechanism is set up properly and a VBScript file with a `.vbs` filename extension runs the WSH engine (specifically, the `wscript.exe` program), then all you have to do is use the `ShellExecute` Windows API function to "run" the `.vbs` file. (That's one cool thing about `ShellExecute`—you can "run" a document file, and the system will locate the correct executable. For example, if you "run" a `.doc` file, `ShellExecute` will cause Microsoft Word to launch, opening the `.doc` file.)

Now if you have lots of money, instead of writing your own macro system you can license the VBA (Visual Basic for Applications) system from Microsoft. This would be for a pretty big project, but in the end you'd have a seriously powerful application. I haven't personally done this, but as I understand it you would still have to expose your product as a COM server. (An interesting side note is that you can actually use the WSH engine and your favorite scripting engine to write your own macros that automate Microsoft Word, for example, and bypass VBA if you don't like Visual Basic for whatever reason. That's because Microsoft Word is a COM server.)

However you want to do it, I do at least encourage you to explore the possibility of a macro programming language for automating your product. It will be one more touch of professionalism and will give your power users much more power (and make them happier users who will *pay you money*, which is the real goal here!).

Building a Minimal Required Usability Vocabulary

When you build your software, you want to accommodate all the users, from beginners up through advanced. This is a difficult job; you want to make your software easy enough for the beginners to use, but at the same time, you neither want to insult your advanced users nor hold them back. How do you do this? Here's how:

- Make the most common and important tasks the most visible tasks.
- Make the less-common tasks easily accessible, such as through menus and toolbars.
- Allow the users to configure the menus and toolbars.

Usability experts talk about the vocabulary that you need for using the software. They talk about different levels of the vocabulary, with the lowest level being the process of pushing the mouse button down, possibly sliding the mouse, and lifting the mouse button, as well as pressing a key. These are like the letters of the alphabet in that they represent the smallest possible piece of a vocabulary.

You can't change this lowest level of vocabulary (and if you attempt to, you'll be making a big mistake in terms of sales potential). And you also don't want to change the next level up, where you find the standard controls such as buttons and listboxes, as well as windows and such. In a language analogy, these are on the word level.

But the level of vocabulary you can change is in how your controls are organized in your window, how your menus and toolbars are laid out, how you make use of the space in your window, whether or not you use status bars and other feedback mechanisms, and so on. Using the language analogy, this is the level of vocabulary where you find sentences and even paragraphs.

While you are free to build as big and powerful a product as you want, on the surface you want your product to be *easy to use*. If you have a great number of features, then the users will need a large usability vocabulary for working with your product. The key, however, is to keep the required vocabulary to a minimum.

Look at a word processor, for example, our old standby product. How do you use a word processor? After starting the program, here's how:

1. Type your document by pressing keys.
2. Print your document by choosing File ➢ Print.

3. Save your document by choosing File ➢ Save As.

4. Exit the program.

And later when running the program again:

1. Load the document by choosing File ➢ Open.

That's only five steps! The program is very easy to use. Even beginners can use it. Yet, if this is Microsoft Word we're talking about, then you can also do a great deal more. But these five steps, I would argue, are the minimal vocabulary required to use the product.

Now think about what you are presented with when you start a word processor such as Microsoft Word. By far the biggest part of the screen is the blank page with the blinking cursor, ready for you to type. You don't have to do anything at all to start writing your document; if you just press the A key, the letter *a* will appear on the screen. Yet, at the same time, all the functionality is there for the power users.

Now the standard word processors we use (such as Microsoft Word) are certainly not perfect in usability, but you have to admit, if you want to type a document, things couldn't be much easier.

To build your own minimal vocabulary, sit down and think about the most common tasks people will do with your software—and make sure you're thinking of your targeted user, not some idealized version of yourself. Make a list, and go through each item carefully. Are these really the most common tasks? Are there more tasks? Are there any tasks that aren't very common that should be removed from the list? Ideally, you should have less than six or seven items on the list.

Then these items will be the focal point when your software starts up. However, make sure that these features are really available and that you're not just starting with some kind of wizard; starting with a wizard, in my opinion, is "faking it." If you need a wizard, then you are admitting that your software is difficult for the beginners to use. Time to go back to the drawing board.

NOTE   One of the hardest things about developing software (similar to writing a book) is remembering what it was like when you didn't know what you know now. Some things that seem like common knowledge to you now are mystifying to less-sophisticated users. Even something as simple as saving a file can be disastrous for the inexperienced. At public computers, for example, it's common for users to work hours on a document, all the while saving it to the computer's hard drive inadvertently. Then they pop out their floppy and leave, only to discover that it's blank when they need to use the document days later. Stupid? Not really. It's an easy mistake for new computer users to make. Even when creating applications for the professional programming market, you know a lot that your users don't. Always keep that at the front of your mind as you develop your vocabulary.

A One-Handed Universe

If you have two hands, consider yourself fortunate. Too much of this world is not engineered for people with one hand. I have two hands, yet I like to use each hand for different tasks. And when you start trying to do certain tasks using only one hand, you start to realize just how difficult it is for people with only one hand.

Here are a couple of examples. When I'm doing the dishes, I like to use the sprayer thing that's attached to the back-right side of the sink, separate from the regular fixtures. The one in my house, however, has a slight flaw that may be adding to my gray hair. Remember how these things work; the nozzle is attached to a hose, and the hose retracts down under the sink. When you use the thing, you pull it out, and the hose extends. But the problem is that when I'm finished using mine, *it doesn't retract!* If I somehow try to push while holding onto the nozzle, the hose just bunches up and doesn't go back in, underneath the sink.

Now I usually use the nozzle only for larger dishes that I can't rinse as easily under the faucet. When I do so, I hold the dish with my left hand, and I use the nozzle with my right hand. When I'm finished spraying, I might do some final rinsing under the faucet after I replace the nozzle. In other words, my left hand is holding the dish the entire time. When I'm finished with the nozzle, I just want to push it back in. *But it won't go back in.* And so I have to set down the dish and use *two hands* to manually feed the hose back in. This is not meant for single-handed usage!

As another example, I prefer to use a book backpack instead of a briefcase. The backpack works great, but like the sprayer in the kitchen, it has a two-handed problem: You can't zip it up with one hand! I've tried many times and it just doesn't work. The cloth holding the zipper needs to be held taut for the zipper to work. But the backpack is too flexible. And once again, instead of zipping up, the whole thing just bunches and the zipper doesn't budge. Grrr. And so I must use two hands to zip it up: one to hold the bag taut and the other to work the zipper.

I'm not a mechanical engineer, so I can't say what the solution for the hose is. However, I suspect it wouldn't be too hard to design some kind of spring system that would easily pull it back in when necessary. As for the zipper problem, that one's easy: All they needed to include was a small wire sewn right into the material that would hold the zipper area taut, without me having to hold it. That's all. And I'd gladly pay an extra couple bucks if it meant saving a few extra, valuable hairs on my head.

Navigation through Toolbars and Menus

I've said this many times before, but I'll say it one more time here: When you build your toolbars and menus, remember that you are providing access to the underlying commands in your system. Here's a tip to get you started:

SUGGESTION

> Do not put extra code behind the toolbar buttons and menus beyond simply calling the command functions.

The reason for this is you don't want to tie functionality directly to a button or menu item; doing so will force you to go outside a generic data structure or class for a particular button, perhaps by subclassing. That will make things messy, and soon you'll have button-specific or menu-specific code throughout your program. And with such additional complexities comes the likelihood of *more bugs*. Remember, simplicity is the key!

But beyond the coding difficulties, one fundamental reason is that if you provide a macro language for your product, you want the people to have complete access to the commands through macro programming, separate from the toolbar buttons and menu items. If you have extra code outside the commands, then users won't have access to that code through the macro language. (Unless, again, you start hacking things and making a mess!)

In the sections that follow, I provide you with tips on creating your toolbars and menus in the light of the programming issues I've just described. But before I get started, remember one final important rule:

RULE

> Save the user's customizations! If the user modifies the menus or toolbars, save the changes and reload them when the program restarts. You can save them in a file or in the Registry. If you use a file, put it in the user's own directory space. If you use the Registry, use the HKEY_CURRENT_USER key.

Laying Out a Meaningful Toolbar

Different usability experts have different feelings on the most effective use of the toolbars. Some people say they should completely mimic the menus. Other people say they should have only minimal functionality. To understand how best to use toolbars in your application, consider this fact: Toolbars are, by and large, used mostly by intermediate-level users.

There are, of course, exceptions to this, but the usability experts tell us this is true, and I've personally witnessed it to be true. However, this doesn't mean you should pack borderline-power-user features into your toolbar. Remember, unlike the menu items, the toolbar buttons are all sitting right out there on display for the users. You don't want to intimidate your beginning users by offering a huge pile of toolbar buttons.

The best way to handle this is twofold:

- First, as I've harped over and over, make your toolbars and menus configurable.

- Second, provide multiple toolbars. At startup, the "standard" toolbar opens, which includes such basic items as New, Open, Save, and so on (as long as these are appropriate to your application). In addition, you can have toolbars that are organized by general functionality. But don't make these other toolbars automatically visible; this will overwhelm beginning users. Let the users choose which toolbars to display, and consider making certain toolbars turn on when they are needed. (For example, an imaging toolbar would come on only during graphics operations, as in Microsoft Word.)

As a case in point, I recently downloaded a shareware program that started up with no less than 10 toolbars, each with roughly 20 buttons. That's 200 buttons! I was incredibly overwhelmed by just the sight of the program, and I wasn't sure I would be able to figure out how to use the program. And even when I learned how to use the basic features, I was still intimidated (and I'm a software engineer!), because I knew there were all these other features staring at me in the form of toolbar buttons, features that were seemingly telling me, "I'm here, and you haven't used me yet, so you're not doing it right." So massive amounts of toolbar buttons can be intimidating to first-time users of your program regardless of how advanced those users are.

What to Put on a Toolbar

This might seem obvious at first, but you put buttons for accessing commands on your toolbars. However, some of your commands might require parameters. That's when you can use items other than buttons. For example, suppose you have a SetFont command, which takes a font name as a parameter. On a toolbar, you could have a drop-down combo box listing all the installed fonts. When the user selects the font, the SetFont command will get called, and the code will pass the name of the font to the command. Easy!

You can also get fancy by creating your own owner-draw drop-down combo boxes. For example, you might include a color box, like this one from Microsoft Word:

Again, when the user selects an item in this drop-down box, the toolbar code would call a command, passing as a parameter the selection (which will likely be a number representing the color or perhaps an enumerated data type).

Also:

Include a ScreenTip for each of the controls on your toolbars, since the controls usually don't have any other text associated with them.

Constructing Sensible Menus

A few years ago, Microsoft came up with a novel approach to the problem of their menus getting longer and longer with each release of the Microsoft Office products. The menus would contain only the most recently used items, and at the bottom would be a double down arrow that you could click to expand the menu to include all its items. The following image shows this:

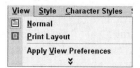

My personal feeling is that I can't stand this dynamic menu capability. I always turn it off.

The reason I don't like the dynamic menus is that the menu items *change*. When I'm trying to quickly find my way around, the last thing I need is for my old standard menus to be changing on me. While the order of the menu items doesn't change, the position on the screen does change since some items aren't showing. And worse, if I use somebody else's computer, the menu items look completely foreign to me. Further, the two stacked down arrows at the bottom of the dynamic menu represent a new idiom for beginners to learn.

Microsoft recognized an actual problem, that the menus are long and unwieldy. Personally, I think the menu customization is a much better alternative (which you can still do through the Customize menu) because it lets me pick which menu item I want displayed and where.

Add to this an easily navigable menu system, and you have two excellent menu features:

- Your menus are customizable.
- In their natural, uncustomized state, they are easily navigable.

How do you make menus navigable? Here are some pointers:

- Use the standard, agreed-upon names for the menus and the standard ordering.
- Avoid cascading menus as much as possible.
- Include keyboard shortcuts to the menus.

Now I just said to use the standard, agreed-upon names for the menus, yet a lot of usability experts suggest a better name for the File menu. That's fine. If you want to call the File menu something a bit more descriptive, then go for it. That's one case where users seem to be fine, and a better name is definitely in order.

As for keyboard shortcuts, remember that menus typically have two keyboard shortcuts. However, one of them is just a keyboard way of accessing the menu (and not really a keyboard shortcut by our definition), and the other really is a keyboard shortcut. For example, in the sample menu shown earlier in this section, you can press the keyboard shortcut Ctrl+N to activate the New menu item, or you can press Alt+F to open the File menu (since the F is underlined in the menu name) and then N to activate the New menu item (since N is underlined in the new item). Pressing Alt+F and then N is not a keyboard shortcut; it's just using the keyboard to activate the menu item.

TIP   Technically speaking, when you press Ctrl+N, you are not activating the File ➤ New menu item. Rather, you are using a keyboard shortcut (Ctrl+N) to activate the New command. Although some programming systems (such as Delphi) let you associate keyboard shortcuts with a menu item, I encourage you to avoid this practice. Instead, a keyboard shortcut can activate a command, and a menu item can activate the same command; the keyboard shortcut doesn't activate the menu (which in turn activates the command). The reason for this distinction is that you want to allow your users to customize the keyboard shortcuts without affecting the menus.

Here are some rules, now, that you can follow in building your own menus:

- Don't modify the menus by adding and removing menu items. Instead, gray out items when they're not needed and reenable them when they are needed. (The various APIs provide functions or methods for graying out and reenabling menu items.)

- If you have a check mark on a menu item, running the command behind the menu should toggle the check mark.

- Avoid cascading menus as much as possible.

- Put an ellipsis (you know, three dots) after the menu text if that menu opens a dialog box. Doing so is customary.

The item about the check mark needs a bit of further clarification. For example, if you have a word processing program, and the ruler is visible, you might have a Ruler item under the View menu, and this Ruler item might have a check mark beside it. When you choose the Ruler menu item, the ruler will go away, and so will the check mark on the menu. When you again choose the Ruler menu item, the ruler will return and so will the check mark.

You might also have a toolbar button for showing and hiding the ruler. A common mistake is to forget to toggle the check mark on the menu item when you click the toolbar's Ruler button. But an easy way to avoid this mistake is by putting the code to toggle the menu item right in the command.

NOTE However, some of the purists out there might disagree, saying the command itself shouldn't be mucking with the user interface. They would argue that the command and the GUI should be separate. But my own experience is that such separations are good in theory but don't really work in practice. Personally, I'm fine putting the check mark–toggling code right in the command code, because otherwise you have to put the same code in multiple places, and further, you have to have check box–toggling code that runs in response to the toolbar button press *in addition to the command code running*. And that, frankly, is messy.

As for cascading menus, here's an example of what I mean by that term:

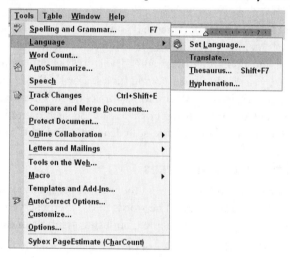

Although the idea behind a cascading menu is sound (the hierarchy adds a nice level of organization), in practice, cascading menus are simply difficult to use. I personally use a Logitech Marble Mouse trackball to help alleviate repetitive elbow motions, and although the trackball works great for almost everything, cascading menus are extremely difficult to maneuver with the trackball. And I find they're even harder to use with the touchpad that comes on most notebook computers. So please, avoid cascading menus if possible.

But all this is fine and dandy for a sunshiny day, but what about the original topic of this section, laying out meaningful menus? While I certainly can't tell you exactly how to lay out your menus since everybody's program will have different menus, I can give you the following tips:

- Try to stick to the standard menus. You've seen these; in Windows these are File, Edit, View, Tools, and so on, plus Window and Help.

- Use a standard ordering of the menus. Don't put your File menu to the right of the Edit menu. Again, that's common sense, and you know it already anyway.

- Since menus are typically used by beginners, place the commands beginners are likely to use more often at the top of the menu.

- Try not to have more than 15 or so items on a single menu. In fact, lean more toward shorter menus, such as seven or eight items. But when you do have several menu items, use a horizontal divider bar to separate similar items.

Be careful when coming up with your own menus besides the standards such as File, Edit, and View. You may have a very good reason for adding a menu, such as an entire category of commands specific to your product, and that's fine; go ahead and add it. But first see if the menu makes sense in a standard menu such as Tools.

However, be careful with the Tools menu. If you have lots of functionality, and you start piling it all under the Tools menu, you may quickly end up with a menu that's just too big and unwieldy. Generally speaking, the Tools menu has higher-level tools beyond simple use cases. For example, in a word processor, you wouldn't put Toggle Italics, Toggle Bold, and other smaller use cases under the Tools menu. (Microsoft Word, for example, doesn't even have menu items for these, although by using the Customize dialog box you can add such menu items. Instead, Microsoft Word has Track Changes and other large-scale features under the Tools menu.)

When to Use Images in Your Menus

In general, I don't care much for images in the menus, primarily because the images people choose are often rather meaningless. The words in the menu serve more purpose than the images. However, that doesn't stop people from using symbols in the menus.

Microsoft has come up with a set of symbols that have basically become standard, and they use these symbols on their menus. I hesitate to suggest that you should use these same symbols, because like most people, I usually don't like the idea that Microsoft makes all the rules and we must all follow them. However, if you're writing software for Windows, the users usually do recognize the symbols. Here's a sample menu from Microsoft Word showing some of the Microsoft standard images:

As you can see, these are the same images that Microsoft typically uses in the toolbars. Therefore, here's a rule to consider:

RULE   If you're using images in your menus, use the same images as in the corresponding toolbar buttons.

Creating Reasonable Pop-up Menus

One particularly useful idiom is the pop-up menu, sometimes called a context menu by some programming tools. A pop-up menu is a menu that appears when you right-click an item or when you press the little Pop-up Menu key on the keyboard. Here's an example of a pop-up menu:

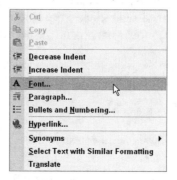

Interestingly, a lot of people I've spoken with (even several power users) *don't know* what that key does. That should be a hint to all of us: People don't always use pop-up menus. Bear that in mind as you read this section.

RULE   First and foremost, a pop-up menu should be short. Don't have more than seven or eight items on the pop-up menu.

One exception to this rule is in programming tools. Programmers seem perfectly fine having lots of items on a pop-up menu for a code editor, for example. However, be careful because if the pop-up menu is too long, it won't fit within the screen's height, and you'll end up with little arrows for scrolling at the top and bottom. That can be *really* annoying because the scrolling tends to be rather slow, even on fast computers.

What do you use a pop-up menu for? First, remember that another name for pop-up menu is *context menu*. In other words, you'll probably have different pop-up menus for different right-click situations. If the user right-clicks a toolbar, a pop-up menu with a Customize item might appear. If the user right-clicks some text, a pop-up menu allowing cut and paste (or whatever) might appear. Generally, however, you'll put pop-up menus only in places where the user spends time working. For example, in a word processing program, a pop-up menu is good in the main editor area. In addition, you can include a pop-up menu on toolbars that can be configured; the users can access the configuration from this pop-up menu. However:

RULE   Don't put functionality on a pop-up menu and nowhere else. Sometimes people don't think of right-clicking the mouse! Always include access to the functionality elsewhere, such as in the main menu bar.

The pop-up menu really is obscure. When you're looking at a screen, you have *no indication whatsoever* that a pop-up menu is available. And for that reason, users really do often miss them. Although I can't remember which program, recently I was using a program I've been using for well over a year, and by chance I right-clicked the mouse and was quite pleased to discover a pop-up menu that I didn't know existed. So don't expect that your users will find the pop-up menus.

Further:

RULE   Don't put cascading menus on a pop-up menu.

Cascading menus are bad enough and you should use them sparingly. But putting them on a pop-up menu is a *really bad idea*.

How do you create a pop-up menu? The various GUI toolkits people use have classes and functions for creating pop-up menus. The worst way in Windows is when you're directly using the Windows API (something I discourage people from doing, because the functions are straight C calls). The API includes a function called TrackPopupMenu, which takes an HMENU as a parameter. Yes, you can do this if you wish. But I prefer the simplicity of tools such as Borland's C++ Builder, which lets me create a pop-up menu object and then attach it to a control. Why spend hours programming something when you can do it quickly?

NOTE   Nevertheless, many programmers I've met over the years still insist on being masochists, although I suspect it's an ego issue: If they find their work difficult, then they feel proud when they've finished, knowing that other people couldn't do what they do. Not to get too far off on a tangent, but this is an issue I have with programmers because it has a direct result on the usability of the code. I talk about this in "Dealing with Egos" in Chapter 15, "Book in a Book: A Guide for Programming Bosses."

REAL WORLD SCENARIO

E-books in a Web Browser: The Next Button Dilemma

A few years ago I was involved with a dot-com startup that was doing e-book software. When we first started talking about the software, we brainstormed though dozens of pretty good ideas. One of the ideas was to simply display the information in a web browser.

But there was a problem, and this problem affects a lot of online documentation software, such as the help system in Windows. The problem is that the forward and back buttons on the browser are not analogous to turning a page forward and backward.

If you're flipping through this book, and you're on, say, page 90, and then you flip ahead to page 100, the analogy of the back button is returning to page 90, not turning one page back. And once you're back on page 90, the analogy to the forward button is to return again to page 100.

In a book, however, a forward button would make more sense to represent moving forward one page. A back button would be more sensible for moving backward one page. This is very different from the meanings of the buttons in a web browser.

One person suggested somehow rigging the back and forward buttons to navigate backward and forward though the pages. But I argued against that, because that would change the fundamental behavior of the web browser buttons (not to mention that it would be extremely difficult to reprogram those buttons without writing some serious hacks). Instead, I proposed that we code our own separate buttons right in the HTML. We finally agreed on this, in conjunction with a tree control on the left that would list the chapters as a table of contents.

But to make matters worse, we still had a problem with our e-books, and that was with the individual pages. When you're looking at a single page in a book, you can see the whole thing at once, and all the pages in the book are the same size. In a web browser, however, a single page can span well beyond the bottom margin of the screen, and you must scroll to see the rest of the page. Further, each page can be a different length. So our question was this: Do we map one page per web page, or do we put all the pages within a single chapter on a single web page?

Other people have been faced with these questions. For example, when you download online documentation for the various free programming tools (such as PHP and MySQL), you can often download all the docs as one giant HTML file or you can download the docs as multiple HTML files along with a single table of contents file. The reason is that *different people have different preferences*. As software developers, then, we can do everybody a favor by supporting the different preferences, thereby accommodating everybody.

Dragging and Dropping

Dragging and dropping is an important feature that you can include in your software, although, frankly, it is not a required feature. But when done properly, it can be a handy feature that adds a professional touch. But before I get started, let me say this:

Whatever drag-and-drop feature you include, make sure you also make the same feature available through some means other than drag and drop!

In the following two sections I cover drag-and-drop operations.

Including a Drag-and-Drop Feature

I'm not going to go into the details of what exactly drag and drop is, because you, as a programmer, already know that. However, here are some tips to follow when implementing a drag-and-drop system:

- Change the mouse pointer to represent that a drag-and-drop action is in progress.
- Change the mouse pointer to indicate whether a drop is allowed or not allowed.
- Enable the Esc key to cancel the drag-and-drop action.

Fortunately, however, if you're using Windows and you use one of the two built-in technologies (Windows Explorer and OLE/COM, which I discuss in the following section, "Drag-and-Drop Technologies in Windows"), then you don't need to change the mouse pointer, because Windows already does it for you. And the same is true for your handling of the Esc key. In other words, when you use these two technologies, some of the work is already done for you!

You might want to allow users to drag items within your program. For example, in Microsoft Word, you can select some text and then use the mouse to drag the text to a different position within your document. Or you might want to be able to drag data items, such as those found in a listbox.

One issue that comes up with drag and drop is that of scrolling. Microsoft has some very strange (and somewhat annoying) guidelines they seem to follow with scrolling in their own Office programs. For example, if you highlight some text in Microsoft Word and drag to the bottom of the editor window, the editor window will scroll. It used to be that this window would scroll way too fast to be practical, although you could apparently slow down the scrolling by not dragging too far out of the window. As of Word 2002, the speed seems to be slower and more reasonable, but the moment you move the mouse outside the editor window, the scrolling stops and the pointer turns into a circle with a line through it, indicating that a drop is not allowed.

Think through the scrolling issue carefully if you have a need for your program to scroll on a drag-and-drop operation. Make sure the scrolling doesn't happen at an insane speed, and make sure your users are able to drop where they want to drop.

You might also want to be able to drag between programs. For this, you will need to ask some questions:

- Can users initiate drags from data within your program?

- Can your program receive drops from other programs?

The choice is yours on each of these issues, but whatever you choose, make sure you document it so your users are aware of the features. And if you're programming for Windows, I provide you with some insight into these issues in the following section, "Drag-and-Drop Technologies in Windows."

Drag-and-Drop Technologies in Windows

If you're programming for Windows, three different types of drag-and-drop technologies are available to you, each with its benefits. Here they are:

- Manual drag and drop

- Windows Explorer drag and drop

- OLE/COM drag and drop

Manual drag and drop simply refers to how you can write your own drag-and-drop system by detecting the mouse-down event, setting a Boolean variable to true, then detecting the mouse-move event, and checking to see if the Boolean variable is true; if so, a drag operation is under way. Then, in response to a mouse-up event, you can again check to see if the Boolean variable is true; if so, the drop operation has taken place. You can also store the beginning coordinates during the mouse-down operation and check the end coordinates in the mouse-up operation. (To make this process work effectively, however, you need to capture the mouse. Different languages and GUI tools have different ways of doing this, but at heart any of these libraries simply calls the SetCapture API function.) Note that if you use Delphi or C++Builder, and you use the drag-and-drop functionality in the controls, the underlying code is implementing a drag-and-drop approach using this method I just described.

The second method lets you *receive files*. This means that if a Windows Explorer window is open (remember, that's Windows Explorer and not Internet Explorer), users can drag filenames from the Explorer window onto your application. Your application can then detect this drop operation and obtain the name of the file. When this happens, your program doesn't actually receive the file; all your program receives is the name of the file (or the list of filenames if the user first selected multiple files in Windows Explorer). Most GUI tools have different ways of allowing you to include this feature, but if they don't, you can easily program the feature yourself by calling into the Windows API. All you do is call the DragAcceptFiles API function, passing the handle for your window that will accept the files, along with a True value. Then, when the user drops a file on your window, you will receive a WM_DROPFILES message.

Using this technique, you can actually do some pretty interesting things. For example, you might not want to accept files on your entire window. Instead, you might want to accept files only in a certain area. To do this, you simply create a child window that is nothing more than a rectangular area (or whatever you want, really), and you then register the child window's handle in the `DragAcceptFiles` call instead of your main window. The only catch is that you have to have access to the child window's message handler (or window procedure). That means writing your own custom control and window class (or, heaven forbid, subclassing a standard control, which is a throwback to the old days of Windows programming).

The third technology for drag and drop is using the OLE/COM system. If you try out the previous technology using the `DragAcceptFiles` function, you may be disappointed when you figure out that users can't drag items from Internet Explorer. For example, you've seen this little icon in the address bar of Internet Explorer:

For many applications (including all of Microsoft Office), you can drag that little icon from IE into the application. The different applications will then handle the drop in different ways. If you drag the icon into Microsoft Word, you will see the address appear in Word, and the address will be clickable. (You have to hold down the Ctrl key, however, to click a link in Word.)

In order to provide for this kind of functionality, you need to make use of the drag-and-drop features of the OLE/COM system in Windows. This is, frankly, a rather complex process if you're programming in straight C++ and beyond what I have room to show you here. (It's easier in other languages such as Visual Basic where you can find controls that implement the behavior for you.) If you're interested in programming this sort of thing in C++, first study a bit of OLE/COM programming, and then do a web search for "OLE drag drop." I've found several pages that talk about it.

Moving Forward

In this chapter I talked about the importance of highly navigable software. Remember, navigation refers to how the user gets to where he needs to be in your software. Don't make the user jump through hoops, or the user will quickly become frustrated with your product. Your product will then find its way into the metaphorical "round file" known as the Recycle Bin. (Although Apple's Trash is probably a more appropriate name in this case!)

In the next chapter I move away from the screen and onto paper. No, computers didn't give us "paperless offices" as people once thought they would. If anything, we now have more papers, except now those papers have pretty fonts rather than illegible handwriting all over them. In the next chapter I talk about how you can make your data and printouts more useable, even when the printouts appear on screen.

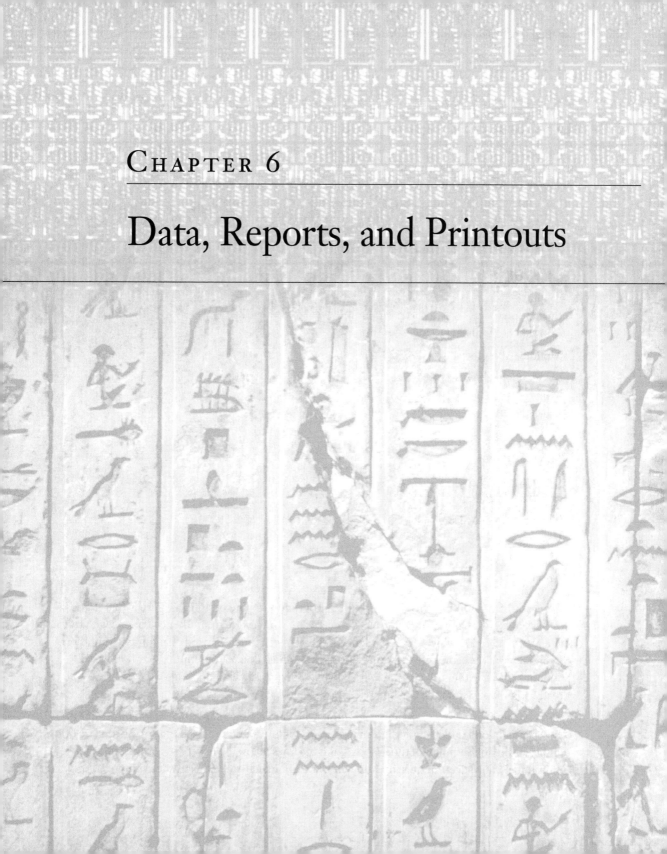

CHAPTER 6

Data, Reports, and Printouts

Quiz time: You're a computer professional. Do you understand your phone bill? Yes, in all fairness, realistically, if you sit down and look it over, you're perfectly capable of understanding your phone bill. You are, after all, a computer programmer. But what about people who aren't? Well, let's start with us computer people. Here's a look at one portion of one of my recent phone bills. It looks something like this:

	Peak	Off-Peak	Weekend	Amount
Current Month's Airtime Usage				
Airtime (minutes)	954	97	303	
Promotional Allowance/Minutes	0	77	243	Included
Monthly Allowance	742	0	0	Included
Cell to Cell Allow. Minutes	212	20	60	Included
Current Month's Billable Airtime	0	0	0	
Current Month's Airtime Charges	0	0	0	0
Total Home Usage and Charges				0
Total Cell to Cell Minutes	233	32	113	

Honestly? I can't follow this bill. And I'm a programmer! The best I can figure is that it goes like this: I talked 954 minutes during peak time, 212 of which were to another cell phone with the same provider, 742 of which were not. During the off-peak times, I talked 20 minutes to another cell phone with the same provider. And during weekends, I talked 60 minutes to another cell phone and 243 to others. And all of this is included in my plan, so I don't have to pay extra. But I really don't know what the last line is all about.

But close enough. As a computer programmer, I can safely say that I understand most of this. The last line I don't understand. But I'm pretty sure I understand the upper part. The top line of numbers is the total amount of time I spoke, and the lines below are how this is broken up among promotional allowance/minutes, monthly allowance, and cell-to-cell allowance/minutes. (I'm not sure why the middle item of these doesn't say "minutes" on it but the others do. Maybe that's an oversight by the people who made the bill.)

And I still don't know what the bottom line means, but that's okay. I'll just pay the bill and not worry about it… I just realized *I fell for it!* Do they want me to just not question it and go ahead and pay it? How do I know the bill is even right?

Well, confession time: I once worked for a company that did billing for cell phone companies. And you know what? We weren't lying. There was no dishonesty at all; nobody was trying to deceive anybody. I can safely say that this bill is correct and honest. So why is it so hard to read? Although the company I worked for didn't print this bill, they printed similar bills. And I didn't work there yet when they figured out the layout of the bills, so I can't say with certainty the steps that took place to come up with the bill's format. But one clue I can see about this bill is the fact that the left column has these three items, which are not described very well:

- Promotional Allowance/Minutes
- Monthly Allowance
- Cell to Cell Allow. Minutes

The first item has a slash in between Allowance and Minutes. The second item doesn't even mention Minutes. The third item has no slash between Allowance and Minutes. My goal, of course, isn't to nitpick the editing (or lack thereof) of the bill, but rather to point out that this bill obviously didn't go through much of a review. Who actually wrote these three phrases? Most likely it was the programmer. The programmer *arbitrarily* decided what it would say, and the programmer showed it to the manager, who approved it and who sent it to the client (the phone company) for review, who in turn approved it, *without doing a usability study.* (I'm only guessing here, but it's likely what happened.) This is indicative of some larger problems in terms of who the decision makers are. (In this case, the programmers made the decisions and the bosses simply approved them!) And that's an issue I talk about later on in this book, in Chapter 15, "Book in a Book: A Guide for Programming Bosses."

In this present chapter, I talk about the issues of not only getting the grammar good—er, I mean *right*—but also about presenting the data in your reports so as to keep people from getting confused, and to keep them from accusing you of dishonesty, as I nearly did with this phone bill.

And incidentally, just for the record, as I was describing the phone bill, I really was going through the actual procedure of figuring out what it all meant. What I wrote was actually my train of thought. And I still haven't figured out what that last line means. So the answer to the question, "Do I understand my phone bill?" is, "Apparently not." After you read this chapter, on the other hand, readers of your printouts and reports won't have to be intimately aware of your database to understand your reports. Even people who aren't programmers will understand them—unlike the situation with my phone bill.

My Arm Is Tired from the Light Pen.

Back in the early days of personal computers, when people owned computers with names such as Commodore-64 and VIC-20, a fancy new gadget appeared in the stores. It was one of the coolest inventions of all time, and it was called a *light pen*. A light pen behaved very much like today's mice, except instead of having a moving cursor that rolled around as you moved a mouse, you would simply touch the light pen to the screen. In essence, the light pen turned your monitor into a *touch screen*, which is something still with us today.

As soon as the light pen came out, people starting making software that not only supported the light pen but required it. I never actually used such software, because I wasn't one of the lucky few who actually owned a light pen, so I don't know exactly what they were doing that required the light pen. But I do know one thing: Soon after light pens came out, people (usually secretaries and data entry clerks) began complaining of extremely tired arms. The act of holding a light pen up to the monitor all day long was just too tiring. And almost as quickly as light pens emerged, they disappeared into the history books and museums.

But what's interesting is that while the final result of the light pen was to turn the monitors into the equivalent of touch screens, touch screens *are still here today*. You see them often in POS (Point of Sale) systems. Go to a restaurant and you'll see the cashiers tapping on the screen to enter the order (which makes me wonder the answer to the Great Question in Life, "How much ketchup can cover a monitor before you can no longer read the monitor?"). Go to an oil change center or a hotel, and you'll sometimes see the same thing. Is this really a good idea? In the case of cashiers, their job doesn't focus on the computer. They don't use the computer all day long. So in this case, the touch screen is probably okay. Further, ketchup on a screen doesn't damage the screen; ketchup inside a keyboard might.

The good news is, then, that while the light pen is left for the annals of science, its offshoot, the touch screen, does still live on, but only in certain situations where the people aren't parked in front of the computer all day long. If you're developing software, then, and are considering a touch screen interface, first ask yourself how much time the users will spend in front of the computer. Will their arms get tired? Will it be easier for them to use the keyboard? But on the other end, will a keyboard even be present? These are all questions to consider. But please don't expect them to use a light pen. Leave that for the time capsules.

Relational Design: Great on the Hard Drive, but...

If you work with reports, you probably work with data. And if you work with data, you probably work with relational design. Relational design, of course, is the way in which you relate your data by breaking it up into *normal form*. I don't want to spend hours giving a lesson on normal form, but suffice it to say that the basic concept is that instead of entering a name, address, phone number, or e-mail address into every field of every sales record (resulting in duplicate data inside a table if a single customer makes multiple purchases), you keep that information in a separate Customer table. With each customer you include a customer number. Then inside the Sales table, you have a customer number, relating each sale to a customer. This keeps your database much smaller. Why have Bill Gates' phone number and address over and over in your computer if you're selling computers to Microsoft? Once is good enough, thank you.

The problem is that just because you design your data in relational form doesn't mean you want to design your reports in relational form. Yes, if you and a couple of coworkers are the only ones reading a report, then fine; you can make them look however you want. But if you're sending reports out to millions of, oh, I don't know, cell phone customers, then you probably want them to be as readable as possible. Why? Many reasons. First, you won't get two hundred thousand angry and confused customers filing a class action suit against you, accusing you of trying to deceive them. And second, you don't want all those two hundred thousand customers plus a half million more flooding your support center needing help understanding their bills. And third, you want to keep your customers and not lose them to the competition.

Here's a case in point: A database for a phone usage system is likely to have a table containing usage information (that is, information on each phone call), which will in turn contain a code describing the type of call, such as whether it's a free weekend call, or an evening call, or whatever. The code can, in turn, be matched up to another table that describes each call.

Suppose the usage data has this kind of information:

From	To	Time	Duration	Type of Call
661-555-1212	405-123-4567	8:35	13	A
661-555-1212	212-999-1111	12:52	17	B
407-111-3535	661-555-1212	22:20	5	C

The type of call is a code with a table that might look like this (of course, the table would have more entries, but this is enough for the discussion):

Code	Call Type
A	Daytime rate
B	Daytime cell-to-cell rate
C	Evening rate

And now the fun begins. You want to print this information in a bill that you send to the customer. What do you do? One way is to follow the same structure as the tables, by printing exactly the preceding two lists. That's pretty simple to program. If the customer wants to find out the type of call, he can simply look at the Type of Call code and then look up the description in the second list. And that's the way many phone bills are printed.

Here are two possible SQL statements that would do this:

```
select * from calls;
select * from calltypes;
```

Easy enough; just dump the data out from the tables. But this has major problems. First, as much as we computer programmers are perfectly fine dividing out information into normal form, the same isn't true for people outside the computer world.

RULE   Normal people don't understand normal form.

(I know, *we're* the normal ones, but I just thought that was a clever way to express it.) As much as this might seem hard to believe, it's true. Ask people what they think of the little "code" part of their phone bills, and you'll quickly discover that they all hate it. Nobody wants to scan through a list and see some strange letter or number and then have to go look it up to find out what it means. (Once again, they think it's dishonest.) And by the way, the list of codes is often printed on the back of the bill, out of the way, making decoding the bill even harder for people.

So why do the bills look like this? Because the programmers are usually the ones who came up with the layout, and the programmers printed them in the way that made sense to them. But:

RULE   The way a programmer thinks isn't necessarily the way everybody else thinks.

To a programmer, the data lives in normal form in the database, and therefore it makes perfect sense to print the data in normal form on the report. But that's simply not the best solution. The best solution is an easy one: Instead of printing the codes, simply print the meaning behind them, like so:

From	To	Time	Duration	Type of Call
661-555-1212	405-123-4567	8:35	13	Daytime rate
661-555-1212	212-999-1111	12:52	17	Daytime cell-to-cell rate
407-111-3535	661-555-1212	22:20	5	Evening rate

Of course, you might run into the problem of this data not fitting on the report. What do you do now? Throw in the towel and go back to the previous, bad solution? Of course not. You barrel forward and fix the minor layout problem.

RULE   Never choose a bad solution simply because the bad solution is easier and takes less time to implement.

Go forward and find a better solution, even if it takes a bit more time. The space problem has a couple of easy solutions. First, you can consider a smaller font, although be careful here because you realistically have to consider customers who might not have perfect 20/20 vision.

But if a smaller font is not an option, then what do you do? Here's a good solution: Abbreviate. Look at this:

From	To	Time	Duration	Type of Call
661-555-1212	405-123-4567	8:35	13	Day
661-555-1212	212-999-1111	12:52	17	Day cell2cell
407-111-3535	661-555-1212	22:20	5	Evening

While I'm not big on *cell2cell*, at least it is a pretty good abbreviation. But if people don't like that, then just use *cell to cell*, still dropping the word *rate* and shortening *daytime* to *day*. But notice I could have fit the whole word *daytime* in the first row. Why did I abbreviate it *day*? Because I used *day* on the next row, and I don't want to be inconsistent. That's all.

But if you want to see some seriously bizarre codes, look at the printout from a car repair shop. I was once involved on such a project (for an oil change center, actually), and I dare say that the people writing the program gave little or no thought to what the customers would want to see in their bills. Car repair statements have codes for the type of car, the work done, whether items are parts versus labor, and on and on. In the interest of space, I won't reproduce a statement here, but take a look at one and you'll see what I mean.

Now a quick point about all this: I can hear some of you saying, "You crazy usage person, you don't know my work, you don't know the problems that I encountered, and you don't know that this was the best solution."

Well, to you I say, "I don't care. Don't tell me it's not possible because I know it *is* possible to do better." Remember the story of how I tried to get my boss to accept the printouts in giant paper because a smaller font wasn't possible. He told me to go fix it anyway, and eventually I did. Often problems like this are really just a matter of spending a few extra hours or a few extra days on them.

RULE   Never say a better solution isn't possible.

Data versus Information

One thing that can help you create reports that are easy for laypeople to read is to recognize the difference between data and information:

- *Data* refers to what's stored on the hard drive.

- *Information* refers to how the data is interpreted by the brain. In other words, information is data with meaning added to it.

WARNING	Be forewarned, however: Not everybody agrees on these definitions. But it's the concept here that I'm talking about, so you can use whatever words you want when I use *data* and *information*.

For example, as I look at this word processor I'm using, I'm seeing words and sentences and headers and other *information*. But the program is storing this information as a bunch of meaningless bytes. By itself, a byte of data has no meaning. Here's an example of a byte of data: 01000001.

By itself, that's just a byte, which is eight bits, with the lowest bit 1, the second-highest bit 1, and the rest 0. But when you add meaning to this byte, you get information. That's a number 65, which is the ASCII code for a letter—small letter *a*. Or, it might be a student's score on a high school remedial math test (not yours or mine, of course!). Or it might be one piece of an entire string of 64,000 bytes of data in a file, and that file contains an encrypted version of a spreadsheet listing employee salaries.

Thus:

- 01000001 is data, which has no meaning.

- The letter *a* is information (on some levels, that is, although by itself it's not particularly meaningful).

- A student's score of 65 on a remedial math class is information (and bad information for the student's parents, on top of all that).

- An encrypted spreadsheet is data, since in its encrypted form it's not directly of much use to us humans.

Remember, then, data by itself has no meaning. *Once you interpret the data, place it in a context, and add meaning to it, you have information.* That means, then, that data is what lives inside the computer. Information exists in our brains. Think about this: I'm staring at a computer screen filled with text and menus and toolbars and so on. But that's just a bunch of bits and bytes inside the computer. My brain interprets this as a document containing the chapter of a book. The computer doesn't know that this is a chapter. The computer doesn't really know anything at all, at least anything with meaning. (I won't get into all the philosophical nonsense about whether computers have existentialism. Yuck.)

So what does all this have to do with reports? Lots. When you create a report for laypeople, remember that the laypeople have no concept of the data behind the information, and they don't want to. That means they don't want to have to deal with mysterious codes and nonsensical data. While such data might have meaning to you, it doesn't have meaning to them.

c

What is that c thing? That's the code for cell-to-cell phone calls. But does it have meaning? Is it *information*? No. It's a code, or just data to the laypeople. That doesn't belong on a report.

RULE   Think about whether you are providing data or information. If you're providing data, get rid of it and replace it with information.

Of course, don't simply provide a legend to your data, as I talked about in "Relational Design: Great on the Hard Drive, but..." in this chapter. By providing a code for the phone call and then providing a separate list, you're simply providing data and not information. Skip the data and get right to the information.

Read It the Way a Customer Would

One of the reasons I'm filling this book with entertaining anecdotes is to remind you that while you might be a programmer developing software, when it comes to other products you're not a designer but a consumer or customer. In this book I complain about all sorts of products that we use on a daily basis. And as you use these products, think about how you, as a consumer, are particularly bothered by the product and what you would do differently if you had designed it.

Then, when you're building your software, do the reverse: Remember what it's like to be the consumer using these non-software products, and then think what life is like for the consumer using your software. Remember, as much as you might not like to think about this, to the consumer you are the evil engineer who designed the product. If you build a bad product, the consumers will be talking about *you* when they say, "Why can't they make their software do this and that?"

Now, of course, my goal isn't to cause you to snap and end up on some heavy psychotic medications because you know all these people out there are talking about you and angry at you. My goal is to help you be more conscious of the needs of the consumers and, in turn, create software that they will actually *like*. And how do the consumers judge the software? If they use the software directly, they judge it through the user interface. If they receive reports and printouts, they judge it through the reports and printouts—but only to a point.

The truth is most consumers who receive reports and printouts (such as phone bills) are not using these sheets of paper to judge the software. They are using the papers to judge the company that sent the papers. If I see a mistake on my bill, I don't blame the computer program; I blame the company. (And if I call and the person on the phone blames the computer, I know better. It's the company's responsibility to send me correct bills, and it's the company's responsibility to make sure the programmers are doing the very best job possible. Garbage in, garbage out, as they used to say.)

When you're designing a report, then, you need to look at the report through the eyes of the people who will ultimately be using the report. Here are some questions to ask:

- Is the information easily accessible and quick to find?

- Will the users spot the most important information first?
- Is the information complete?
- Is the information clear?
- Does the information provide the users with the answers to any questions they might have and help them accomplish their goals?

These are things the customers will look for. Remember, if a customer receives a phone bill, she isn't going to say, "Wow, what a nice *sans serif* font they used on this bill, and look at how they made good use of an eight-character tab." Instead, she is going to *first* look at the *amount* due and then, usually, the *date* that the bill is due. She could care less about the font or if the report includes the officially trademarked corporate logo.

She's also going to want to easily find a way to contact the company if she disagrees with the bill. Is the 800 number easy to find? Is the website available? (And please, have a website.) Can she pay the bill online? Is the account number clear? (Sometimes I've seen bills with an account number as well as other numbers, and the bill isn't clear to me as to which number I need when I go online to pay!)

Then you should show the additional information, such as a breakdown of the amounts. But remember, for amount breakdowns, customers don't want to see the kind of abomination I started this chapter with. For example, customers don't want to see this:

Total carried over from pg 2:	$35.25
Federal tax	$2.25
State tax	$1.05
City tax	$.75
Total tax	$4.05
Additional fees	$2.52
Total taxes and fees	$6.57
Interest	$8.97
Total due	**$50.79**

Do you see what's wrong with this? The second, third, and fourth lines are all added up, and the total is on the fifth line. The next line is then added on, for a new total shown on the following line, as Total taxes and fees. Then an Interest amount is shown, followed by the sum of Total taxes and fees, Interest, and the Total carried over from pg 2. That's too darn confusing! And worse, some bills with this kind of a format will have some items in bold and maybe a few underscores to try to make it clearer. Try as they might, they're not helping. The bill is a mess and impossible to read. Consumers hate this kind of bill (and again accuse the company sending the bill of trying to deceive them).

One slightly better way is to indent, like so:

Total carried over from pg 2:			$35.25
Federal tax	$2.25	
State tax	$1.05	
City tax	$.75	
Total tax		$4.05	
Additional fees		$2.52	
Total taxes and fees			$6.57
Interest			$8.97
Total due			**$50.79**

But I would argue that this still isn't great. It's better, but not great. While indentations such as this are easier for somebody with a bookkeeping background to understand, laypeople still aren't accustomed to multiple levels of indentation. I'd limit it to just a couple levels, like this:

Total carried over from pg 2:		$35.25
Taxes and fees		$6.57
(Taxes and fees are broken up into the following)		
Federal tax	$2.25	
State tax	$1.05	
City tax	$.75	
Additional fees	$2.52	
Interest		$8.97
Total due		**$50.79**

This is looking better. But I still don't like some parts. For one, I don't like the "Total carried over from pg 2" item. Here's why:

RULE Don't have several rows labeled *Total*.

I would argue from my own experience that one reason phone bills are so hard to read is they have a million items with the word *Total*, when, in fact, the bill can only have one total, the amount due. Further, the phrasing of "Total carried over form pg 2" is stiff. Instead, I would propose the front page have a list like this:

The amounts on page 2 add up to	$35.25
The amounts on page 3 add up to	$15.54
For a grand total of	$50.79

Then, page 3 (which is the page I was working on before) would have something like this:

Federal tax	$2.25
State tax	$1.05
City tax	$.75
Additional fees	$2.52
Interest	$8.97

And don't include a sum on this page. The reason is that the person questioning the bill who sits down with a calculator may accidentally add up all the numbers and then add in the total as well, doubling the amount for that page. Then the value won't match up with the amount due, and he will have to go back and do it all over again. That causes a frustrated and confused customer. If she wants to see the total for page 3, she can add it up with a calculator and then compare the number to the $15.54 shown on page 1 after the words "The amounts on page 3 add up to...."

In my opinion, these final two lists are the best for dealing with itemized details. The reader can clearly see how they add up, and she won't accidentally add in an extra total or two, and the question of where the total came from is clear.

But before I close this section, let me include one final note and some thoughts:

RULE   If a number is supposed to be subtracted from a total, show it with a minus sign.

Don't have this kind of thing:

Previous amount due	$97.35
Payments	$80.00
Current amount due	$57.36
Total amount due	**$74.71**

Instead, fix the wording problems (...amount due, ...amount due, ...amount due, each with a different number!), consider reordering with a bit more chronology, and get a minus sign in there, like so:

Amount of this month's bill	$57.36
Amount you owed last month	$97.35
Amount you paid last month	-$80.00
Total amount due	**$74.71**

Earlier generations might have frowned on words such as *owe* and might have liked to see the words *Thank you* after the amount you paid last month. Skip it. People these days know very well they owe the money and don't see it as any more negative than the word *due*. In fact, I'd argue that people today are less intimidated by the word *owe*, since *due* has the connotations of "You will pay me NOW!" And further, people aren't impressed with the words *Thank you* showing up on their bill. Nobody today believes some sweet elderly secretary with photos of her beautiful grandkids on her desk sat and carefully typed up the bill and was putting a personalized "Thank you" note on it. People know that a giant printer in an operations center spit out the bill and that no human hands even touched it. The words *Thank you* are as much of an insult as a mail-merge program printing out reports in a handwriting font to make us think somebody wrote something by hand.

But not to harp too much on phone bills, let me talk about some other reports people receive. Almost everybody shops at a grocery store. And our cash register receipts are getting longer and longer. And to make matters incredibly complicated, in some states, food is not taxed while other merchandise is.

The other day I went to the grocery store and spent $132.92. My receipt was really long. And it's broken up into several sections. Here are some highlights (I won't list the whole thing here):

General Merchandise

Map	4.59	CT
Snowbrush	5.99	CT
Gen Mdse Sub (before tax)	10.58	

Grocery

Tomato Sauce	.39	F
BBR CKN BRST	1.49	F
1 @ 2 / 3.00		
Carrots	1.50	F

Toothpaste	2.94	T
Spaghetti	1.39	F
1 @ 2 / 3.00		
Soup	1.50	F
Total		
Total Ad/In-store savings	14.34	
Total Tax	2.66	
Total	132.92	

This one isn't too bad; I've seen worse. But the part I want to draw your attention to is the lines that say 1 @ 2 / 3.00. That's saying I bought one item that's priced at two for three dollars. (And so now I know, looking at this receipt, I didn't have to buy two to get the deal!) The first 1 @ 2 / 3.00 line is between the breaded chicken breast and the carrots. Which does it apply to? One is 1.49 and the other is 1.50, both conceivably two-for-three-dollars (give or take a penny). Now at first I thought the line applied to the item just before it. But that's not right, because look at the second 1 @ 2 / 3.00 line. The item before it is 1.39 and the one after it is 1.50. Apparently the 1 @ 2 / 3.00 refers to the item that follows.

But notice also that some items have a T by them, and some have an F. In this state, food is not taxed, apparently. And so the F probably stands for Food. Since the toothpaste is not food, it's taxed and gets a T by it. But these are more secret codes! As a programmer, I was able to easily figure out what T and F mean. But what do those two letters mean to most people? True and False, of course!

And why do some taxed items appear under General Merchandise? Probably because the store divides the items into two distinct accounting units. But why should that matter to me? All I know is that I bought a bunch of things. I don't care about the accounting. They're just confusing people.

Maybe instead they should have two sections for the receipts, non-taxed items and taxed items. Then they wouldn't need to have a little T or F beside each item.

Then, of course, we have monthly credit card statements. These in general aren't all bad; however, the part I want to talk about is where they figure the interest. I won't reproduce one here, but take a look at one of your own statements and see what I mean. How clear is it? Did they really think of you when they printed it? Are you a bit suspicious of them? Now go back to your engineering hat. Do you want your customers to be suspicious of you? Probably not.

Wasted Paper in Your Mailbox

The days of dumping piles upon piles of paper that was touched once and viewed maybe twice are quickly going away. People are tired of seeing the trees getting destroyed, and they want to save paper. Think of all the bills and bank statements you've received in your life. (And I'm not talking about junk mail, either.) The landfills are getting deeper and deeper, and companies are also spending millions of dollars on the paper that's ultimately ending up in the landfills.

And so today, often phone bills don't come with a detailed list of each and every call. Instead:

SUGGESTION

> If you want your customers to have access to the details, include an option to provide it online. (Don't automatically provide it online, however, as not everybody has Internet access!)

The Web is a good thing, although I shouldn't have to tell you that. Put the information online. Don't give all the details in the report if they're not absolutely necessary in printed form.

Spelling, Grammar, and Word Usage

I feel like I shouldn't even have to include this section, but I'm continually amazed at how many reports and printouts I receive in the mail or see on websites that have spelling and grammar problems. (And that doesn't include signs I see, marketing brochures, and on and on.)

Nobody is perfect. But that doesn't excuse you from having spelling and grammar problems in your reports. Book publishers, for example, know that nobody is perfect. Although I consider myself a good writer, I know that I still make mistakes, and that's why the publisher has a staff of editors who will go through this book with a fine-tooth comb, fixing the problems. Yes, occasionally problems squeak through in a book. But a book is big. A one- or two-page report isn't. Don't allow grammar and spelling errors into your reports. It cries out, "Unprofessional!"

Remember the Usual Gotchas

We all have our pet peeves, but the two biggest errors I see again and again in reports, in web pages, in advertisements, and on signs are the *your* versus *you're* and *its* versus *it's*. (In fact, I'm not kidding; just today I saw "it's" when "its" was intended.) You know the rules for these four words; I'm not going to insult your intelligence by reiterating them here. (And if for some reason you've been left behind, I suggest you go look up the difference as soon as possible and start using the correct terms.) Everyone makes these and similar errors on occasion. I recommend that you get a copy of the little book *The Goof-Proofer: How to Avoid the 41 Most Embarrassing Errors in Your Speaking and Writing* by Stephen J. Manhard (Fireside, 1999). In fewer than 100 pages, you'll learn to steer clear of the most common "gotchas."

Also, if you're serious about learning the ins and outs of good English usage, then I suggest you pick up a copy of the classic book *The Elements of Style*, fourth edition, by William Strunk, Jr., and E. B. White (Allyn & Bacon, 2000). Even if you're not serious but do any writing whatsoever, you should own a copy. Everybody should. Add to that *The Elements of Grammar* by Margaret Shertzer (Pearson Higher Education, 1996), an excellent reference for the points of grammar, punctuation, and capitalization.

In truth, there's no shortage of books on usage, style, and grammar, but with the three short volumes described here, you'll have everything you need to look professional in print.

Avoid Talking Shop

Remember that your work is filled with *shoptalk*. When you're with your coworkers, you're perfectly allowed to say, "The problem is the UDP packets weren't making it to the DNS server, preventing the client system from being able to resolve the IP addresses." But if you're dealing with customers and laypeople, that's the last thing you want to say. (Yes, we all like to impress people, and confusion is always a good start, but let's keep the confusion off the reports that our customers will read.) Instead, say, "The computers had trouble connecting." Good enough, and it allows customers and laypeople to understand the problem.

NOTE   Of course, if you're dealing with corporate customers, they may require a technical answer. In that case, go for it.

We've all been faced with the situation where somebody wants to know what we do for a living. We're very aware that these people see us as some kind of high-tech superhuman with brain abilities that far surpass anything they could ever dream of. We can comprehend things that they'll never understand in a million years. (Hey, I'm on roll here!) In their eyes, we can leap tall buildings...well, you get the idea.

Yet, at the same time, they really would like to have at least *some* idea of what we do when we drive to work everyday. The skill of translating our technical knowledge into simple terms is exactly the skill you need to put into place when designing reports for laypeople.

Here's an example:

- Real answer: *I developed the portion of the software package that resolves IP addresses by sending out UDP packets to a DNS server.*

- Perfectly good answer: *You know how when you're online and you type in www.cnn.com, and somehow your computer is able to take that name and from there figure out how to connect to CNN's computer? I wrote the part of the software that helps the computer figure that out.*

There's always an easier way to express something. You can even make it simpler, depending on how much detail you want, for example: *I wrote the part of the software that helps your computer figure out how to connect to another computer when you type in www.cnn.com.*

TIP   Not yet convinced? Then think of it this way: If Albert Einstein can explain his theory of relativity to the general public in a mere 157 pages—as he did in his book *Relativity: The Special and the General Theory* (Crown Publishing, 1995)—then we can certainly explain our jobs to our in-laws in simple language.

What is the key to simplifying everything? I removed the *shoptalk*. I got rid of the junk about IP addresses and UDP packets and DNS servers. People don't know what they are, and they certainly don't want a lesson first. Imagine if, when asked what you do on your job, you answered, "Well, in order to understand what I do, let me first take a few moments to explain to you how information travels about the Internet using two different protocols, one called TCP/IP and one called TCP/UDP." Blah, blah, blah. I can see the listener's eyes glaze over. In other words, don't fall into the engineer's trap of explaining how to build a clock just because someone asked the time of day. Or for that matter, if somebody asks a simple question, don't answer with, "Okay, but first I have to take a half hour to teach you a bit...."

TIP   Remember, even some words you use every day might be shoptalk. In the phone world, for example, the word *usage* is part of our everyday language, and it's easy for me to forget that it's not a common word everybody knows. Or, in the publishing world people refer to *front matter* for the introduction, table of contents, and all that other good stuff that comes at the beginning of a book before the first chapter. And, of course, the computer world is filled with shoptalk, as you already know.

And on to reports. While all this information I'm giving out might help make your life easier when meeting people at a singles bar or when talking to Aunt Emma at the annual family reunion, a more practical use of this is in the world of reports. If you are sending out reports to customers, keep your information in plain English. Don't say:

Total usage during cycle

Instead, say something like this:

Here is the total amount of time you spent on the telephone for this month.

Notice several things:

- I used a complete sentence.
- I chopped the shoptalk.
- I allowed myself to use the slightly less-accurate term *month*, even though a billing cycle isn't always an exact month. Customers are okay with that.

Now you might not be able to fit that whole sentence on the report if you're really tight for space. In that case, you can forgo the complete sentence. But don't allow the shoptalk back in. You might write this, for example:

Total phone time for the month

This is every bit as clear as *Total usage during cycle* and far easier to understand. And for every thousand people who understand the bill more clearly, you will save yourself possibly hundreds of support calls from confused people.

RULE   The goal is to communicate to the users, and doing so means speaking their language, which is probably different from yours. Attempt to capture the way the users would express an idea.

Making Data Available Online and on the Screen

Often you have two views of your data: what you see on the screen and what you see in the reports. For example, a checkbook program might have a transaction view of the data where you can enter your transactions. Then it might have a reports view where you can see, for example, all your transactions organized by category.

This report view might be available both as a printout and on the screen. But if you make it available on the screen, don't confuse it with Print Preview. Print Preview refers to drawing on the screen exactly what the user will see when printing the document. Showing the report on the screen, on the other hand, should be more powerful than a simple Print Preview, since the users have, after all, a computer at their disposal that can let them customize the view.

For example, the checkbook program might allow the user to customize the report by choosing which categories appear in the report. However, that's still not taking the online report to its full potential, since after the customization, the user might be presented with a static report.

Therefore, think in terms of dynamic versus static: A printout (and Print Preview) is a static report. On the screen, however, you can make your reports dynamic. Here are some possibilities:

- If the report has text, the user might be able to highlight certain parts of it, copy it, and then paste it into another program.

- The user might be able to sort the report based on different columns by clicking on a column header.

- The user might be able to collapse certain parts of the report, showing no detail for the collapsed section, only, for example, a total amount.

- You could include a filter so the user can see only specific data. For example, in an e-mail program, the user might want to set up a filter so she could see only messages from a particular user. An accounting program might allow the user to show only expenses within a particular dollar range, for example.

- For the advanced users, you might include a 3D chart. Such a chart might include controls the user can manipulate to rotate the chart and view it in different ways. You would want to put this in an advanced features area of your product, however, since studies have shown that people not skilled in math have a difficult time with 3D information.

You can see where I'm going here: I'm taking the concept of the report and making it dynamic and *interactive*, using electronic capabilities that aren't available in a printed report.

RULE   If you make your reports available on the screen, make them dynamic so that the users can get the most out of the information. Don't create just a poor excuse for a Print Preview.

Putting Your Data on the Web

If you want your data to be available on the Web, remember that people surfing the Web expect data to be slightly different than in a regular program. For example, if you're writing banking software and want to allow people to access their accounts online, instead of just printing the equivalent of a bank statement on the screen, think in terms of links.

First, you might have a page that lists the different accounts the customer owns, such as a checking account and a savings account, like so:

Account	Balance
Checking	5.37
Savings	2.52

Each of these accounts would be clickable. When you click on an account, a new page comes down showing the transactions for the account. But this list might be simple, including, for example, the date of the transaction, the amount, and a description, like so:

Date	Description	Amount	Balance
1/1/04	Safeway	$25.35	$100.25
1/2/04	Exxon	$72.42	$27.83
1/3/04	7-Eleven	$22.46	$5.37

(Yes, gas was expensive that week.) At the top of each column in the list might be a link (for example, the word Date might be clickable) that lets the user relist the data sorted by that column, either ascending or descending. And each transaction might also be clickable, which might, for example, open a new window showing more detail about the transaction, if such information is available.

Backwards Odometers and Mile Markers

I do a lot of traveling, and I enjoy going on long drives across multiple states. In the United States, most of the highways have mile markers on them. These come in handy when the exits are numbered similarly. (Georgia and Florida used to not have exit numbers that coincided with the mile markers, but they recently changed that. California still doesn't even have any exit numbers on most of its highways, which makes trip planning that much more difficult.)

While the mile markers let me know how far I am from an exit, they also serve the wonderful purpose of knowing how far I have to go until the next state. (No, I'm not running from anything and need to get out of state; I just like to drive places!) If I'm heading west on Interstate 40, and I see the mile marker 140, I know I'm 140 miles from the next state. At 70 miles per hour, that's two hours of driving.

That works out well, as long as I'm going in the right direction. If I'm going the opposite direction, I'm at a loss. Unless I know what the maximum mile marker number is, I can't know how many miles I have left. And even if I do know, for example, that the maximum number is 432, I still have to do a subtraction in my mind every time I want to know how far I am from the state line.

Maybe I'm abusing the mile marker system and "they" never meant for me to use it to figure out how far away the state line is. But I do use it for that purpose. And a simple solution would be to have a small number at the bottom of the mile marker with the opposite mile marker, showing how far away the other state line is. This number could be smaller and at the bottom, so there's no mistaking the actual mile marker in case somebody has to call 911 to report an accident.

But in addition to the mile markers, I make heavy use of my odometer. My Honda has three odometers: one that tells me the mileage on the car and two trip odometers that I can reset to zero. But these odometers suffer the same problem as the mile markers: They go only one way.

Now an odometer that counts backwards still wouldn't be much help. If I know I have 50 miles to go and I reset the odometer to 0, counting next to 999999 then down to 999950 would cause some mental anguish in figuring out how far I have to go. (Although I could just ignore the 9999, but that's annoying.) Better would be if I could somehow type in five-zero (like on the timer on a microwave) and then watch the odometer count backwards, telling me how many miles I have to go! I would love that!

Now having spent a lot of time behind the steering wheel, I've given a good bit of thought to how you would type in five-zero without swerving off the road into a giant oak. A keypad would be impractical near the odometer and other gauges, and that would be hard to type on, since the steering wheel is in the way. Instead, right on the steering wheel could be 10 little buttons where I could type in the desired number. But a keypad arrangement (or a phone arrangement, which is upside down) wouldn't be practical, since typing while driving isn't a good idea. Instead, the steering wheel could have 10 buttons arranged across the front of the wheel from left to right, with 0 on the leftmost, and 9 on the rightmost, and I could press the buttons with my thumbs.

Continued on next page

That would be ideal! And it's not like I'm typing a 450-page book while driving down the road. (Don't give me any bad ideas, now!) I'd prefer to let my car move straight ahead, following the lines on the road…while the car easily tells me how much farther I have to go. (Of course, someday all cars will have GPS systems with such information, but that's a separate usage issue altogether!)

However, don't go overboard with the clicking! Just as you don't want to make the user jump through hoops in your software to get to where they want to be, you don't want to bog them down as they try to get to the information on your site. If you have further data for each transaction, you can easily use a smaller font and list the details below the transaction, for example.

Accessing Up-To-Date Information Online

The company carrying my cell phone lets me access the current bill online. That's a good thing; I can pay it online and see the current bill. Unfortunately, the information gets posted on the Web at the time the bill is printed, and I can't see any phone call data until the next bill posts. The website, then, is serving as nothing more than an online version of the phone bill.

Come on, folks, the information is there in the database. Why can't I see the calls I made yesterday on the website? Why do I have to wait three weeks until the *next bill posts*? Probably because of some computer limitation.

Nonsense. The data is there on the computer; let me look at it! But if you're concerned about the website hitting the database, then mirror the database, make the mirror available to web users, and, if necessary, update the mirror only once every 24 hours. That's good enough. And then I can look online and see all the calls I've made since the previous bill, and I'll have an idea of how far I am into my allowed minutes. And I can go through and see what day I called my editor, and I can find out what day my sister called me with a great book idea. The information is there, and the company has no reason not to put it online. (Don't tell me it's not possible, and don't make up technical excuses why it's too complex. I'm paying you a lot of money every month.)

Including Print Features in Your Software

If you're shipping software rather than reports, chances are your software will include at least some form of Print feature. In this section I share with you some tips on making the best Print feature possible.

Choosing the Best Menus

I get frustrated if I can't find the Print Preview and Page Setup features of a program. Some people have separate menu items for these; some people have them embedded all inside the Print menu. Other people put them other places, and those are the programs that frustrate me.

A lot of usage experts have strong opinions about whether you should have a single Print menu or more than one Print menu. I personally am fine with either approach, since I see both so often. Therefore, I recommend that you choose one approach or the other, and stick to it, and don't veer off and use some strange approach. Therefore, if you have separate menus, please use these three menus, all grouped together, and all under the File menu (or whatever you call your first menu):

- Page Setup...

- Print Preview

- Print...

The first menu item, Page Setup, should have an ellipsis after its title as I show here (which means a dialog opens). The item opens the Page Setup dialog. Every Page Setup dialog will be different depending on the software package, and so I can't give you specifics on what to include. But I can give you these general tips:

- Allow the user to set the margins.

- If your program is a graphics program, allow the user to choose the size of the graphic and whether it's centered on the page.

- *Don't* allow your user to choose which pages to print in this dialog; save that for the main Print dialog!

- Let the user choose Landscape or Portrait orientation, and *use the setting accordingly*.

The final item needs some clarification. In most operating systems, the print drivers can specify Landscape or Portrait. The problem is that the application software might not know about this choice and might try to print in the wrong mode, causing the pages to end up printed sideways, possibly taking up more pages than expected. The solution, then, is for the application software to be aware of whether Landscape has been chosen or not and to write the text and graphics appropriately for the choice.

RULE   Your application shouldn't just always print for Landscape and let the print driver choose which way to orient the printout.

The next menu item, Print Preview, opens up the Print Preview portion of your application. I talk about this in "Including a Print Preview," later in this chapter.

The final menu item, Print..., opens up the Print dialog box. Most operating systems have a built-in Print dialog box, and you're welcome to use this. However, these dialog boxes don't give your users much control, and for that reason I encourage you to consider creating your own Print dialog box, *but only if the built-in dialog box doesn't give you everything you need.* Your

Print dialog box should include these options (all of which belong here and not in the Print Preview dialog box):

- Which part of the document to print, such as which pages
- How many copies to print
- Which printer to print to

In addition, you should allow the users to open up the driver-supplied Print Options dialog boxes. What I recommend you do is look at the built-in Print dialog box and model your own Print dialog box after the built-in one, adding additional necessary features, such as which part of the document to print. However, remember to do this only if the standard Print dialog box doesn't offer you what you need; no reason to reinvent the wheel!

As an alternative, some people prefer to have only one menu and make the Print Preview and Page Setup features available from the main Print dialog box. That's fine, but these should perform the same options as I just described, except they're accessible from the dialog box rather than from the menu bar. Be careful, however, with the problem of cascading dialog boxes. You don't want the screen to look messy. Some people handle this by closing the dialog boxes in back and then reopening them when the front dialog closes. For me, that's also a bit messy, and that's why I personally prefer three separate menu items.

Including a Print Preview

A Print Preview feature is easier to implement than you might expect. Most operating systems these days (Windows is one example) let you create a canvas at print time, draw on the canvas, and then send the canvas to the printer as the page. A Print Preview is easy, then: Use the same drawing methods, but after you've finished, copy the canvas to the screen. Quick and easy. You have two things you need to worry about, however:

- You might have multiple pages to print; therefore, in the Print Preview feature, let the user select a page to view without having to exit out of the Print Preview and restart it.
- Printers have drastically different resolutions than a screen.

If a printer has 2400dpi resolution, and the drawing area on a sheet of paper is 8 inches by 10.5 inches, then the page has 19200 dots across by 25200 dots down. That's a lot more than the 1024 across by 768 down on a typical computer screen. The solution, then, is to scale the printout. But in writing the code to do so, you're actually opening up an extra feature that the users will appreciate, the ability to *zoom* the document in Print Preview mode.

Scaling is actually easier than you might expect. Most operating systems let you perform all your drawing routines based on inches rather than pixels. To scale, you simply adjust the dots per inch and redraw, done deal. In Windows, this is accomplished through what is called a Window Port and a View Port. You can read up on these in the API manuals.

RULE   Before writing all kinds of high-powered scaling routines, investigate which routines are available to you that provide scaling.

Remember, however, that fonts are sized not in pixels but in inches. A 12-point font takes up $12/72$ of an inch. When you draw a 12-point font on the screen, the operating system attempts to draw the font so it takes up $12/72$ of an inch, or .16666 inch. When you print to the paper, then, your font will also show up as $12/72$ of an inch. If you don't use the operating system's scaling mechanism and instead use your own calculations, you might be surprised to find that your fonts didn't scale. Be sure to read in the API manuals how the operating system handles font sizes as well.

Wasted Paper in Your Printer

I'd like to wrap up this chapter with a little pet peeve of mine about software in general. Too often, software doesn't let me choose what to print! If you, the programmer, created a software package that deals with text (such as a word processor), and I, as the user, select only a few characters, then let me choose to print only those characters I selected.

Microsoft Word 2000 and higher lets me do this, and that's a good thing. In the Print dialog box, there is an option to print the selection. That way, if I want to print only a single sentence in a 300-page book, I can do so. Internet Explorer lets me do this too, and it's in the "page range" option.

RULE   Don't make your users print the entire document every time.

Moving Forward

Getting your reports right is just as important as getting the general usability right in the rest of your software. Don't skip corners and forget that users are reading your reports and that the reports have their own usability issues.

In the next chapter, I take the notion of displaying data on the screen to the next level and talk about what issues you're going to be dealing with when adding a full web interface to your product. You have many options in doing so, such as embedding a web browser right in your application or having your application read HTML pages from the web and process them accordingly. And as usual, remember as you're reading forward that the goal here is designing highly *useable* software.

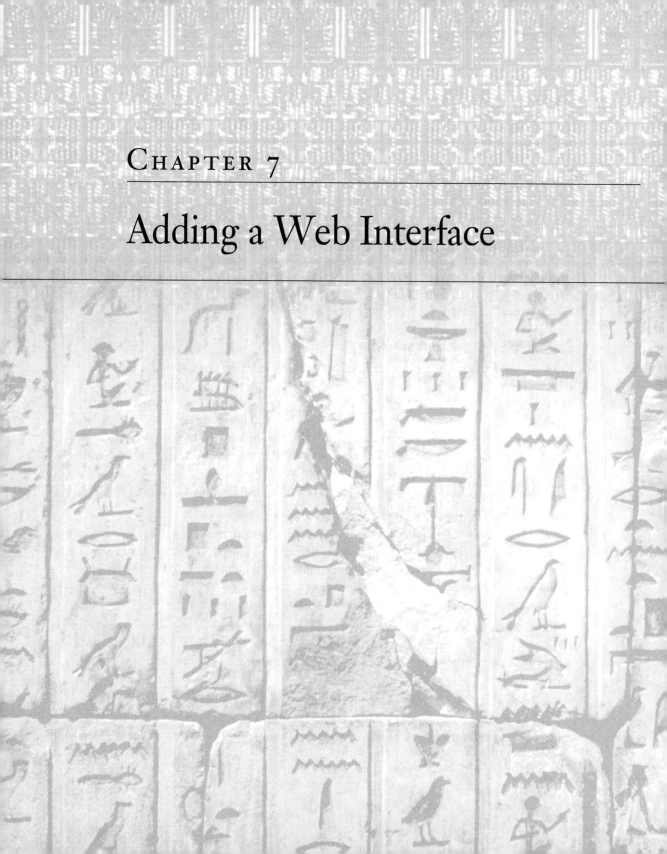

CHAPTER 7

Adding a Web Interface

T he Web has given us a whole new way of looking at software. Not only can you browse web pages, but you can create software that actually puts the Web to use; such software can grab files off the Web, process them, or whatever you want. From a technical perspective, creating software that interacts with the Web is pretty easy, thanks to the abundance of helper libraries. I would argue, however, that creating software that is highly useable is actually much harder. Read on for the details.

Accessing Data over the Web

In this first main section, I talk all about the issues of accessing data that's out there on the Web. Although I do provide a tiny bit of code here, the focus, of course, is on usability. Let's get started with a fun anecdote, and then you can move on.

Embedding a Browser (Yawn)

Microsoft made it easy: Want to add a web browser window to your program? Turns out, the center window in Internet Explorer (the part of the window that holds the web page) is an ActiveX component. That means that you can embed a web browser in any application *without* having to write your own! And because every Windows computer includes Internet Explorer, you can be assured that the users will have the ActiveX component already on their computer. What could be easier! If you want a web interface in your program, all you have to do is embed the Internet Explorer ActiveX component in your window.

But why? What would you gain? Would you like the users to be able to surf the Web right from within your application? What would be the point? Not much.

Now, in all fairness, including a web browser inside your program does have its places and benefits. For example, for the last couple of years, Intuit's fine product TurboTax has included a web browser inside it for the purpose of allowing you to set up your bank accounts. The assumption, of course, is that your bank provides a website for setting up your accounts, and you can access the site from within TurboTax, without having to switch over to a web browser.

But such examples are few and far between. Instead, the web browser component is useful for displaying data that is encoded in HTML. And more likely, your application can benefit from accessing data over the Web and processing the data, rather than just displaying browser web pages.

Even though to the average user the Web consists of billions of web pages, in reality those web pages are *data*. Further, the web servers hosting the web pages can have web services, which are, at the most fundamental level, suppliers of more data.

Paper Towel Fun

Ahhhhh, paper towels. Gotta love them. They cover the floors of our public restrooms, while allowing us the convenience of drying our hands without the hygiene problems of sharing cloth towels as we do at home.

While paper towels may be a great invention, the real ingenuity comes from the devices that dispense the paper towels. Now I don't mean to diss any Paper and Pulp Engineers who might be reading this book (yes, that's a real major; they had it at my university). I'm sure they're very talented people. But right now I want to talk about the dispensers. These are the works of our friends, the mechanical engineers.

The other day I was at a local franchise of a popular bookstore chain (its name starts with a *B*), and in the men's room they had a paper towel dispenser that was simply a tall, thin metal box attached to the wall. The paper towels were all stacked neatly inside the box, and the box was sized such that they fit perfectly. The hole for grabbing the paper towels was on the *bottom*. And what happened when I pulled out one paper towel? The one came out and stayed in my hand, and a dozen or so over-eager paper towels promptly climbed on out in hopes of joining their comrade but instead ended up *on the floor*.

But the solution to this remarkable device isn't straightforward! Suppose the hole were instead on top. Then soon the only people who would be able to reach the paper towels would be those with really long, narrow arms as the stack inside gets lower and lower. The rest of us would have to make do with wet hands. And you certainly couldn't just leave the front of the device open, for two reasons: First, the towels would probably fall out. And second, this device would qualify too closely as a shelf, and people might not respect it for the original invention that it was.

But a funny thing happened: The young college students who worked at this store seemed to come up with a pretty good solution: They just stacked a few towels on top of the dispenser. Yes, that's not all that different from the version of the dispenser that has no front. But it works. In fact, here's an even better solution: Skip the dispenser altogether and just leave a stack of paper towels on the counter.

But wait; that's not the best either: People with wet hands before me end up getting *my* paper towels wet. Gross.

What to do? I guess we'll just have to wait, and as our planet's culture evolves, maybe some sharp young minds of the 22nd century will come up with the best paper towel dispenser. Until then, I'll just keep my complaints to myself.

The data that consists of web pages is, of course, in HTML format. The data dished out by web services, however, is in whatever format the developers of the web services choose. (Most likely, the data comes down encoded in XML, and on your end you use the SOAP protocol to decode it.)

This book isn't a tutorial on web services. Instead, I want to share with you how web services can fit into your application, while providing you with a bit of background on web services, if you're not familiar with them. And if you are familiar, you might find that my suggestions are a bit unusual and out of the ordinary. That's okay; I'm not your typical engineer. I myself am a bit unusual and out of the ordinary.

In the sections that follow, I talk about how you can access data that's in HTML format using the HTTP protocol and how you can access data in other formats using web services. But the goal isn't to teach you how to code; the goal is to demonstrate how you can do these things while creating the most useable software possible.

TIP   One particularly interesting use of a web browser control is in displaying local files. This is most often done for online help and e-books. Using this method, you can actually create a sophisticated user interface completely in HTML. However, you want to be careful, because if you're using the Internet Explorer control on Windows, you could inadvertently give your users the ability to surf the Web from your program if you allow them to somehow enter a URL or if your local web pages include a link to a page such as a search engine. That might seem a bit strange to the users.

Requiring an Internet Connection?

These days, you can be pretty sure that the majority of your users will have an Internet connection. Therefore, you're safe in writing software that expects an Internet connection. However, remember the following:

RULE   Your users might not always be online, so don't require that they stay online. What if they're using your software on a laptop on an airplane or on the subway?

And on a similar note:

RULE   Many users still have slow dialup connections. Don't require them to have high-speed Internet yet.

But on the other hand, don't write your software strictly for the lowest common denominator, assuming that they don't have high-speed Internet or any Internet at all. Instead, write your software to have additional features that can support the high-speed Internet, but include features that also allow for a slower connection or no connection at all. In other words:

RULE   Write software that caters to everybody: those with a high-speed Internet connection, those with a slow connection, and those with no connection at all.

Of course, you will find exceptions to these rules. If you're writing a streaming audio program, then the software can't really function without an Internet connection.

TIP   However, I can think of a way around that one, too: Let the users download the streams beforehand and listen to them without a connection, provided the copyrights of the audio files allow for downloading. See, there's always a way, and never say *it can't be done.*

How do you make allowances for this varying crowd? Here's how. For starters, your software can detect the connection speed. If it finds a high-speed connection, then include the extra features. Is your software downloading images? Then the high-speed people can download higher-quality images. If the connection is slower, give the users an option: Would they like to download a poorer image, or would they like to download a higher-quality image? But don't ask this question every time the program wants to download an image; that would be a major annoyance. Instead, consider asking it only once, and include clear instructions about how to change the preference later on in your Options dialog (which you will have, right?).

If your application is downloading general data, not just images, then if it detects a high-speed connection, it can download larger batches of data more quickly. If it detects a slower connection, it can download only the absolute minimum data and grab more data as it is needed.

Your application can also behave in a hybrid mode: If the user is on a high-speed connection, in the background your application can download large amounts of data very quickly, save it to the hard drive, and then have the data available later if the user is working offline. (This is especially useful when your software runs on a laptop computer.) And again, make this hybrid mode an option.

And what about the people with no connection at all? Some software, of course, requires an Internet connection. But for other software, you might provide default data that the user can work with. Here's an example: Suppose you're writing a specialized word processing tool or graphics layout tool that includes templates for helping the users get started. Here are three different things you can include all at once within your program to cater to the different users:

- Default templates that are easy to use

- The option for downloading more templates

- The option for high-speed users to download even more advanced templates, with megabytes of sample images and text

These features would be available in a single software package. And there's nothing new here; I'm just laying it out in plain human language. Think of an e-mail program. When you're traveling, you might use Hotmail or Yahoo! Mail to check your e-mail, forgoing the downloading of huge attachments. Once home, you might download all your e-mail to your laptop while on the high-speed connection. But you might not be ready to read all the massive PDF files somebody sent you until you're back on the airplane, headed for your next destination.

Retrieving Data on the Web

Web servers usually offer their web pages as HTML files and then transfer the files using the HTTP protocol.

TIP   Remember, HTTP is just a protocol, and when you specify a URL, your prefix of `http://` is not actually part of the address but rather a directive to the browser to use the HTTP protocol.

Using various libraries, you can retrieve data from the Web using HTTP. For example, I've seen some weather programs that download files from The Weather Channel site (`http://www.weather.com`), process the information to extract the current temperature and forecast, and then render the data in their own format. (I find it hard to believe that this happens with The Weather Channel's blessing, but to each his own. Be careful if you choose to use this method using data from somebody else's website.)

Files on a web server, however, don't *have* to be in HTML format but can still be accessed via HTTP. The HTTP protocol specifies that in addition to the HTML file (or whatever type of file it is), the client software will first get a list of headers. These headers specify information about the file. *This is how your browser knows that a PDF file, for example, is a PDF file even if it doesn't have a* `.pdf` *filename extension.* Here's an example of the headers from my own website:

```
HTTP/1.1 200 OK
Date: Mon, 08 Sep 2003 02:17:10 GMT
Server: Apache/2.0.46 (Unix) mod_perl/1.99_09 Perl/v5.8.0 mod_ssl/2.0.46
OpenSSL/0.9.6g DAV/2 FrontPage/5.0.2.2634 PHP/4.3.2 mod_gzip/2.0.26.1a
Last-Modified: Sat, 09 Aug 2003 15:50:57 GMT
ETag: "14011503-c32-eb3e1a40"
Accept-Ranges: bytes
Content-Length: 3122
Connection: close
Content-Type: text/html
```

This includes a lot of blah-blah information, but the important part is the final header, which says that the content type is `text/html`. That means the file is text with HTML markups. For a PDF file, you'll see this header (in addition to others):

```
Content-Type: application/pdf
```

This data is all used by the browser. However, if you're using an HTTP library to access data via the HTTP protocol, your own client application is free to ignore all this information. In other words, you don't have to embed any specific content type header. I recommend that you do, however, in case somebody happens across the link and tries to access it with a browser. For example, suppose you have data on your web server for a popular program you have written, and you save that data at `http://www.Sybex.com/mydata.abc`. The `.abc` file format is your own special file format. If you put this file on your server, and you have an Apache web server, for example, Apache will not know what type of file it is, and will, by default, send it down with a basic text header of type text/plain. If web surfers happen across a link pointing to this file, and they type the address into their browser, they'll see the file rendered in text format.

> **TIP**   For sensitive or secure information, however, I hope you wouldn't just make it available via nonsecure HTTP; for that I would recommend more security.

By default, Apache uses the filename extension to make an assumption about what type a file is. You can, however, easily configure Apache to do otherwise, or, if you're not the administrator and can't modify Apache's configuration files, then I recommend that you create a CGI script that specifies the headers. Here's an example in Perl, which sends down four bytes (1, 2, 5, 10):

```
#!/usr/bin/perl
print "Content-Length: 4

print "Content-type: custom/abc

$data = pack("CCCC", 1, 2, 5, 10);
print $data;
```

> **TIP**   Instead of hard-coding the data into the script, however, you could have the script read the data from a file.

Now your client program can easily access your data via this CGI script. And if somebody tries to access the file via a web browser, the browser won't display the file as corrupted text, *at least in theory*. Netscape, in fact, responds by saying it doesn't recognize the file type and wants to know if it should download the file. Internet Explorer, however, makes a fundamental assumption: If it can't figure out the file type, then the file must be plain text. Oops! That's bad, unfortunately.

A slightly modified solution, then, is to cheat. This is nothing more than a hack; I admit it, but it works: Make the content type image/gif. Make sure you include a length header as I did here, and make sure it matches the data size. (Otherwise the browser will hang waiting for more data, although that, I suppose, would also prevent people from looking at it.) Then the browser will display just an icon representing a corrupted image. (Hey, it works; you have to admit it.) You can use this line for the Content-type line:

```
print "Content-type: image/gif
```

> **WARNING**   Now remember, however, I want to reiterate that this is not a secure method. This will not prevent people from gaining access to the data. Instead, it will just stop them from looking at the data in their browser.

Talking Cars: Shut Up, I'm Trying to Drive!

Back in Chapter 2, "Modeling the Real World," I told a story about the car that had the all-digital dashboard and what a disaster that was. I briefly mentioned the fact that the car talked. And now I want to tell you more about *that*. My dad owned a talking car, and this car had a whole host of usability problems, um, *waiting to be complained about*.

If the car was running low on fuel, the car would loudly announce, "Your fuel is low!" It would then do so every 10 miles or so. "I know, I know, give me a minute to get to the stupid gas station!" This was the mid-1980s, and if you remember back then and recall seeing a bunch of people driving down the roads, hands tightly clenching their steering wheels, and they seemed to be angry and shouting at nobody, then you know what they were doing: They were yelling at their talking cars!

But it wasn't just the fuel the car talked about. He (I mean *it*) had all kinds of things it liked to discuss. If you started up the car while somebody was still climbing in, the car would proudly announce, "A door is ajar." Now I clearly remember my young cousin Leah, who at the time was maybe six, heard this and said, "Why does the car say a door is ajar?" We all explained that it's saying so because the door is opened. Then suddenly we realized what she was *really* asking: "Why does the car say a door is a *jar*?" Oops, noun trouble. She heard the word *jar*. And we then had to explain what this new word *ajar* meant.

Talking Car Usability Rule Number 1: If you're going to make the car talk, at least use common words!

Then there was the day my poor mother was driving the car home from work when suddenly the car shouted, "Urgent! Severe engine problem occurring! Please get the car in for maintenance immediately!" She managed to drive the rest of the way home (apparently the problem wasn't *that* bad), walked into the house stark white, and my poor dad thought she'd had a heart attack. (I think that's when she took up smoking again, but I'm not sure.)

Talking Car Usability Rule Number 2: DON'T.

Forget the talking cars. And talking software? I turn on my speakers only when I want to listen to a CD. If your software talks, you better have it give me feedback in other ways, too, because otherwise I won't hear it. Seriously? Make it an *option*. Low-vision people can benefit from talking software; deaf people would not need the option. People who can both see and hear might want it or might not. Yes, an *option* is good, unlike the talking car, which wouldn't let us turn off the sound. (We got rid of it.)

And before I finish this story, while on the topic of annoying sound, don't even get me started on those websites that have annoying (and often cheesy MIDI-quality) music playing in the background. One editor of this book had a problem where he was shopping for a gift for his wife, and when he got to the website, he got bombarded with sound that gave away what site he was on. As a result, his wife, who was in the other room, couldn't help but know what he was buying for her!

Once you have your CGI script in place, your client program can easily download the data using any of the widely available HTTP libraries. (And please, don't write your own HTTP library unless you're an HTTP expert. Your job is to focus on your client program, not on writing an HTTP library. You want to ship your software on time, right? This is a book about usability, after all, and I want to encourage you to keep your software shipping on time and without bugs.)

Since this book isn't a coding book, I'll stop here on the data transfer methods, because you get the idea.

Auto-updates

The idea of auto-updating software is not very new; since modems have been around, several software packages have made use of auto-updates, where the software automatically downloads new data and software. America Online is one such program that has, for a very long time, done auto-updates. I was also involved in a project back in 1993 that did auto-updates. There are two types of auto-updates:

- Updating the software executables and libraries
- Updating the data

Regardless of which type of automatic updating your software employs, some common usability points exist between the two:

- Allow the users to cancel an automatic update.
- Include a timeout check in case the file stops responding, and let the user choose whether to resume.
- Allow for resumable downloads if possible.
- If the downloaded file is corrupted, discard it! Don't overwrite a perfectly good file. (This should go without saying, but I'm mentioning it here just in case.)

In the following two sections I cover the usability issues surrounding both types of auto-updates.

Automatically Updating Your Software Itself

Of the two types of auto-updates, auto-updating software is the touchiest. The reason is you don't want to be messing around with the very executable files that encompass your running program! Windows systems, for example, will not let you overwrite or delete files that contain currently running code. Unix is a little friendlier on the way it does file locking, in that it will actually temporarily maintain two different versions of the file: The programs that have the file open will see the original until they shut down and restart. Other programs will see the new file.

But you can still run into problems with Unix if you are modifying several libraries: You might have five shared libraries that you are modifying, and you've so far downloaded and modified three of them. Just then another user might start another instance of the software and load all five shared libraries. Three are new; two are old. That could be a mess.

From a safe programming perspective, then, you want your software to change itself only when convenient for the user. In general, here's a good rule of thumb regarding convenience:

- Windows users are likely to tolerate auto-updates of software.
- Unix users are *not* likely to tolerate auto-updates of software.
- Macintosh users *might* be willing to tolerate auto-updates of software.

As for the Unix situation, if you're a programmer, you probably have worked with Unix systems administrators. Do they really seem like the type of people who would want their software downloading automatic updates to itself? I didn't think so.

From a usability perspective, consider the following when updating the software:

SUGGESTION

Wait until the users have finished using the software before updating. In other words, wait until they want to exit the program.

I made that a suggestion and not a rule, because you might have times where you absolutely must update right away, such as in a stock program or some program with legal issues. Now here's another one:

RULE

Let the users decide if they *want* the update. (They might not be interested in the new features.) And further, let the users choose if they want the software to *never* update itself; they might, after all, be happy with the current feature set.

I can think of at least one program that updates itself when you exit, and then it restarts automatically. Let the users specify whether they want the program to restart. Don't automatically restart the program for them, especially if they're exiting. And finally, when downloading an update:

RULE

Warn the users how long the update is going to take, please. (This is especially true with dial-up connections.)

Automatically Updating the Data

Because a lot of people have "always-on" Internet connections (such as cable modems), your software can take advantage of the Internet and automatically download revised data right while the users are working. For example, Microsoft Streets and Trips has a really nice feature where it can download all the latest road construction information from across the United States.

If you are going to include such data auto-updates in your program, please follow the suggestions I've outlined throughout this chapter about not assuming that the users are online and so on. But also consider these points:

SUGGESTION

Don't require the users to automatically update. They might not want to do it right now!

And on a similar note:

RULE

Don't sneak around and update behind the users' backs. Ask before downloading an update, whether directly or through a user scheduling the update.

The second point is especially important in this day and age of viruses, Trojan horses, and other dangers. If I see some Internet activity going on in the tray section of the taskbar of my Windows system, I get extremely suspicious. If I see that my computer is downloading data, then I get worried. So don't be sneaky about the downloads.

You might also let the users schedule downloads. For example, if their computer is always on, you might give them a way to configure your software to download the data updates at midnight every night. But again, include a safety check: If for whatever reason the Internet connection is not active, handle the problem accordingly, such as by simply skipping the download and kindly notifying the user.

TIP

If you choose to notify the user, please follow all the good usability suggestions; don't freeze the computer by putting up a system-wide modal dialog box, for example. I'd personally opt for a message in the status bar, perhaps—something very innocuous.

After your program downloads the data, it can handle the data appropriately. Sometimes when you're writing a program that downloads data, you might have no choice but to restart the program. But please *try* to figure out a way that you don't need to restart the program. Can you unload the old data and then reload the new data? Only in extreme cases should your program require a restart. Don't force a restart simply because you, as a programmer, find that to be the easiest option. *Choose good software over programming ease!*

But also, if the users are in the middle of working with the data, don't force them to stop what they're doing. And don't interrupt their work with a modal dialog, loudly announcing to them that new data is available. (Don't you love it when you're typing along and a dialog suddenly and mysteriously opens just as you happen to press the Enter key, and the dialog takes the Enter key, instantly shuts, and you're left wondering what on Earth happened?) Instead, save the data away, and wait until a logical and gentle time to let the user know that new data is ready—if you even *need* to let the user know. If you don't have to, then don't!

For example, suppose your software calculates some financial data, and it periodically downloads various rate tables. The user might be entering some checks or whatever, and while doing so your software happened to download the new data. As soon as the user is ready to run an analysis, you can go ahead and let him use the new data you just downloaded. Why announce it to the user?

Or, you might do this: When the user is ready and clicks the Calculate button, you might open a dialog box asking whether to check for new data. Include on the dialog box one of those "Don't show this dialog box again" check boxes in case the user doesn't want you to ask each time.

Or, don't even bother: Include a separate "Download the latest rate tables" command, and let the user choose when to download the tables. With any of these options, you're not sneaking around, and you're not halting the user's work.

Synchronizing Data

This whole Internet business has opened up some fascinating ways of letting users manage their data, but it has also created a bit of a mess. For example, when I'm traveling, I want to be able to send and receive e-mail. And when I'm back home, I'd like to be able to have access to the same e-mail that I received and, if possible, the e-mail that I sent while I was traveling.

As programmers, we can do ourselves and others a favor if we recognize the problems of data synchronization. E-mail programs are just the start. As somebody who travels a lot, I've worked hard to come up with ways to keep my data synchronized.

In this section instead of laying out some rules and suggestions, I'd instead like to lay out some ideas for you to ponder. Software that makes heavy use of the Internet is still relatively young, and we, as engineers, need to really consider how we can get the most out of the technology. Consider these scenarios:

- I want to be able to send and receive e-mail from my laptop while traveling and then have access to the same e-mail from my desktop that I sent and received.

- I want to store all my files somewhere on the desktop and still have access to them when I'm traveling. (And please don't make me use version control software.)

- I want to save all my bookmarks and favorites in one place and have access to them no matter where I am.

What I'm about to say next isn't intended to make me sound like a walking advertisement. Instead, I want to use this a starting point for a solution to many of these problems. Here goes: The closest I've come to a central solution to all this mess is the services offered by *Yahoo!*. Yahoo! lets me store my bookmarks on its toolbar, which is a downloadable add-on to Internet Explorer. The bookmarks are all stored remotely on the Yahoo! server. Thus, if I make a change, the next time I log in from another computer, I'll see the change. I don't have the problem of storing separate versions.

This solution isn't ideal, however. The biggest problem that keeps me from using this is that I have more than one Yahoo! e-mail address. I paid extra for the additional storage, and I use that address for some of my professional work. Another one I use for friends. And the Yahoo! toolbar works per e-mail login. If I switch to another login, I lose my favorites. But it's a start, and a very good one.

The e-mail problem also has a solution in Yahoo!, but again, it isn't ideal. I have my own domain name, and I use that for my main e-mail address in addition to the e-mail accounts on Yahoo!. I have my Yahoo! e-mail set up to check the POP3 e-mail on my own domain. That works fine. But recently I discovered that my hosting provider includes web access to my e-mail. And that works well, too. Both of these work well for when I'm using somebody else's computer, and I have both set up to *leave the e-mail on the server*. That way, when I return home to my main desktop, I can download all my e-mail and still get copies and have them all stored neatly in my main e-mail program. Similarly, when I'm traveling with my laptop, I have an e-mail client on there that can send and receive e-mail through my own domain's server, again leaving the incoming mail on the server.

The problem, however, is the outgoing e-mail, and to this day I don't have a solution. When I'm traveling, if I'm using Yahoo! to compose e-mail or use the web e-mail on my domain or my laptop, the outgoing e-mail gets stored in the system that I'm using to compose the e-mail. And when I return home to the good old desktop, the outgoing e-mail doesn't end up on the desktop. Bummer. Sometimes for an important e-mail, I forward it to myself. But that's not good, because then I can't find it as I would expect it to be in the outgoing e-mail, but instead it's in the incoming e-mail with my own name as the recipient.

Storing my files is a separate problem. Because I'm a programmer, I'm well aware of version control software. But that's just too cumbersome. When I run out with my laptop, I don't want to have to first check my files back in from the desktop and so on. As I mentioned in "My Own Hourglass Problem Solved" in Chapter 4, "Managing Your Software's Time," the best solution I've come up with is to keep all my work files on a single CompactFlash card, which I normally use for my digital camera.

Now add to all this mess the "Wireless Revolution." I love wireless. I have two aspects to my own wireless world: Not only do I pay for a service that lets me be online at various coffeehouses, I also have for $6 per month web access on my digital cell phone. Using the cell phone, I can check my e-mail…through none other than Yahoo!. (I won't go into the Yahoo! e-mail interface on the cell phone; however, it could stand some improvements.) Fortunately, the cell phone doesn't really make the mess worse, because the cell phone doesn't store any e-mail; instead, it's just like using Yahoo! from any other web browser. But the cell phone *is* a factor in all the excitement.

Tear Here to Destroy the Instructions

I like to cook. The best way to cook is to go buy one of those nice spice packets, because then you don't have to mix your spices yourself. Okay, I'm just kidding. That might not be the best way to cook (I know at least one person who graduated from the Culinary Institute of America, and he doesn't use spice packets). But you have to admit, over the years, the spice packets have gotten pretty darn good.

But somebody somewhere made a mess. This time, however, the problem didn't originate with engineers but more likely with graphic artists. (See, we're not the only ones to blame for all the world's problems!) Here's the problem: When you tear open the end of the spice packet, you also tear off the top of the instructions!

Really, now. Did these people even consider this situation? This isn't a matter of designing the best protocol to transfer information over lines that may have a poor signal-to-noise ratio. No, this isn't a major engineering feat. Instead, it's a matter of spending just a wee bit more time laying out the graphics and text on the back of the packet so that I can still read the instructions.

The solution? It's an easy one: Don't put the instructions at either end of the spice packet! (Okay, I know, I could just tear the other end, but most humans by nature open things at the top. So don't sue me.) Just put the instructions in the middle. (Not that I expect that the graphic artists at these places will actually be reading this book, but if you happen to know one, could you mention this to him or her? Please? I'll cook a nice spaghetti dinner for you in return. Thanks.)

Moving Forward

Now we, as software engineers, designers, programmers, or whatever we call ourselves, need to start thinking about ways to build software that interacts with the Internet—both through wireless and more traditional methods—while maintaining high usability. Is it possible? Yes. We just have some work to do. This field is young, with lots of new software on the horizon, and now is the time to start thinking about usability, before the software is released and before the ideas are even generated. And if you follow all the rules and suggestions that I laid out in this somewhat short chapter, you'll be one step ahead of the competition.

This wraps up Part I of the book, "Keeping It Simple"! I've gone through a lot of issues dealing with the presentation of your software: the GUI, the reports, the web interface, and so on. The next chapter starts Part II, "The Lonely Engineer," where I talk about the programming side of usability. Usability extends far beyond just the obvious visual elements of a program. I start everything out with Chapter 8, "Under the Hood," where I talk about a miscellany of topics such as dealing with dynamic memory allocation. When done correctly, such programming practices as I describe shortly will greatly improve the usability of your software.

PART II

The Lonely Engineer

CHAPTER 8

Under the Hood

Part I of this book dealt with usability issues from the GUI perspective. Now it's time to shift the focus to what's under the hood—the innards, the guts of your software. Some people might be surprised to learn that the inner workings of your software have just as much of an impact on usability as the more visual GUI aspects of your programs.

In the following sections I provide you with some general issues that you should concern yourself with in your software development; handling these issues correctly will help you prevent bugs in your software and create better, more useable software.

REAL WORLD SCENARIO

Unscrew the Bottle Cap? No Thanks, I Like My Epidermis Just the Way It Is.

Some bottles—particularly beer bottles, but this is a family book (so be sure to read it to your kids)—have caps on them that are supposedly screw-off. Right. Yup. I can just hear the skin on my thumb and index finger ripping off, shred by shred. Isn't that a nice thought?

What in the world would possess somebody to make such a terror? Those old can tabs that you pulled off were a problem because they would sometimes fall into the soda cans (or get thrown out beside the highway), resulting in either choking or littering. Didn't we learn from that? No, today we have the screw-off bottle caps.

Ever since I was introduced to these some time back, I have opted for the bottle opener approach to opening them. And it works. So I suppose we could argue that the engineers did us a favor by providing us with an *option*. (Are there bottle engineers? I'm not sure, but I suppose somebody had to design these things.) The option is that I can either screw off the cap (no thank you) or take it off with a bottle opener.

Maybe the idea is that if you're in a place where you don't have a bottle opener (like driving down the road? Not a good idea if it's beer!), then you'll still be able to open the bottle, albeit at the minor cost of a few layers of epidermis and possibly a small amount of blood. But if you're really thirsty and stranded in Death Valley and all you have is a bottle of America's Finest Brewskie, then maybe this little pain and bloodshed would be well worth it. (Although they say drinking alcohol while you're dehydrated only makes it worse.)

Recently, however, I did discover that if I hold a rag in my hand, I can unscrew the cap without tearing my skin. However, I must admit, the truth is I've never actually tried unscrewing the cap with my bare hands. Maybe I would surprise myself and discover my own inner Superman abilities. Or maybe not; I am a piano player, after all, and like to keep my hands reasonably intact.

Fortunately, writing software rarely results in actual damage to one's person. And maybe we can take a lesson from the bottle engineers: They developed a device that serves two types of users: the manly men out there with thick, rugged skin (quite literally) and those of us goofy people who do things like, oh I don't know, *play the piano and program computers*. Now that's usability in a bottle!

Dealing with Dynamic Allocation

I like cars. No, actually I don't like cars, but I accept them as a fact of life, especially speaking as a guy who lives in the U.S.A. And that's why I use the car in so many of my examples in this book. Love them or not, they are a part of most people's everyday lives. But on top of that, the automotive industry has had a good 60 years or so to figure out a lot of issues that the computer world is still figuring out. (For example, I haven't tried to figure this out, but I wonder how long it was until they realized *brake lights* might be a good idea for a car.)

Now suppose you just bought a brand-new car, and you're running errands on a Saturday morning, trying to get everything done. You're at the bank, just leaving. You climb into your car, and when you try to start the car, you hear these words coming from some sort of (annoying) talking device in the car: "I'm sorry. You have started this car 17 times today. You'll have to wait until tomorrow to start it again."

Ridiculous, right?

Now imagine if the users of your software tried to open a document and your software announced this rule in the form of an angry message box: "Too many documents open. Please close one before opening another."

Exactly how many documents can your software open? 10? 16? 32? 64? 100? And what's significant about *these* numbers? Well, everybody knows that 10 and 100 are significant. And 10 is a very famous number. Lots of people have heard of it. I'm pretty sure it's famous because that's how many fingers a person has. And 100 is just about as famous as 10, because it's 10 multiplied by itself. As for 16, 32, and 64, these numbers are famous in the computing world because they're powers of 2. All good numbers.

But let me ask you this: What in the world do these famous numbers have to do with the number of *documents your software can open*? Nothing! Absolutely nothing! They're completely arbitrary. But you do have to pick something, right? Suppose you have a Document class, and you have an array that holds pointers to Document objects, like so:

```
Document *Docs[100];
```

This, of course, creates an array that holds 100 Document pointers. But that 100 is what some people call a magic number. It's a number hard-coded into your software that you or another programmer picked arbitrarily. Here are some of the excuses:

- "One hundred documents is more than anyone would ever need open." (Famous last words.)

- "I don't want to make the array too big, you know. Memory is expensive." (No, actually these days memory is *not* expensive, and arrays of pointers aren't very big.)

- "It sounds like a good number." (Magic, right?)

I'll get to the point:

Don't hard-code arbitrary limits in your software.

Instead of using a fixed-size array, use dynamic allocation. You can either code your own linked list, for example, or—better—use one of the container classes in the C++ Standard Library (or the library and types of whatever language you choose). I like to use the vector type:

```
std::vector<Document *> Docs;
```

That's it. This creates a container to hold the Document instances. And the container doesn't suffer from arbitrary limits. (Really, however, the container holds *pointers*. Please don't stuff the actual instances into a vector using, for example, std::vector<Document> Docs;. If you do, you'll end up with *copies* of the instances inside your container, resulting in copy constructors getting called, new instances getting created, and a big mess.)

NOTE If you're using one of the newer languages such as Python, creating a dynamic array is even easier. In Python, you can simply use the built-in array type, denoted by brackets, [ ]. Or, Borland's Object Pascal (found in Borland's Delphi language) has a TList class that works like a charm and has since the day Delphi 1.0 was released in the early 1990s.

Watch Those Pointer Variables

In the previous section I talked about how you can use pointers in your container variables. But as they say, with such power comes a certain responsibility. Pointers can be a mess if you're not careful.

You know the old story: Delete every object you create. But sometimes this is easier said than done. What if you're creating a library that other people will use, and one of your functions creates a new object and returns a pointer to the object? Who is responsible for deleting the object, you or the user? If you delete the object eventually, will the programmers making use of your library know that the object got deleted? And if you don't delete it, will the programmers think you deleted it, leaving it hanging around, using up memory? Before I move on, I'll go ahead and solve this one for you.

RULE The choice is yours as to whether you want to delete the object or you want the programmer using the library to delete the object. But whatever you choose, document it and make sure the people using your library are aware of your decision.

Ultimately, when dealing with pointers, you should have one goal in mind: to make the absolute best software that has no errors and no problems. All your efforts in worrying about memory allocation and handling orphan objects are for naught if your program isn't highly useable.

What difference does it make? Junk that's slightly better than other junk is still junk. And who decides if your software is junk? The users, of course.

Some of you might think I'm being a bit harsh here, but I would guess that at least in the world of C++ programming, pointer problems are the single biggest contributor to bugs in software, particularly crashes. Want to see a really easy way to crash your program? Here goes:

```
int main() {
    int *x = 0;
    *x = 0;
}
```

This tiny program, of course, tries to write the byte 0 to the memory address 0. And with the virtual memory systems of today's processors, that memory 0 probably isn't even mapped into the physical memory. Or if it is, who knows where the operating system mapped it to in physical memory. The end result? A big ol' crash.

Now, of course, you wouldn't write code like that, but you might find yourself writing code like this:

```
int main() {
    MyObject *inst = AllocateObject();
    inst->value = 0;
}
```

where MyObject and AllocateObject are part of a third-party library you obtained. Why is this code bad? It's not, unless AllocateObject returns a 0 or NULL pointer for whatever reason. Maybe AllocateObject requires an Internet connection, and during development and testing you and the testers all had Internet connections, but you forgot to test what might happen if the Internet connection goes down. And then you send out your software, and it works fine on 99 out of 100 systems. But that 100th system is struggling to get a connection in the dial-up on the old co-op phone system in the rural areas. Alas, the connection fails, so AllocateObject can't get the data it needs, and it simply returns a NULL pointer. Then your program will crash and you'll have an unhappy customer.

The solution, of course, is good error checking, like so:

```
int main() {
    MyObject *inst = AllocateObject();
    if (inst) {
        inst->value = 0;
    }
}
```

Easy! But of course, you need to handle this error and not just end the program as my little sample does. If the object is NULL, you'll want to ask the user how to proceed, whether to use some presaved data or whatever. (Look at what Internet Explorer does: If it can't get a connection, it offers to load the data from the cache if present.)

But this brings up a troubling question: Should you test a pointer every single time you use it? What if you call a routine, passing the pointer in, and you don't know but that routine might have just wiped it out? Let's consider that for a moment. Look at this line of code:

```
Wipeout(inst);
```

The `inst` variable is a pointer to an object. Can `Wipeout` wipe out the pointer? Maybe. But to be sure what `Wipeout` does, look at the prototype. Suppose it's this:

```
void Wipeout(MyObject *someinst);
```

You're a little bit safer here, because `Wipeout` doesn't take a reference. Therefore, whatever `Wipeout` does is on a copy of the pointer, not the original pointer. But that only means you're a *little* bit safer, because while `Wipeout` may be getting a copy of the pointer, that copy still points to the same object you're working with, which *isn't* a copy. In this case, `Wipeout` can still corrupt the data in the object *or call* `delete` *on the object*. (Don't forget about `delete`!)

If `Wipeout`, instead, takes a reference, then you still want to be suspicious, although in some sense you're actually a little safer. Here's a sample prototype:

```
void Wipeout(MyObject &inst);
```

To call `Wipeout`, of course, you need to de-reference your pointer:

```
Wipeout(*inst);
```

This is indeed safer, because your pointer never even makes it into `Wipeout`. `Wipeout` gets a reference to the object (which internally is really the function's own pointer variable totally separate from your pointer variable). Thus, there's no way for `Wipeout` to change the value stored in your pointer. `Wipeout` *can*, however, corrupt the object by maliciously (or accidentally) putting bad data inside the object.

Another really nasty thing that `Wipeout` can do is delete your object, which is something you might not expect it to be able to do considering it doesn't even take a pointer. Here's a sample `Wipeout` routine that deletes the object:

```
void Wipeout(MyObject &inst) {
    delete &inst;
}
```

This is particularly nasty because the calling routine really has no way to test whether this action took place without using some advanced memory management libraries. The reason is the original pointer is still intact and nonzero, even though the object is no longer valid. *Yet I have seen libraries with code like this frightening Wipeout sample.* And really, a `Wipeout` function that takes a pointer can do the same thing, of course. However, deleting a reference by taking the object's address is especially bad because you don't have to pass in a heap object; you can pass in an object that's on the stack, like so:

```
MyObject inst;
inst.value = 10;
```

```
Wipeout(inst);
cout << inst.value << endl;
```

No routine I call should even be attempting to delete this `inst` object! Yet, the compiler allows this code to run just fine. Yuck!

But do you want to know what's even scarier about code like this? The calling routine *might* be able to continue using the object for awhile! This, of course, depends on the runtime library, but the runtime might not have cleared out the object's memory. Instead, the runtime may have just left the memory there but noted that the memory is available for use elsewhere. This means your program might happily go along and only much later (after another call to `new`, most likely) your pointer will suddenly point to bad data and you'll get a crash. *My personal experience is that this is the absolute hardest possible bug to track down.* I'm not exaggerating; memory corruption takes hours upon hours to track down because you can't immediately identify when the corruption takes place. (For what it's worth, the gcc compiler and library I tested did clear the object's memory to 0 after deleting the object if the object was on the heap but not if the object was on the stack; however, values of all 0 for the data members might not cause your program to crash just yet.)

But the good news is this: This kind of evil code doesn't necessarily occur just in third-party libraries where you have no control. It can occur in your own code. When you're grinding out hundreds of lines of code a day, it's easy to forget exactly what you did in some function. Or, if you're working on a team, it's very easy for one of your less-experienced teammates to include such evil code.

My recommendations, then, are these:

- Be extremely conscientious of your `new`s and `delete`s.
- Document your functions carefully so people writing code to call into your functions know whether your functions will be deleting the objects.
- Consider purchasing a memory management tool that provides *instrumentation*.

As for the final point, several vendors create memory management tools that can be lifesavers in helping you track down problems. The way they work is that they start up in the background, and when your program starts, the utility performs an *instrumentation*, which means the utility analyzes your software for the function calls. Then you just use your program as you normally would. Once you finish using your program, you look at the utility's report. It will tell you if it found any problems, such as attempts to access an object after the object was deleted. It will tell you the line where the access occurred and provide a call stack showing the function flow that led to the line.

In addition, you can find various libraries that you link into your program that track all your `new` calls and `delete` calls, saving everything to a log file. Or, if you're ambitious, you can write your own such library by overloading the new and delete operators. Since this isn't a book on C++, I'm not going to show you how to do this; instead, I recommend doing a web search because I found lots of websites through Yahoo! that have tips on overloading the new and delete operators. (However, I did actually have a need to overload the new and delete operators in Chapter 9, "When Your Software Starts, Stops, or Dies a Quick Death," in the section "What About Exceptions in Constructors and Destructors in C++?" So you can find an example there, although I don't do any logging.)

Mucking with the System Directory: Keep Out!

If you're creating Windows software, here's a word of wisdom:

SUGGESTION

Stay out of my Windows directories!!!

Don't dump garbage—er, I mean files—in my Windows directory, or in my System directory, or in the System32 directory, or anywhere under the Windows directory (which I collectively call the *system directory*). I know a lot of people like to put DLLs there in the belief that their software won't function otherwise. But that's not true. If you put your DLLs in the same directory as your executable, Windows will find them. (At least one shareware program I downloaded put a file called SYS.DLL in my system directory; it took me all of 10 seconds to figure out that this file was a text file containing a number that represented how many times I could run the program.)

There are lots of good reasons to avoid the system directory beyond me griping about it:

- Some corporate users on Windows 2000 and XP don't have access to the system directory. Do you want them to be unable to install your software?

- You run into major versioning issues, even with your own DLLs, if people install multiple versions of your software.

- You might inadvertently name your DLL the same name as some other company's DLL that's already there. That would cause their software to malfunction. But what do you care? What if the user installs their software after installing yours, causing your software not to function?

If you're working with the new Microsoft .NET system, Microsoft has given you permission to put assemblies (which are really DLLs that make use of the managed system) in the system directory inside the global assembly cache. The global assembly cache is a set of directories under WINDOWS\assembly\gac. This directory includes various version directories; that allows you to have different versions of your own assemblies. However, before you get all gung ho about putting your assemblies in the global cache, remember that the only reason you should do this is if your assemblies will be used by multiple applications. Otherwise, put them in the same directory as your executable, and Windows will find them just fine.

> **TIP** Check out this link for more information on assembly placement: `http://msdn`
> `.microsoft.com/library/default.asp?url=/library/en-us/cpguide/html/`
> `cpconassemblyplacement.asp`. (If you don't want to type all that in, go to `http://msdn`
> `.microsoft.com/library/default.asp` and search on the string `Assembly Placement`.)

All Kinds of Mistakes Your Coworkers Make

Nobody likes to be told they're not perfect. So instead of telling you what mistakes you're making (because I can't know for sure), instead let me tell you about some of the mistakes your coworkers are making (like trying to burn up the poor processor). In the following sections, I talk about some problems your coworkers might have that can have a direct impact on the users.

Tight Loops and Burning Up the User's Processor

I've occasionally heard programmers make fun of the coworker who occasionally includes a line like this in his code:

```
sleep(1);
```

The typical response (while laughing) is, "What, sleeping for 1 millisecond is going to have an effect on the program?" Well, in fact, *yes*. By carefully placing this line in your code, you can greatly reduce the chances of setting your user's computer on fire (or, more likely, of causing the computer to melt). Pentium chips run hot. Have you ever opened up your computer and actually looked at the Pentium? You can't really see it because it's buried in the biggest heat sink this side of Jupiter, which is usually, in turn, underneath a fan blowing right down onto the heat sink. And the computer's case will have at least a couple of fans, too. We're talking *hot*.

The human heart is an amazing device, and sometimes people wonder, if the heart is just a muscle, how come it doesn't get tired? Doctors (or, more likely, trivia buffs) like to point out that the heart does, in fact, rest a lot. The heart muscle is a special kind of muscle tissue that relaxes in between each beat. The amount of relaxing time is greater than the amount of beating time. If the heart didn't get a chance to rest, we would probably live our lives like the hummingbirds, racing along at a hundred miles per hour and dropping dead after only a short time. (Hummingbirds live about three years.) Thank goodness for the resting time in between beats!

Today's microprocessors, like the human heart, need a rest. If you have a laptop computer, you've probably been surprised and even a bit alarmed to hear the auxiliary fans come on occasionally. What caused that? This program might do it:

```cpp
#include <iostream>
#include <stdlib.h>

using namespace std;
int main() {
    long long sum = 0;
    for (long long i=0; i<100000000; i++) {
        sum += i;
    }
    cout << sum << endl;
}
```

Now actually, this program probably won't make the fan come on, because it ends too quickly to really make the processor heat up. But if you were to put the inner loop inside an outer loop and perform this complex calculation, say, 50 times, then you probably will hear the fans come on. (Please don't try it.)

If you're on a Windows computer, try this: Type in the preceding program (without the extra 50-times loop), and start up Windows Task Manager. Click the Performance tab. You might also consider making the Task Manager "Always on Top" by choosing Options ➢ Always On Top.

Then compile and run your little test program. Watch the CPU Usage! There's a screen capture in Figure 8.1 if you don't care to try it yourself. The Usage is at 100%. You'll also notice that the processor jumped to 100%, dropped a bit, and then jumped back to 100%. The first jump wasn't caused by my program; rather, it was caused by the gcc compiler! I once nearly burned up a notebook computer trying to do an hour-long build with gcc. Bad program, bad! Fortunately, pressing Ctrl+S paused the compiler, and I was able to let the computer rest periodically.

What's causing this? Your program is running in a tight loop, without yielding to the operating system. Yes, you have a multithreaded operating system, and so the other threads do run. But you're not giving the processor a rest. And if you're writing scientific software, for example, that goes through lots of calculations, you run the risk of overheating somebody's poor laptop (like mine).

The solution is to throw in a `sleep` statement, which allows the thread to rest a bit while the operating system tends to the other threads. But you don't need to sleep with every iteration; that would slow your program down too much. Try some different numbers. For this sample program, I found that a sleep every 10,000 iterations worked well. Here's the fixed code:

```cpp
#include <iostream>
#include <stdlib.h>
```

```
using namespace std;
int main() {
    long long sum = 0;
    for (long long i=0; i<100000000; i++) {
        sum += i;
        if (i % 10000 == 0) {
            _sleep(1);
        }
    }
    cout << sum << endl;
}
```

FIGURE 8.1

The program runs the processor to 100%. That's bad.

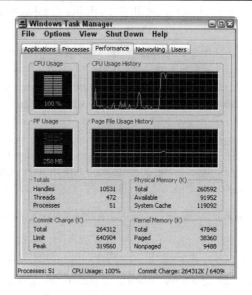

The implementation of the gcc compiler's libraries that I used has _sleep instead of sleep; you can check the header files to see what your compiler has.

With this quick change, the Task Manager no longer shows the processor running at 100%.

But there's a problem: Now the program runs considerably longer. Bummer. And so you have a trade-off. If you're writing software that is extremely calculation intensive, you might consider a user option that allows for the presence of the sleep function. Some people have computers with really good cooling devices that won't have a problem.

Invisible Programs Running in the Background

Programs that run in the background can be a problem to users. On a Windows system, for example, users can open up the Task Manager and look at what programs are running. Unfortunately, the Applications tab of the Task Manager shows only the programs that have a window. Any programs running in the background without a window show up only in the Processes tab. Unix users tend to be a bit more savvy and are more likely to use the ps command to see what processes are running, rather than just look at what windows are open.

Regardless of the operating system, a program running in the background can be troublesome, for many reasons:

- Users might not know the program is running.

- If users know the program is running, they might not know how to end the program.

- Users might know a program is running because they see its process name but not know what the program is or what it's doing. This is especially a problem today with the huge number of viruses out there.

Be careful before shipping software that runs in the background. If I find that a program is running in the background and it has an obscure filename or process name, I worry that it's a virus. This usually causes me to go to http://groups.google.com (formerly Dejanews) and start searching for information on the process name.

TIP   On Windows, I use an advanced program called Process Explorer, which shows information about each executable running, including the full path to the executable file. You can find this free software at the SysInternals site at http://www.sysinternals.com. Also, note that I say *free*, but licensing rules are applicable, including commercial licenses.

If your software must run in the background, here are some ways to make sure the users stay happy:

- Make it clear during the installation that the software will be running in the background.

- Include good documentation that explains how to use the software.

- Provide the users with a way to open a window to configure the software, even if this window is nothing more than a way to stop the program.

- Always include a way to stop the program.

- If you're writing a program for Windows, seriously consider including a tray icon on the taskbar.

One really great example of this is the open source Apache HTTP server. On Windows, the Apache server follows all these rules. Here's an example of the tray icon I presently see on my Windows computer:

The Apache server is represented by the icon on the bottom left. Above that is the icon for Zone Alarm, a firewall software package that also follows all these rules.

Unfortunately, way too many software packages *don't* follow these rules. I won't name names, but if you create and distribute such software, please consider the rules here. If nothing more, do you really want people to be afraid that your software is a virus?

Programs that Run upon Startup

Programs that start automatically when you start your computer are as troublesome as programs that run silently in the background. (In fact, often programs that run in the background also start automatically.)

I Love That Car Alarm That Goes Off Every Night

Ahh, car alarms. You've got to love them. They go off all the time. I recently did my civic duty and called the police because a car alarm was going off for about six hours early one Sunday morning. I even drove by the owner's apartment, and there was the car, its headlights blinking for the world to see. Other neighbors were standing around looking at the car, complaining about it. (And I lived a good quarter mile away and it was terribly loud!) And so the police took care of it: *They towed the car.* I didn't know that's what would happen, and I'm glad the owner didn't know I was the one who caused this. But then again, his little device caused me a great bit of frustration, too, so maybe fair was fair.

How many times have you heard a car alarm and immediately thought, "Somebody's car alarm is acting up again." Shouldn't you instead be thinking, "Oh, no! Somebody is breaking into a car! Call the police! Call the FBI! Send in the Mod Squad!" But no, we don't react that way. We have a modern technological version of the little boy who cried, "Wolf!"

Have you used a software program that was so unreliable that you got so you would expect it to crash—yet you had no choice but to use it because your boss required it of you? I can think of one in particular, but I'd rather not say what it is for fear of being sued. And the problem with this kind of software is that the disdain for it gets so bad that the disdain turns into pure, raw, unadulterated hatred. And from there, the people actually start laughing and joking about the software. "Yeah, I hate _____ software, too!" (Fill in the blank.)

Now imagine if you were on the team that developed that software. Sure, your bosses are getting rich. But what about you? Would you really want that on your resume come time to find a new job? I would think not. Therefore, make your software dependable. Make your software good, even if you're not in charge of the project. Good software really is possible. (And maybe if all else fails, leave a copy of this book on your boss's desk opened to this page. That might do the trick.)

The problem is often that during installation programs set themselves up to launch automatically at system startup *without the user's permission*. That leads to the first rule for this section:

RULE   Always have your program ask permission before setting itself up to launch automatically at startup.

A surprisingly high number of software packages are guilty of this. Yes, it's fine to have your software start at startup, but please ask for permission first. But that leads to a second tip:

RULE   Give the users a way to disable the automatic startup of your program.

Often users might like the feature at first but grow tired of it. And believe me, if you don't give me a way to disable the automatic startup, most likely I will uninstall your software and throw it into the trash. Or, if you don't include an uninstall option, I will delete it. (And I'm good. I will spend a half hour searching through the system Registry, wiping out all traces of your software!)

TIP   Time for a user tip: If you're a Windows XP user and you want to see what software launches automatically on your system, you can run the `msconfig.exe` program, found in `C:\WINDOWS\PCHealth\HelpCtr\Binaries`. In addition, you can download a great free program called Startup Control Panel (which is especially good for pre-XP systems). You can find this program at `http://www.mlin.net`.

Writing Overly Complex Code

You might be surprised to find this heading in a usability book. After all, what does code complexity have to do with usability? *Everything*. The reason is that if the code is terribly complex, chances are great that the person on your team suffering from a complexity complex didn't necessarily know what he was doing, and bugs can easily creep in. I'm very serious here. My experience is that true programming experts are few and far between, especially when dealing with a language such as C++, which allows code such as this:

```
template<typename _Item, typename _Traits, typename _Alloc>
    my_class<_Item, _Traits, _Alloc>
    operator*(const my_class<_Item, _Traits, _Alloc>& __a1,
    const my_class<_Item, _Traits, _Alloc>& __b1)
{
    my_class<_Item, _Traits, _Alloc> __ptr(__a1);
    __ptr.append(__b1);
    return __ptr;
}
```

Yes, if you look this over you can figure out what it does. But do you *really* trust your coworkers to write code like this? And what's going to happen after they quit and you're stuck maintaining this code? (Unfortunately, the various implementations of the C++ Standard Library are usually filled with code like this.)

Here's a quick tip: If you're using C++, you can easily `typedef` your sophisticated templates, and that alone will make your code easier to read and maintain and, most important, *debug*.

SUGGESTION

Have code reviews, and if you see overly complex code, encourage the author to rewrite it in simpler terms. In C++ this means breaking up complex lines into multiple lines and using plenty of `typedefs`.

Implementing an Undo System

In this section I give you pointers and tips on how to implement your own undo system. Because every software program is unique, I can't simply give you code here to drop into your system while you step back and watch your new undo system run. Instead, as usual, I'll give you some starter code that you can work with.

The best way to implement an undo system is by extending the command-based system I've discussed a great deal in this book. Since you're already implementing your software using a command-based system (you are, right?), this shouldn't be a problem. (Remember, a command-based system is nothing new; I didn't invent it. Most people attribute its invention to the *Design Patterns* book (Gamma et al.)

With the command pattern, you implement a new command for each feature in your application. To add an undo capability, you add an undo to each command. For example, if you're creating a graphics program and you have a command that applies a particular filter to an image, then you include an undo with that command that undoes the filter.

But how do you undo a filter? Well, you could try to actually run the filter in reverse, but that wouldn't work if you lost data in the filtering process. Instead, you store the previous version of the image. Yes, that can get costly in terms of memory, but a multilevel undo is extremely important in a graphics program.

Back in Chapter 1, "The UUI: The Useable User Interface," I provided you with a very simple way to execute commands. In that sample, each command is a function. A better and more useful way to make this work is to make each command an object instead. One way is to use templates; however, to keep this sample easy, I'll start with a `Command` class that contains a `run` method and an `undo` method. From there I will derive some commands. I'll also have a `CommandList` class that contains a list of the commands, an undo stack, and a redo stack. As I execute a command, I'll push the command onto the undo stack, provided the command can be undone. (Some commands, such as Print, usually aren't undoable.) Then when somebody issues an undo, I'll pop the command off the undo stack, call the command's undo method, and push the command onto the redo stack.

Quiz time: How many levels deep should I allow for the undo stack?

Answer: If you've read this entire chapter, you know the answer is that I shouldn't specify a fixed level.

However, suppose you're writing a graphics program and each level saves a copy of the image. That could eat up memory in a hurry. In that case, you'll want to monitor how much memory is available and make a rough estimate of how much space you can allow for the undo stack. Then, make this number clear to the users in one of two ways: either by choosing the level of undo for the users and noting it, perhaps right on the undo menu item itself, or by allowing the users to choose how many undo levels they want while telling them how many levels are available. But never just hard-code a magic number, saying, for example, "Twenty undo levels is good."

Now here's the sample code:

```
#include <iostream>
#include <stdlib.h>
#include <stack>
#include <map>

using namespace std;

// Base class for all commands
class Command {
protected:
    bool undoable;
public:
    bool isUndoable() { return undoable; }
    virtual void run() {}
    virtual void undo() {}
};

// Sample command
class ApplyFilter : public Command {
public:
    ApplyFilter() { undoable = true; }
    virtual void run();
    virtual void undo();
};
```

```cpp
// Sample Command
class PrintPage : public Command {
public:
    PrintPage() { undoable = false; }
    virtual void run();
};

void ApplyFilter::run() {
    // ApplyFilter code goes here!
    cout << "Running filter..." << endl;
}

void ApplyFilter::undo() {
    cout << "Undoing filter..." << endl;
}

void PrintPage::run() {
    // PrintPage code goes here!
    cout << "Printing..." << endl;
}

typedef stack<Command *> CommandStack;
typedef map<string, Command *> NamedCommands;

class CommandList {
protected:
    NamedCommands Commands;
    CommandStack UndoList;
    CommandStack RedoList;
public:
    void AddCommand(string name, Command *cmd);
    void CommandList::DoCommand(string name);
    void Undo();
    void Redo();
    bool HaveUndo() { return UndoList.size() != 0; }
    bool HaveRedo() { return RedoList.size() != 0; }
};

void CommandList::AddCommand(string name, Command *cmd) {
    Commands[name] = cmd;
}

void CommandList::DoCommand(string name) {
    // Do the command
    Command *cmd = Commands[name];
    cmd->run();
```

```cpp
    // Add the command to the undo list
    if (cmd->isUndoable()) {
        UndoList.push(cmd);
    }
}

void CommandList::Undo() {
    if (HaveUndo()) {
        Command * cmd = UndoList.top();
        UndoList.pop();
        RedoList.push(cmd);
        cout << "UNDO::";
        cmd->undo();
    }
}

void CommandList::Redo() {
    if (HaveRedo()) {
        Command * cmd = RedoList.top();
        RedoList.pop();
        UndoList.push(cmd);
        cout << "REDO::";
        cmd->run();
    }
}

int main(int argc, char *argv[])
{
    // Create the commands
    CommandList Commands;
    Commands.AddCommand("ApplyFilter", new ApplyFilter());
    Commands.AddCommand("PrintPage", new PrintPage());

    // Run a couple
    Commands.DoCommand("ApplyFilter");
    Commands.DoCommand("ApplyFilter");
    Commands.DoCommand("PrintPage");

    // Undo
    Commands.Undo();

    // Redo
    Commands.Redo();

    return 0;
}
```

You can easily adapt this code to your own needs. Remember some pointers, however:

- *Your commands usually won't have parameters.* Instead, those commands might open a dialog box that will allow them to gather information on the parameters, or they may gather the parameters from other means.

- *A dialog box should be undone as a single unit.* If the user configures a bunch of settings in a dialog box, clicks OK, and then chooses Undo, the state of your software should go back to just before the dialog box.

This second item shouldn't be an issue when you recognize that a dialog box is opened by a command, meaning that an undo will undo the entire command, including the results of the dialog box.

For example, if a command displays a Font dialog box, and the user sets the height to 10, then to 15, then to 20, then to 25, and finally back to 15, and then clicks OK, she would intend the Font size to be set to 15. She would be a bit disconcerted, however, if choosing Undo took the height back to 25, then another Undo action took it back to 20, then 15, and finally back to 10.

Moving Forward

With this chapter, I moved away from the more obvious usability issues such as GUI design and into the less obvious, but equally important, usability issues of good code design. I really did try to compile a huge program with gcc on my notebook computer, and the fan did come on, and the computer got incredibly hot. Would the computer have burned up? Possibly; I wasn't about to test it to find out. Remember, then, that usability isn't just for the people designing the GUIs. Usability impacts every aspect of programming.

In the next chapter, I work from both ends of the usability stick, the GUI end and the coding end, and talk about the issues of software startup and shutdown. And with this I also talk a bit about exceptions, because they can cause your program to die a sudden death. And if you've been reading this whole book up to now, you already know why a sudden death is so bad: It will cause frustration and, in turn, lost sales. Read on!

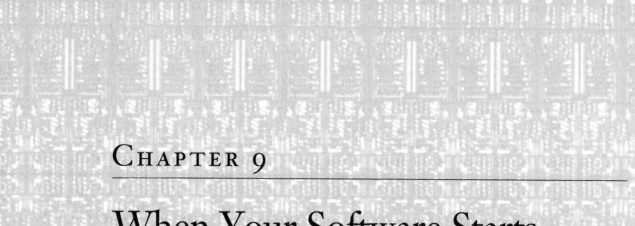

CHAPTER 9

When Your Software Starts, Stops, or Dies a Quick Death

S ome programs take a very loooooooong time to start up. Other programs start up instantly. Some programs seem like they take just a tiny bit longer to start each time you open them. Other programs take forever to shut down. Other programs shut down quickly. And some programs stop too quickly, in that they suddenly crash and shut down. Really, users are the happiest if a program starts quickly (preferably instantly) and shuts down immediately when they shut it down. And, of course, users don't want a program to crash. In this chapter, I talk about:

- Starting up your program (as well as starting with different options and allowing multiple instances of your program or not)

- Shutting down your program

- Dealing with exceptions

Starting Up

The best kind of software is software that starts up as quickly as possible. But sometimes an instant startup isn't possible. Your software might be linking to dozens of dynamically linked (or shared) libraries, which could take many seconds to load. Or it might need to scan a database or look up some data on the Web…or whatever. In this section I talk about ways you can minimize your startup time, as well as ways to make your startup as useable as possible. (Yes, usability even affects the starting of your application! You cannot escape!)

Minimizing Startup Time

Minimizing your startup time involves a fine line between keeping startup time as short as possible and not making the user wait for libraries to load periodically while using the program. The way most people minimize their startup time is by simply waiting until later into the program's running to do certain tasks, such as loading dynamic or shared libraries.

But on the other hand, you don't want to make your users sit and wait every time they try to do something while your program goes about its business, loading libraries, downloading data, and so on.

Your goal here should be to get the best of both worlds:

RULE   Try to keep the startup time within two seconds, and set other startup tasks to happen later on but without making the user wait at various times while using your program.

I would say that a pretty good limit for startup time is two seconds; anything beyond this is likely to frustrate the users. (And please don't say I'm being overly picky here. How long do you want to wait to start up that wonderful IDE that you use for developing your software?) In the world of computers, two seconds isn't bad. You can accomplish a lot in those 2000 milliseconds. You should be able to load plenty of libraries in that amount of time.

But you probably won't be able to check for an Internet connection. You might be able to connect to a database and briefly verify some data. But maybe not. And what do you do if you can't accomplish these tasks in two seconds? Then you don't do them during startup.

I don't like to pick on software programs in this book, but I will say that one particular web browser takes a very long time to load. (I won't say which one, but it's one of the "big two.") If you are a programmer who worked on this particular browser, you might like to know that that is the *single* reason I do not use the browser. It's true! Surely some of those tasks it's doing at startup could wait until later, right?

> **NOTE**   Although I'm raving about the importance of software that starts up quickly, I'd also like to point out that exceptions do exist. For example, a large-scale software system that runs on an enormous computer with many users might need rapid response time once the software is running. In such cases, you might see a need to let the software take as long as necessary to boot up. Use your best judgment, and base such judgment on the needs of the users.

Reading the Command-Line Arguments Even in a Windowing System

Yes, you're using a windowing system. But you really do need to make sure your software reads command-line arguments. Sound crazy? No! Whether you're using Linux or Windows or any of the others, if your program opens files, then it must read the command-line arguments.

The reason is that even on Windows you can launch a program from the DOS shell, specifying a filename. Try this from a DOS prompt on Windows:

```
notepad abc.txt
```

(You might want to substitute a real filename, but you don't have to.) Notepad will try to open the file called abc.txt, and if the file doesn't exist, Notepad will ask if it should create the file.

But don't ask this question like Notepad does. Come on, that's ridiculous. Here are some of possibilities that would result in the file not existing:

- You were in the wrong directory.
- You typed the filename wrong.
- You're creating a new file.

As programmers with a great understanding of usability, you and I now know that one of these is going to be the most common situation, and therefore the program should make an assumption. Yes, creating a new file is the most common reason why the file doesn't exist. Therefore, don't ask, "Do you want to create a new file?" Just do it! Make the file. (And besides, you don't have to actually *save* the file until the user saves it.)

Yes, on rare occasions you might be in the wrong directory or you might type the wrong filename. But these occur a lot less often than when you want to create a new file, and you can handle closing the program and trying again.

Back to the issue at hand: Notepad is smart; it reads the command-line arguments. Typically a command-line argument will be a filename. But not always; you might want to also accept command-line options.

This feature is useful, however, not only when running the program from the command line. In Windows, you can create a shortcut to the program on your desktop (or in any folder, or on the taskbar, or wherever) and include command-line arguments right in the shortcut.

Of course, when you're dealing with shortcut icons, you don't even need the program name; you can simply specify the document name, and Windows will open the correct program. But you can include command-line parameters if you wish.

But do users even know this? Some do; some don't. But enough power users are out there that chances are good that many people are going to expect you to accept command-line parameters. When I run a program from the command line, I expect the program to accept a filename as a parameter (if the program is one that opens files).

Here then are some suggestions for dealing with command-line parameters to make your software more useable:

- If your program opens files, then accept a command-line parameter of a filename, and open the file when the program starts.

- If your program can have multiple files open simultaneously, then accept multiple filenames from the command line.

- Decide how to handle the situation of the user specifying a filename when that file is already open in another instance of your program. Do you simply activate that other instance, or do you start a new instance that also has that file open?

- Consider using wildcards; if the user opens *.cpp, then open all the files matching *.cpp in the working directory.

- Consider including some command-line options if you think the users will have a need for them. If you have different views in which you can display a file, then maybe the user can specify the view in a command-line parameter, such as -v fullscreen.

NOTE   The debate is still going on as to whether you should use -v or /v for your command-line options (that is, a hyphen or a slash). Most Windows programs use a slash, although a lot more are starting to use a hyphen. Unix programs almost always use a hyphen.

Regarding the item about the user choosing a filename while the file is already open in another instance, you will want to give this some serious thought. Should you just switch to the instance already running? Or would it make more sense to open the document again? A lot of text editors open a document again, but frankly, you can run into some serious problems here. I take on this issue in the next section, "Allowing Multiple Instances of Your Program (or Not)."

Allowing Multiple Instances of Your Program (or Not)

You've seen how some programs won't let you run multiple instances. On Windows, I can think of dozens of programs that do this; Microsoft Word is one of the best examples.

Think very carefully about whether or not you want your program to allow multiple instances. On one hand, this can be handy. Microsoft Outlook, for example, lets you run multiple instances. You can then have one instance showing your Inbox and another instance showing your Calendar. This makes sense, since Outlook doesn't let you open up two separate windows like Microsoft Word does. (However, Microsoft Word has an option where the documents can either all be in a single main window or they can occupy separate windows. When the documents are in separate windows, the screen looks like the windows are separate Word instances, but they're not; only one instance of the WINWORD.EXE process is running.)

The developers of Outlook went to great lengths to make sure that you can run two or more instances of Outlook. For example, if you use one instance to send an e-mail message, and that window shows a message in the lower-right corner saying that Outlook is sending your e-mail, the other instances will also show this message. And then when you've finished, your Sent folder will update in all instances. Clearly there's some interprocess communication of sorts going on here. (Showing you how to do such interprocess communication would be beyond the scope of this book; however, you can find plenty of information in the various SDK documentation.)

Different operating systems have different ways of allowing you to detect whether an application is already running. On Windows, you *used to* be able to check the hPrevInstance passed into your WinMain. But in the more recent versions (Windows 2000, XP, and so on), this parameter is always 0. The official way on Windows now is to create a named mutex (make sure it's unique, like the name of your program followed by a bunch of numbers). If you get back an error that the mutex already exists, then you'll know that somewhere out there on the same computer another instance of your program is running. That's easy. Then you can just call FindWindow to locate the main window of the other instance and call ShowWindow. Then shut down, leaving the original instance running.

But what about a command-line argument? As I mentioned, Word allows only one instance. Suppose I'm running Word and I type this into the command prompt:

```
winword c:\letter.doc
```

If I open up my handy-dandy system spy tool called Process Explorer (available from Sys-Internals at http://www.sysinternals.com), I can see a second instance of Word start up. That's cool; it's doing what I just described. But then I see the second instance stop, and then the first instance loads the c:\letter.doc document. How did that happen? I talk about this in the next section, "Accepting Files and Opening Them While Your Program Is Running."

NOTE   Since Windows 95, you have been able to launch a program based on a document. If I create a shortcut, I can point the "command" to a document such as `c:\letter.doc`. Now really, `c:\letter.doc` isn't a command, but the Windows Shell system doesn't care; it will locate the correct program based on the filename extension and run the program.

One major issue about running multiple instances is whether you want to allow users to have two instances of the program modifying the same file. Although Microsoft Word does not actually run multiple instances, if you do try to run another instance while specifying a command-line argument of a filename that is already open in Word, Word doesn't try to open the file again. Instead, Word activates the window containing the document.

Most text editors do allow two separate instances of the program to run, each modifying the same file. This is dangerous for the user. I've allowed myself to open up one code file in multiple instances of my favorite text editor on Windows, and then I'll forget that I have two open and go my merry way modifying the code in one of them. I'll save that code, test, change it, save it, test some more, and so on. Then later I'll accidentally switch to the other instance, type something in, save...and kablooey, all my earlier changes are lost. Fortunately, if the instance where I made all the changes is still running, I can go back and rescue my code. Otherwise, I'm toast. (And yes, I'm speaking from experience.)

For this reason, I usually encourage programmers to follow this rule:

RULE   Do not allow multiple instances of your program to open the same file if the users can make changes to the file.

This, of course, doesn't include a read-only program such as a web browser, where you don't use the software to save files, only open them.

Accepting Files and Opening Them While Your Program Is Running

Suppose you allow only one instance of your program, and the user types the name of your program followed by a filename, expecting your program to open. Then what? *The answer is that the running instance should open the file.*

If I have Microsoft Word open and I open the command prompt and type

    winword myfile.doc

then the currently running instance of Microsoft Word will open the document. Really, however, I can do any of the following to see this behavior:

- Type `winword myfile.doc`.
- Type just type the document name without the program name: `myfile.doc`.
- Double-click the document in Windows Explorer (or a shortcut to the document).

All three of these options work the same way; however, Microsoft apparently used two different methods to make these work. If Word is already running and you type just the filename, `myfile.doc`, without the program name, or you double-click an icon for the file, the Windows Shell system initiates a DDE (Dynamic Data Exchange) conversation with Microsoft Word and tells Word to open the file. DDE is a method of interprocess communication that has existed since before Windows 95, all the way back to the 16-bit days of Windows.

If you type `winword myfile.doc`, on the other hand, a second instance of Word momentarily starts up. This instance then communicates with the existing instance, telling that instance to load the file. Then the new instance shuts down. For this process communication, Word uses COM (Common Object Model, formerly called Object Linking and Embedding, or OLE).

Don't Open Two Drawers at Once (Severe Bodily Injury Could Result).

Now who in their right mind would design a huge object like a file cabinet that goes in every office on the planet and create it in such a way that if you use it wrong you could be seriously injured or killed! (For some reason, the word *automobile* just popped into my head. I'm not sure why. But back to our scheduled program....)

A file cabinet, by itself, seems rather benign. Unlike a car, you don't actually get inside it and project yourself down an interstate at 70 miles per hour. But, if you fill the file cabinet with so many books and papers that it weighs hundreds of pounds, and then you open two drawers at once, it could become front-heavy and fall forward right onto you (or your unsuspecting help from the local temp agency).

For some time, these file cabinets just came with instructions, apparently (in some minds) absolving the manufacturers from all liability claims. But since then, I admit, they have designed better file cabinets. Most just have a contraption inside that prevents more than one drawer from being opened at once. I imagine some engineer won an award for that one (perhaps saving millions in lawsuits?).

But I can think of some other options; maybe somebody else did too. For one, a file cabinet could be bolted to the floor. (This, of course, has the added benefit that some seriously determined robbers couldn't just haul off the entire file cabinet, waiting to pick the little lock in the comfort of their own living room. Don't laugh. I've heard that automated teller machines used to have this problem.) Another option is to include a counterweight. Of course, this might make delivering the thing kind of difficult.

Regardless, we, as software engineers, can learn from this example. Don't let your software suffer from bugs that are easy for the users to accidentally run into, with catastrophic results. Cover all your bases. For example, suppose a user happens to type a strange set of keystrokes that inadvertently causes your program to run a macro that in turn shuts down the program without saving the files. Wouldn't your support people like to take that phone call?

The topics of DDE and COM/OLE are big enough to fill an entire book. Thus, I'm not going to give you the whole rundown on how to use these to add interprocess communication to your application. (Besides, you're an advanced programmer; you don't need step-by-step handholding.) Instead, I'll point you in the right direction. If you want to implement DDE and COM/OLE, hop over to the MSDN website at

```
http://msdn.microsoft.com/default.asp
```

and type DDE or OLE or COM into the search box. I recommend that you find some of the technical articles, download the sample code, play with it, and then work it into your own application. (That's the way I learned this stuff, after all.)

Shutting Down

If you're using an older compiler, then strange things can happen when your program exits. The newer compilers don't seem to suffer from this problem, but I know that in the late 1990s, when you would create a new object and then let the object run out of scope at the end of your program, you had no guarantee that the object's destructor would get called. Here's the situation I'm talking about:

```
int main() {
    MyClass inst();
}
```

A simple program like this in the past had no guarantee that the inst instance's destructor would actually get called. However, I did test this out on three compilers—gcc, Microsoft Visual C++ 6.0, and Microsoft Visual C++.NET—and all was fine. The destructors do get called when an automatic instance inside main goes out of scope.

That aside, I won't lecture you on the importance of cleaning up after yourself. Remember when your program closes to:

- Close database connections.
- Close any files you left open.
- Delete any temporary files you left around.
- Free any memory you allocated (don't rely on the operating system to free the memory, even though it probably will).

You know the routine. From a GUI perspective, in addition, you'll want to make sure you don't just close the program without saving important information (such as the file your user was working on). All this should go without saying. Enough said.

Correctly Using Exception Handlers

A lot of computer scientists warn us not to use exception handlers as general error handling. I disagree. Why not? They work, and they work well. And the last thing you want to do is manually propagate an error out of a function call stack that's eight levels deep. The exception mechanism already does this for you!

My goal here is not to teach you how to use exceptions; plenty of good programming books offer that information. Instead, what I'm doing here is giving you tips on how to use exceptions most effectively with the end goal of creating good software that handles error situations appropriately by:

- Not dying

- Not issuing angry messages directed at the user

- Not leaving resources open and causing memory leaks

Now in theory, the final bullet item shouldn't be a problem if your program is shutting down. (But experts argue over how much the popular operating systems—most notably, Windows—really do clean up after a program shuts down.) However, where you run into trouble is if you handle an error situation appropriately and therefore your program *doesn't* shut down. But what if the error keeps happening, and each time you're allocating more and more resources? Then your user's computer could eventually run into a low-resource situation.

In the following sections are some tips that will help you make exceptions work for you.

Handle All Exceptions

Please make sure you handle all your exceptions. This includes exceptions generated by any third-party library you might be linked to. If I forget to handle an exception, here's the error I see using gcc:

```
This application has requested the Runtime to terminate
it in an unusual way. Please contact the application's
support team for more information.
```

The bold emphasis in this error is my own. Wouldn't your support team love to get a phone call like this:

Angry customer: "Hey, dude, your software shut down and it told me to contact you."

Support team member: "Tell me exactly what happened."

Angry customer: "I dunno, I was just using it and the program died, and I saw this message that says I need to call you."

Support team member: "What were you doing when it died?"

Angry customer: "What, you sound like you're blaming me for this problem?"

Support team member: "Uh, no, uh, I just need to know what situation was taking place when the software died."

Angry customer: "I already told you! I was *using* it!"

Support team member: "Okay, let's try a different approach. What do you see on the screen?"

Angry customer: "Nothing!"

Support team member: "So your screen is blank?"

Angry customer: "No, you idiot! I see a message…"

You can see where this is headed. And you can also imagine the bug report you'll receive, and you can see having to fill in the "cannot reproduce" check box in the bug report after you've messed with it. And then a week later another customer calls with the same problem. And then another, and another, and soon the VP of Engineering is coming down on you and the other programmers to *find* the problem and fix it. But how do you find the problem if you can't reproduce it? And worse, imagine this thought that will keep you up in the middle of the night: *Where is that message coming from?*

> **WARNING**   If you're a Windows programmer, don't think that you're immune to mysterious messages. I placed the same code that caused gcc's runtime library to dump the preceding message inside a nice, unsuspecting MFC application. Figure 9.1 shows the error I received inside a message box.

Remember, if you're just not sure what exceptions could be called, use the catchall exception handler of an ellipsis, …, in C++.

Clean Up Resources Appropriately

One common mistake in exceptions is that people forget to clean up their resources. Cleaning up can be tricky at times, so you'll want to spend some time to make sure you get it right. The general idea is to put cleanup code inside your exception handler.

FIGURE 9.1
Windows programs also generate a message that's not exactly user friendly.

But think about this scenario: You have a function that opens a file, and then the function opens another file. But during the second file opening, an exception occurs. Inside your exception handler, you have code that closes both files. The problem is the second file's handle is not valid, since the file never opened. Oops!

One way to code around this problem is by wrapping exception blocks around exception blocks. I'm not particularly fond of that approach, however, as it makes for code that's hard to read. Instead, a simple solution is to initialize your file pointers to 0 (or NULL) and then inside the exception handler, first check to see if each file pointer is 0. If the file pointer is not 0, then close the file. Otherwise, skip it.

Unfortunately, this causes another coding problem that I'm not fond of: duplicate code. You want to clean up your resources if an exception occurs but also if an exception doesn't occur. The following complete program (which I used gcc to compile) demonstrates a simple solution to this problem:

```cpp
#include <iostream>
#include <string>
using namespace std;

class SomeException {
public:
    string filename;
    SomeException(string afilename) : filename(afilename) {}
};

class FileInfo {
public:
    string filename;
    FileInfo(string afilename) : filename(afilename) {
        cout << "Opening " << filename << endl;
    }
    void Close() {
        cout << "Closing " << filename << endl;
    }
    void Process() {
        cout << "Processing" << endl;
    }
};

FileInfo *MyFileOpener(string filename) {
    // Force a demo exception
    if (filename == "another.dat") {
        cout << "Forcing exception..." << endl;
        throw new SomeException(filename);
    }
```

```
        cout << "Opening " << filename << endl;
        return new FileInfo(filename);
    }

    void FileStuff() {
        FileInfo *file1 = 0;
        FileInfo *file2 = 0;
        try {
            file1 = MyFileOpener("testfile.dat");
            file2 = MyFileOpener("another.dat");
            file1->Process();
            file2->Process();
        }
        catch (SomeException *e) {
            cerr << "LOG FILE: Unable to open " << e->filename << endl;
        }
        // Clean up!
        if (file1 != NULL)
            file1->Close();
        if (file2 != NULL)
            file2->Close();
    }

    int main() {
        FileStuff();
    }
```

I'm assuming you're fluent in C++, so I won't walk you through this code line by line; instead, I'll make some general comments about the code. (However, I would like to point out—in case you're not aware—that the 1998 ANSI standard of C++ now supports initialization of object members by following the constructor name with a colon, then the member name, then the initial value for the member; you can see I do this in both the SomeException and FileInfo classes.)

As you can see, this code includes a class that simulates the opening, processing, and closing of a file. (I like to create my own classes for such work to help with encapsulation; a real program would actually open the files, of course, rather than just print out a silly message as this sample does.) To simulate an exception, I've hard-coded a test for whether the filename is a certain value, and if it is, I throw the exception. This, of course, occurs inside the routine that is supposed to create a new instance of the FileInfo class. Thus, when this line runs

```
    file1 = MyFileOpener("testfile.dat");
```

I will get an exception, causing file1 to remain at its initial value of 0. I next catch this exception and write it to an error log. But thanks to the beauty of the exception-handling system, the code will continue running after the exception handler. Thus, whether I get the exception or not, I can clean up. I do so by checking the value of file1 and file2 before calling each object's Close method.

TIP   Some languages (notably Java and Borland's Object Pascal) have a construct (called `finally` in Java and Object Pascal) that gets called whether the exception occurs or not. This is a great place to put your cleanup code. The idea is that you put your throwable code inside a `try` block. Then you put cleanup code in the `finally` block.

What about Exceptions in Constructors and Destructors in C++?

If you use exceptions in constructors and destructors, you need to be extremely careful to get it all right. And part of the problem here isn't just what you do but rather what the experts all say. The experts disagree on how and whether to use exceptions in constructors and destructors:

- Should an exception throw an exception? And if so, what's the best way to handle it?

- Should a destructor throw an exception? And if so, what's the best way to handle it?

I know that if I take sides on this issue, I'm going to get letters from people telling me I'm wrong, no matter what I say. But let me point out some things:

- Not all compilers handle exceptions thrown inside constructors the same way.

- I've heard from people that some compilers might allocate the object itself without deallocating the object if you throw an exception inside the constructor. (But see my point following this list!)

- None of the compilers call a destructor in response to an exception handler.

NOTE   Regarding the second point: I ran a test and found that the gcc does indeed deallocate the object by calling `delete` if you throw an exception inside the constructor. The compiler does *not*, however, call your destructor in such a case. I then tested this out in Visual C++ 6.0 and Visual C++.NET, and both of these compilers also deallocated the memory. Apparently doomsayers abound.

Now just to get you thinking here, let's say you allocate some resources inside your constructor, and toward the end of the constructor something causes an exception. Suddenly you're back out of the constructor and inside your exception handler. How do you clean up the resources? The object doesn't exist (or does it?) and so you can't call the object's destructor!

I think everybody would agree with me that this is a mess. Therefore, I suggest clients do either of the following:

- Don't allow exceptions to be thrown inside constructors. Instead, include in the class a member variable that holds a status, and check the status after the constructor.

- Don't do anything inside the constructor. Instead, have a separate `Init` member function (or some similar name) that you can call; this `Init` function can throw an exception, and then you're free to call the destructor yourself.

- Put a `try/catch` block inside the constructor to catch any problems, and then do the cleanup inside the `catch` block. Then, inside your `catch` block, rethrow the exception, allowing the code that created the instance to catch the exception.

Regarding the final point, you don't have to actually rethrow the same exception. Instead, you can make your own exception class called something like `ConstructorFailed`, for example. And as for cleaning up your resources inside the constructor, you can manually call the destructor function, if you want, simply by calling `~MyClass()` but not by calling `delete`. (Yes, theoretically you can call `delete this` inside your constructor, but come on, do you really think that's clean programming style?)

Here's kind of a silly little program that throws an exception inside the constructor, catches it, does some cleanup, and rethrows the exception. (Now really, you would probably catch an exception that was generated by a function call made by the constructor, as opposed to just throwing the exception as I did here.) You can see in this code how I called the destructor function without deleting the instance. (The gcc compiler required that I use `this->` before the destructor name.)

```cpp
#include <iostream>
using namespace std;

class MyException {
};

class Failable {
public:
    int x;
    Failable() {
        try {
            x = 10;
            throw (new MyException());
        }
        catch (MyException *e){
            this->~Failable();
            throw (e);
        }
    }
    ~Failable() {
        cout << "Cleaning up..." << endl;
        x = 0;
    }
};

int main() {
    try {
```

```
        Failable x;
    }
    catch (...) {
        cout << "Oops..." << endl;
    }
}
```

Incidentally, if you're wondering how I tested whether the compilers deallocate the object if you throw an exception inside a constructor, here's how. I included these two member functions in the preceding class declaration:

```
void * operator new(size_t s) {
    cout << "new..." << endl;
    return malloc(s);
};
void operator delete(void * mem) {
    cout << "delete..." << endl;
    free(mem);
};
```

When I ran the program, I saw the messages "new..." and "delete..." appear on the screen, meaning the C++ runtime did indeed clean up everything on gcc, Visual C++, and Visual C++.NET.

But what about destructors? Can and should you have exceptions inside destructors? The answer is yes you can; as for whether you should, it depends on your particular situation. Generally I try to avoid exceptions inside a destructor, because you do have one big problem: On most compilers (including gcc) if you throw an exception in the destructor, the C++ runtime library will not finish deallocating the memory for your object. (You can test this by overloading the new and delete operators as in the preceding new and delete samples, creating an instance on the stack, and then throwing an exception inside the destructor.)

Therefore, I usually recommend the following:

- Do not throw exceptions inside a destructor.

- If your destructor calls functions that could throw an exception, wrap the call inside a try /catch block, and handle the exception right inside the destructor. In addition to assuring that your object's memory will be deallocated, you can also be assured of continuing with your own cleanup code inside the destructor.

Specifying Exceptions in Function Headers in C++

Be careful if you use the throw keyword inside a function header like so:

```
void b() throw (ExceptionA) {
```

C++ gurus encourage us to use this construct because it provides good documentation for what exceptions the function can throw, and it doesn't allow any additional exceptions to propagate out of the function. Well, if you're not careful, you can end up with a problem if your function calls other functions that throw other exceptions. Look at this code:

```
class ExceptionA {
};

class ExceptionB {
};

void a() {
    throw new ExceptionB;
}

void b() throw (ExceptionA) {
    a();
}
```

Look closely at what this code does; if you call function b, then b will call function a, which in turn throws an exception that b refuses to propagate. The C++ standard says that in such a situation the C++ runtime library can terminate the application.

Not a good situation. Here's how you prevent this, regardless of your compiler: Handle all exceptions! In this case, using the throw keyword in the function header is actually a good thing when used properly, because it prevents your function b from being the evil function that threw an exception others weren't prepared to handle. The key in making this all work, however, is in making sure your function handles any exceptions it receives. The solution is to put an exception handler inside b and include the ellipsis exception handler, like so:

```
void b() throw (ExceptionA) {
    try {
        a();
    }
    catch (ExceptionA e) {
        throw e;
    }
    catch (...) {
        // Handle the exceptions yourself!
        HandleSomething();
    }
}
```

This code rethrows the ExceptionA exceptions that it receives and *handles all others*. The end result is that your users won't see a horrible message.

Oh, and by the way, what do you do if you're using a third-party library that you purchased, and you call a function in the library that has a `throw` keyword in its function header, and that function doesn't handle some exception it receives from another function within the same library? You get to call the third-party's support team and give them a hard time! Because try as you might, you cannot coerce the function into passing the exception outside it. Changing the header file won't work; you need to change the original source, which is typically a bad idea when dealing with third-party libraries. If you change just the header file, and you're linking to an object file, the gcc linker will be fine, but you won't change the behavior of the function. So you're stuck. Call the support team (and tell them about this really great book you're reading about usability!).

Moving Forward

How your software starts, ends, and even dies has a huge impact on its usability. Remember that I refuse to use a certain web browser because I don't like the way it starts up.

Give careful thought to the issue of how your software handles errors and whether it dies a sudden death. Remember the users. And fair is fair; I know a lot of people who refuse to use the other main browser because of the way it handles errors: It opens a message box asking if it can notify the manufacturer. That irritates more people than the manufacturer probably realizes. (Hint: If that bothers you, you can disable the feature by removing a certain file. Search `groups.google.com` and you'll see how to do this. I don't care to say it here, however, because I don't want to be responsible for your removing system files!)

In the next chapter, I take on the topic of libraries and modularity. That's a topic that rarely occurs in a book on usability. Yet think how many times software has dumped DLLs all throughout your hard drive, making a mess of your system. I'd say that qualifies as *poor usability*. Read on.

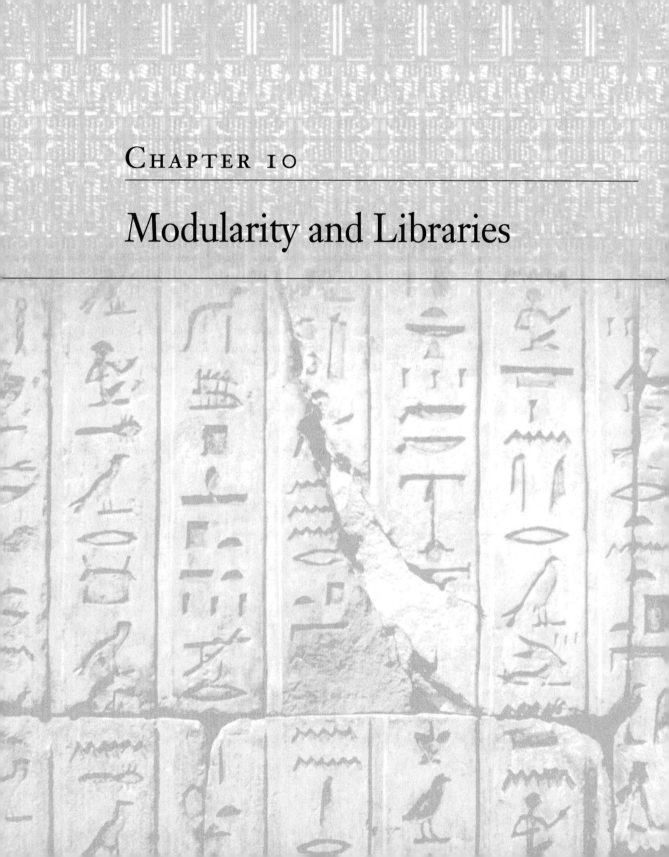

CHAPTER 10

Modularity and Libraries

As a programmer, you're well aware of the importance of breaking certain parts of your code into libraries. Further, you're aware of how to do that. But what are the usability issues of libraries? Does usability even stretch into the domain of libraries? Sure it does! And in this chapter I talk about such issues. I do not, however, talk about how to create a library, since that's a topic you can find in introductory programming books and online help documents.

Dividing Your Product into Libraries

Libraries are a touchy issue. Some developers prefer to break up their code into numerous dynamic libraries, while other developers prefer to keep the whole program in a single binary executable file. And as for those who combine everything into a single binary executable file, some people prefer to divide the code into multiple static libraries that get linked into the final executable.

I'm not about to tell you what's right and wrong in this regard from a developer perspective (primarily because each approach has its pros and cons). However, I am going to tell you how the users perceive libraries and what effect they have. Therefore, I'm going to assume that your projects either:

- Include dynamic libraries
- Link to static libraries

Unless you're creating a rather small application, rarely will you develop a product that has no libraries, whether shared or dynamic.

> **NOTE**   In this chapter I use the term *dynamic* for the type of library that lives in a single file separate from the binary executable file. This dynamic library gets shipped with your product. Unix people know this type of library as a shared library. On Windows, the library gets a .dll extension. On Unix, the file gets a .so extension.

Static versus Dynamic?

Before I get into the details of the usability differences between static and dynamic libraries, I'm going to sum it up with these two important points:

- Static libraries make for larger executables.
- Dynamic libraries allow for smaller executables but more files.

These two points can be either good or bad for the user. A single but large executable:

- Can be easier to uninstall or move to a different directory
- Can be difficult to download, since even a compressed .zip file containing the library can be large

If I Only Knew Who Invented Coax Cable

Quick: What engineering design do you despise more than anything else on the planet? For me, the one I can't stand is coax cable—you know, that kind of cable that goes between your cable TV and the wall jack. Yes, you've seen it; it's that cable that has a little screw-on end.

Here's the main problem I have with coax cable: It takes two hands to screw it in! One hand to hold the cable, and one hand to screw the end on. Why does one hand have to hold the cable itself? Because so often the screw-on part is too tight (due, perhaps, to corrosion or something), and if I try to turn the screw-on part without holding the cable in place, the cable will spin, *too*. And the moment I let go to reposition my hand for another tightening, the tension causes the cable to unwind, undoing my previous tightening!

Then I have another problem with coax cable: Trying to unscrew it, I encounter the same difficulties of trying to screw it in, only it's usually sticking even worse, and again I need to somehow reach two hands down behind that VCR (as if one hand could fit, much less two).

I'm only going to say this once, and I'm going to scream it at the top of my lungs: WHO ON EARTH INVENTED THIS THING!!!! It's clearly the work of the devil, straight up from that place in the center of the earth with eternal fire and brimstone.

Look at USB cables. They just snap right in. Why does coax have to be the way it is? No reason. No reason at all other than to frustrate honest, hard-working citizens such as myself who never did anything wrong to the engineer personally responsible for this abomination. My glasses are starting to steam up just typing this. I can feel smoke coming out my ears. I better go take my blood pressure medicine.

One day, as it happens, I stumbled across something that was so incredible I would almost happily trade in every last slice of pizza for some guarantee that this invention would replace every coax cable on the planet. This was a special, new kind of coax cable with no screw-on cap. Instead, it had a plastic cap that doesn't screw, and the cord just slides onto the jack! It was amazing! It was truly amazing! I would say I was so thrilled by this invention that I hung the thing on the wall over the mantel for all to see. But that would have been a travesty to let it go to waste. Instead, believe me you, I put it this wonder cable to use! This cable is on the back of my VCR, transporting tiny little happy electrons from one end to the other as they eagerly do their work carrying data and information for my eyes and ears to behold.

Why would somebody make something so difficult to use? Using coax cable without the happy aforementioned invention is akin to making the user hold down the left mouse button while typing a paragraph with both hands. Imagine that. I don't have to imagine it; I have experienced coax cable.

Be a good programmer and don't do to your users what the coax engineers have done to me. You want your users to live long and prosper and purchase more of your products so you, too, can prosper, right? Make only good inventions with your computer.

Dynamic libraries, on the other hand:

- Allow for easy code sharing between applications

- Allow users to download just the executable if they already have the dynamic libraries

- Can make for a cumbersome installation when your user's computer has to manage possibly dozens of files

- Can also make for a difficult time when your user's computer needs to locate the dynamic libraries

The Trouble with Dynamic Libraries

I'll be blunt: In general, the whole issue of managing dynamic libraries has, since the early 1990s, been, frankly, *a disaster*. So you wrote a really great static library that you use in your application. Do you really believe that other developers will use this library? And further, what kinds of usability issues are present if another developer uses your library, in addition to the legal and financial issues?

Think about this: You created a great library, and another developer is using it. That developer distributes a program. Do you allow the developer to ship your library with his application? And do you require the developer to pay you a flat rate for using your library, or is it free? Or, heaven forbid, are you charging royalties on each copy the developer sells?

RULE   I say *heaven forbid*, because, frankly, don't do that. Don't sell a library and then demand a cut of every copy the developers sell. The reason is developers *hate* this kind of arrangement, and the moment they cross paths with your competitor who doesn't require royalties they will ditch your product and go with the competition faster than you can say, "Pay me, please!"

And, of course, you might run into legal issues. Let's say your library has a bug in it whereby if the other developer uses a certain routine wrong (in other words, goes against your documentation and requirements), it ends up wiping out a user's database. The user promptly files a lawsuit against the developer, who tracks down the problem as being within *your* library. The developer then blames you, even though he used the product incorrectly. And although you feel you're in the right, anybody can sue anybody, and before you know it you're being sued as well. Can you say *long, drawn-out court battle*? Nice try. Frankly, I'd rather stay clear of that.

Those are just two of the financial and legal issues that could come up. But what about usability issues? Some developers might expect that your library is so incredibly popular that it will already be installed on every user's computer. (Face it: that's only going to happen if your company's initials are MS.) But worse, what if the users do have your library, but it's a different version from the one the other developer is expecting? Imagine if a developer's product manages to link to the different version, and all is fine until one day the program crashes, displaying a message that there was a problem deep down inside a file that you created. Soon the other developer will be getting tech support calls and then will be routing the calls to *you*.

Many things can go wrong when a third-party developer uses your libraries. Here are some of them:

- The third-party product's installer might overwrite another version of the library that's required for another product.

- The third-party product might locate the wrong library.

- The third-party product might simply use the library incorrectly for whatever reason, resulting in bugs that you get blamed for.

- The third-party developer might not know that your library, in turn, requires certain other libraries, and then when the developer does a mass distribution of software, half of the installations won't work because that other product isn't present.

Regarding this final point, such a situation should not occur if the third-party developer did her homework on the installation process. The developer should have tested the software on a clean machine. Further, the developer should have used the various binary dump tools to determine exactly which libraries are present and whether or not such libraries are typically already installed on an end user's computer. Still, if the developer doesn't do all this, you could get blamed for the resulting problems!

But even though the developers (including you) end up getting into battles with each other, the person who ultimately gets the brunt of the punishment is the forgotten end user. Here this user has just paid good money for a software package, and the user might need the package for a business purpose. Meanwhile, as you and the other developer are fighting over who is at fault, the end user is growing more and more frustrated by the day as the product does not function. Remember, software is for the end users. Yes, you may be in it for the money, but the software itself ends up on the end user's computer, and that's the person who must live with this potential garbage.

But even if a third party isn't using your dynamic library, users can still run into problems. Here are some issues:

- You happen to name your library the same as somebody else's library. Two programs end up on a single computer, each requiring a different library that has the same name, and at least one program picks up the wrong one.

- A user installs two programs, and both require the same library. (Both programs might have been written by you!) Later the user uninstalls one of the programs, and oops, the dynamic library got uninstalled as well. Now the remaining program no longer functions.

But things can get worse:

- Your library uses certain resources (such as a log file or a hardware port) and two programs use your library. A single user runs both programs simultaneously, and one of the programs crashes.

- And one final usability issue that I can think of (among many more, no doubt) is this: The user's computer ends up with dynamic libraries thrown every which way, piled in every directory imaginable, making for a Royal Disaster of a Hard Drive.

For what it's worth, Microsoft has even identified the realities of this Royal Disaster, and the marketing people at Microsoft have even informally adopted the term *DLL Hell* to describe the situation. (Microsoft has attempted to solve this problem with their .NET architecture, confining the dynamic libraries to the private bowels of the system directory known as the Global Assembly Cache. Dante would be proud.)

Frankly, life need not be this way. I would like to think that my software never runs into this problem. Why? Because back in the 1990s, I worked for a software company that did something right: They spent a lot of time carefully organizing their libraries. (They did this because they created libraries for use by third-party developers.) There I learned how to make dynamic libraries *right*. All these problems I'm describing in this section need not occur. Therefore, please don't think I'm saying you shouldn't use dynamic libraries. I'm not at all. Instead, in the remaining sections of this book I talk about the correct way to create and use dynamic libraries, in addition to shared libraries.

What Makes for a Highly Useable Library?

In the previous section I talked about all kinds of things that can go wrong with dynamic libraries. Unfortunately, some of these problems can even occur with static libraries, such as the point about two libraries vying for the same resource. (What difference does it make if the code is linked into an application or sitting in a dynamic library? If two copies of the code are running, and both vie for the same resource, you will still have problems.)

Therefore, in the following sections I talk about some approaches you can take to ensure that you will create a library that is *good*. And, of course, this being a book about usability, I'm talking about libraries that are highly useable. (Would you expect anything different?)

A Unique Naming Convention

Choosing a unique name for your libraries helps make sure they don't clash with other libraries. This section applies primarily to dynamic libraries, although if you're creating a library (either static or dynamic) to be used by other developers, you want to make sure your names don't clash then, either.

It would be crazy for me to try to give you a naming convention and then tell you to stick with it. However, what I can do is offer suggestions. First, the days of 8.3 filenames on Microsoft systems are a thing of the past. For some time even after Windows NT and Windows 95 both came along, some network servers still had trouble with long filenames. That's not a concern anymore. You now have plenty of room to work.

Therefore, with all that extra space in a filename, consider using a naming convention that includes your company or product name, or an abbreviation of your company or product name. For example, instead of this name

```
comm.dll
```

for the communication portion of your software, try something like this

```
abccomm.dll
```

where abc is the name of your company. And if you want to embed version numbers (something I talk about in a later section, "Proper Handling of Versions"), you might do something like this

```
abccomm03.dll
```

for version 3, for example. Or, you might even make a name that's especially clear to end users, such as

```
CompanyName_CommunicationsLibrary_v03.dll
```

Thus, remember:

RULE   Pick a name that you're reasonably sure will be unique.

Loading the Dynamic Library Now or Later?

On most modern operating systems, you can choose whether to have a dynamic library load automatically by the operating system when your application starts or to have your program load the dynamic library itself, manually.

You can read about all the technical details elsewhere on what exactly takes place when the operating system's loader loads a dynamic library for you as it loads your application. The process involves loading the library into memory, obtaining the memory addresses of all the exported functions, and then loading your application, filling in the memory addresses of the function calls. Although complex, this process is easy for the programmer, because you don't have to do anything at all; the operating system takes care of the hard work.

But, like everything in life, you get what you pay for. With this minimal work comes minimal power. If you want the loader to load the libraries for you, you're limited on where those libraries can be located on the hard drive: They can be in the same directory as the executable, or they can be on the system path. (At least, that's the case for Windows. Unix uses a very different approach, which I'll describe shortly in this section.)

If you want to load your dynamic libraries from places other than the same directory as the program or the system path, you can instead manually load the libraries, specifying the full path and filename for the library. But that's just the beginning; you then have to manually obtain the memory address of each function in the library you wish to call and then call the function through a pointer. If you attempt to just call the function directly, then when you build your program, the linker will not complete, because it will be unable to find the function you're calling.

To locate the functions in your library at runtime, you use the GetProcAddress procedure, which is part of the Win32 SDK. This is a well-documented procedure, and therefore I won't be showing you here how to do this.

In the sections that follow, I talk about different issues surrounding dynamic libraries, and in many issues I compare the pros and cons of letting the loader load the library versus loading the libraries manually.

Proper Handling of Versions

Microsoft Windows allows you to embed version information in your DLLs. *It doesn't work.* Yes, you can embed the information, and yes, you can hope that the installation program you're using is smart enough to look at the versions, and you can hope that other developers have used installation programs that look at version numbers. And you can also hope that if a user installs your program first and then installs somebody else's program that uses one of the DLLs that your program installed, that other program's installer will be smart enough to not overwrite your file if the version is older.

At least you can hope. And while you're at it, you can hope that all disease, famine, and war will end.

Or, better, you can become an activist and try to help end disease, famine, war, and DLL problems. I can't give you many tips on the famine thing, but I can give you some tips on dynamic libraries, whether on Windows, Unix, or any other system, regardless of whether the system supposedly supports versioning information.

But in case you're curious, here's the rundown of versioning information on Windows. First I'll give you the old version approach, and then I'll talk briefly about the way Windows does versioning under the newer .NET architecture. And then after that I'll show you how you can implement your own versioning system, regardless of operating system.

The Old Windows Versioning System

Although the older versioning system on Windows is pretty much useless in a practical sense, I do recommend using it if for nothing more than to embed version information in your files in case anybody (including some wiser installation programs) looks at the files.

When you link together a binary executable on Windows (whether the executable is an EXE file or a DLL file), you can include resources in the final file. Such resources can include bitmaps, menus, dialog boxes, icons, string constants (for international programs, you can embed translated strings in place of your native language), and yes, version information.

Figure 10.1 shows an example of a project in Microsoft Visual C++ 6.0 where I'm setting the version information. You can see from this figure that the version information resource includes:

- File version

- Product version

- Operating system

- File type (which can be VFT_APP for application, and other names for such types as DLL, device driver, virtual device driver, and font file)

In addition, you can enter the following information:

- Comments: Some general comments by you

- Company name: The name of your company

- File description: A description of what the program does

- File version (this is just a copy of the file version in the upper part of the screen)

- Internal name (such as Competition Killer 1.0, I suppose)

- Legal copyright: Such as Copyright (c) 2003 Me, Inc.

- Legal trademarks: Such as The Me logo is a trademark of Me, Inc.

- Some various build numbers and product versions; the product version is a copy of the product version in the upper part of the screen.

FIGURE 10.1
Visual C++ lets you
create a version
resource for your
executables.

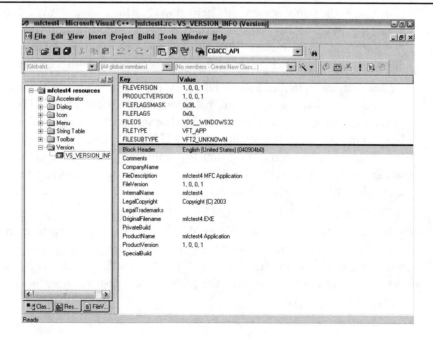

You can treat every bit of information in this version screen as strictly *comments*. You can put whatever you want in them. What is the information used for? Very little. The biggest problem is that even though you might have two versions of the same DLL, you might well use the same filenames for the two versions. But here's the big problem: *Windows doesn't allow two files in the same directory to have the same filename, even if the two files have different version information.*

Some smarter installation programs use the FileVersion field, and some system utility programs display all the version information. But beyond these uses, this information really isn't valuable. However, if you are using Windows, I still recommend that you create a version information resource. The reason is that some power users (such as me) will use various spy tools to see which executables are running on our computers. Such spy tools will list information from the version information resource, if the information is present; otherwise the tools will list just the filename. And if I see something like this

```
ea.dll
```

(or `ea.exe`, or `ea.vxd`, and so on), I'll be suspicious and will begin searching the Web under the assumption that I'm looking at a virus. But if I see with the entry an entire description of the program, then I'll feel a little bit better. (Of course, the virus makers could lie and claim their file comes from Microsoft, for example. However, if I see no information at all, I automatically assume *virus*.)

The New Windows .NET Versioning System

The Windows .NET architecture takes a very different approach to versioning. You can put your files in the Global Assembly Cache (GAC), which is really just a directory on the computer, usually `C:\WINDOWS\assembly\GAC`. But you *don't* just dump your files off inside this directory. Instead, you have to either make use of the installer tool that ships with Visual Studio.NET or use the `gacutil.exe` program that also ships with Visual Studio.NET.

Now remember, in .NET, your DLLs are called assemblies. (Technically, an assembly is a type of DLL that contains additional information used by .NET.) I briefly mentioned the GAC in Chapter 8, "Under the Hood," in the section, "Mucking with the System Directory: Keep Out!" But here are more details: The GAC includes a separate directory for each assembly. (That's why you don't dump your assembly into the GAC's directory; you need your own subdirectory.) Under each subdirectory lives a separate subdirectory for each version of the assembly. The subdirectory is named for the version. Finally, inside each version subdirectory goes your actual DLL file containing the assembly.

The Visual Studio.NET installer tool is the tool you use to create an installer for your end users. The end users use your installer to install your product, and you can set up the installer to insert assemblies into the GAC. Or, if you're installing a product manually (such as on a developer computer), you can use the `gacutil.exe` program by simply typing

```
gacutil /i myfile.dll
```

(The online help entry for `gacutil` describes all the command-line parameters, such as one for listing the contents of the GAC.)

In order to put your assembly in the global cache, you need to make sure your assembly is a *strong-named assembly*. A strong-named assembly is simply an assembly that has a public key and digital signature attached to it, combined with information about the assembly, including its name and version number. (There's that version stuff I've been talking about.) I won't show you the steps for creating a strong-named assembly; instead, open up the Visual Studio.NET Combined Collection (that's the name for the online help) and type **strong-named** into the index. There you'll find all the gory, er, I mean *helpful* details. After you create a strong-named assembly (even if *strongly named* sounds better), you can insert the assembly into the Global Assembly Cache.

But you don't have to always put your DLLs in the GAC. In fact, in general you should not put them in the GAC. Put them in the GAC only if you expect them to be used by multiple applications. For your own private assemblies that will be used only by your program, simply put them in the same directory as your executable file.

Now just to make sure I'm not blowing smoke here, I created a sample project in Visual C++.NET. The project is a Managed C++ Class Library. I then created a key pair (which is required in order to create a strong-named assembly); I typed the key pair name into the Key File Attribute section of the `AssemblyInfo.cpp` file; I then included a version number in this same file. The version number I specified is 1.0.1. (By convention, that means version 1.0, build 1.) I built the library and then opened up the .NET command-line prompt (which is available from the Start menu under Visual Studio.NET tools), and from the directory containing the built DLL I typed

```
gacutil /i UsableAssembly.dll
```

Then, I returned to Visual C++.NET, changed the version number to 2.0.1, and rebuilt the project. I went back to the command-line prompt and typed the same `gacutil` command.

Next, I looked at the GAC from the command prompt. Here's what I saw:

```
C:\WINDOWS\assembly\GAC\UsableAssembly>dir /s
 Volume in drive C has no label.
 Volume Serial Number is 9090-6698

 Directory of C:\WINDOWS\assembly\GAC\UsableAssembly

09/28/2003  12:48 AM    <DIR>          .
09/28/2003  12:48 AM    <DIR>          ..
09/28/2003  12:48 AM    <DIR>          1.0.1.0__9aed7bce1e438dd5
09/28/2003  12:48 AM    <DIR>          2.0.1.0__9aed7bce1e438dd5
               0 File(s)              0 bytes

 Directory of C:\WINDOWS\assembly\GAC\UsableAssembly\1.0.1.0__9aed7bce1e438dd5
```

```
09/28/2003  12:48 AM    <DIR>          .
09/28/2003  12:48 AM    <DIR>          ..
09/28/2003  12:48 AM                252 __AssemblyInfo__.ini
09/28/2003  12:48 AM            122,880 UsableAssembly.dll
              2 File(s)        123,132 bytes

   Directory of C:\WINDOWS\assembly\GAC\UsableAssembly\2.0.1.0__9aed7bce1e438dd5

09/28/2003  12:48 AM    <DIR>          .
09/28/2003  12:48 AM    <DIR>          ..
09/28/2003  12:48 AM                252 __AssemblyInfo__.ini
09/28/2003  12:48 AM            122,880 UsableAssembly.dll
              2 File(s)        123,132 bytes

   Total Files Listed:
              4 File(s)        246,264 bytes
              8 Dir(s)   9,818,222,592 bytes free

C:\WINDOWS\assembly\GAC\UsableAssembly>
```

Inside the GAC directory I can see a UsableAssembly directory. (That's what I called my assembly.) Under that directory, I see two version subdirectories, each containing a different version of the DLL. (The name of each version subdirectory is the version number followed by some hex numbers that are related to the public key portion of the key pair.)

For the most part, this system works and is much better than the previous Windows versioning system. The idea is that you can have multiple versions of your DLLs on a single computer, and the .NET system will help each application locate the version it needs.

The Unix and Linux Versioning System

On a Unix system, life is very different from Windows. The various modern breeds of Unix automatically support versions of shared libraries. For example, here's a list of some files I found on a Linux system in the /lib directory:

```
lrwxrwxrwx  1 root  root      12 Jul 17 11:09 libdb.so -> libdb-3.1.so*
lrwxrwxrwx  1 root  root      15 Jul 17 11:09 libdb.so.2 -> libdb1.so.2.1.3*
lrwxrwxrwx  1 root  root      11 Jul 17 11:09 libdb.so.3 -> libdb2.so.3*
-rwxr-xr-x  1 root  root 525905 Oct 12  2002 libdb-3.1.so*
lrwxrwxrwx  1 root  root      15 Jul 17 11:09 libdb1.so.2 -> libdb1.so.2.1.3*
-rwxr-xr-x  1 root  root  62620 Oct 12  2002 libdb1.so.2.1.3*
-rwxr-xr-x  1 root  root 289204 Oct 12  2002 libdb2.so.3*
```

At the top of this listing are three dynamic library files, libdb.so, libdb.so.2, and libdb.so.3. At runtime, a program can request to link dynamically to version 2 of this library (specified as libdb.so.2), version 3 of this library (specified as libdb.so.3), or whatever is the current version (specified as libdb.so).

But all three of these are symbolic links to other files. The first, `libdb.so`, is a link to the current version, `libdb-3.1.so`. The `libdb.so.2` file is a link to `libdb1.so.2.1.3`. And the `libdb.so.3` file is a link to `libdb2.so.3`. The files these links link to, in turn, are the actual shared libraries, not links.

This versioning system on Unix allows the application developer to choose whether the application should just always load the current version of a library (such as `libdb.so`) or to always choose a particular version of a library (such as `libdb.so.2`).

But this system has a strange caveat: Notice the heavy use of symbolic links. The reason is that the versioning system doesn't allow for minor versions. You cannot, for example, choose version 2.1.3 instead of version 2.1.2. Instead, you can choose only version 2, which is the major version. Or you can choose version 3, but nothing in between. If you choose version 2, you'll get whatever minor version is currently on the system.

Implementing Your Own Versioning System on Windows

If you want to implement your own versioning system, you have several options for doing so. Remember, our goal is to make the application as useable as possible. Therefore, as I list these possibilities, I present them in the light of usability. Here are three possible approaches; you can probably think of some others:

- Putting the dynamic library files in the same directory as the executable
- Using the Registry (when on a Windows system)
- Using a common area in conjunction with version information

The first item is by far the simplest: Just drop the dynamic libraries in the same directory as the executable. If different programs are on the system that require different versions of the same library, then each program will have its own version right in its own directory.

In the past, this might not have been a very good idea, since hard drive space came with a premium. If you have a 500MB hard drive, and you have a DLL that takes up, say, 1MB, and 15 programs need the DLL, then that would mean the 15 copies would take up 15MB. But today that's not even an issue. What's 15MB in a world of 80GB hard drives? Therefore, this is a viable option.

But on the other hand, suppose the user decides to clean out her hard drive, and she stumbles across the file called `abccomm.dll`. She then does a full search of the hard drive and finds 15 copies of this file scattered all about the system. I know that I, personally, would be a little distraught: Why are there 15 copies all over the place? Are they really necessary? And worse, I might be rather troubled if I find that they all have different timestamps and sizes!

But this approach also has another potential problem: What if this library is used by many different developers, and some of the applications put the library in their own directory, and at least one dumps the file into the system directory? What will happen? Well, by default, Windows will first look in the same directory as the executable. (I tested this out and found it to be true; I created two different versions of a DLL and put one in an application directory and one in the `c:\windows\system32` directory, and the application located the one in its own directory.) Therefore, if some rogue developer decides to put all his dynamic libraries in the system directory, your application will be safe if you put the dynamic libraries in your application's own directory.

Another option on a Windows system is to use the Registry. Remember, you have two ways to load a dynamic library: You can let the Windows loader load the library when it loads your application, or you can have your program load the library manually. If you're willing to load the library manually, you can make use of the Registry to locate the library. The idea is simple. During installation, save a key in the Registry that holds the name of the directory containing the library.

Using this Registry approach, you can build your own versioning system. Here's how to do this: For saving the location of dynamic libraries, you will want to use the `HKEY_LOCAL_MACHINE` tree. (That's as opposed to `HKEY_CURRENT_USER`, since the location of the library will be the same regardless of which user is logged in.) Under this key is the Software key; under Software you create a key for your company name. Under your company name you have some choices: You can create a product key and put the library information there. Or, you can create a key specifically for the libraries. I recommend this approach; that way, you can have multiple applications (that you wrote) that use the same library but only one copy of the library and only one key pointing to the library.

Suppose, then, that your company is named Me, Inc. Your library is `mecomm.dll`, and your two applications are AllMe9000 and MeMeMe2000. Here's how you might arrange the keys in the Registry:

```
HKEY_LOCAL_MACHINE
    Software
        Me, Inc.
            AllMe9000
                options
            MeMeMe2000
                options
            LibraryLocations
                mecomm.dll
                    1.0
                    2.0
```

The 1.0 key would have the a string value containing the path to version 1.0 of the `mecomm.dll` library. (Remember, each key can have a set of named values as well as a default value. You can either have the default value for the 1.0 key contain the path or you might, for example, have a value named Path hold the path.)

Then, each application can simply grab the key `HKEY_LOCAL_MACHINE/Software/Me, Inc.` `/LibraryLocations/mecomm.dll/1.0` to obtain the path to version 1.0 of the library and then load the library manually. Or, the application can drill down to 2.0 to locate version 2.0 of the library.

This Registry approach has an important benefit: You don't need to mess with the system path! Personally, I am upset when an application installs itself and then adds its location to the system path.

The third option for rolling your own version system deals with using a common area in conjunction with version information. By this I simply mean you create a directory that contains several subdirectories, one for each version. Each version subdirectory contains a different version of the DLL.

This is the same way .NET handles its Global Assembly Cache, and in a sense this method mirrors the Registry approach. On Windows, you would typically create a directory for your products under the Program Files directory. For example, if you again have a company called Me, Inc., and you have two products, AllMe9000 and MeMeMe2000, and finally a library used by both applications called `mecomm.dll`, then you might create a directory structure like this:

```
Program Files
    MeInc
        AllMe9000
        MeMeMe2000
        Libraries
            1.0
            2.0
```

In the 1.0 directory you would place the 1.0 versions of your libraries. In the 2.0 directory, you would place the 2.0 versions. Or, if you have drastically different versions, you might do something like this:

```
Program Files
    MeInc
        AllMe9000
        MeMeMe2000
        Libraries
            mecomm.dll
                1.0
                2.0
            another.dll
                6.5
                7.2
```

NOTE   I chose to leave out the comma, space, and period in the name Me, Inc., although you're perfectly allowed to use these characters in directory names. On Windows, however, if you end a directory name with a period, that period won't show up. If you create a directory called `abcdef.`, then the final dot won't make it into the directory name.

In the mecomm.dll\1.0 directory you would have mecomm.dll version 1.0, and in the mecomm.dll\2.0 directory you would have version 2.0 of the library. In the another.dll\6.5 directory you would have version 6.5 of another.dll, and in the another.dll\7.2 directory you would have version 7.2 of the library.

Finally, remember this:

> **WARNING**   If you create a directory structure or a Registry structure pointing to the various versions of the libraries, the system loader will not be able to locate the libraries (as I describe in the following section, "Placing Libraries in the Correct Locations on Windows.") Your program must, then, manually load the libraries.

Placing Libraries in the Correct Locations on Windows

If you don't want to manually load your dynamic libraries, then you must rely on the system loader to load the libraries for you. Of course, doing so is much easier, because you don't need to locate the functions inside the library. But with this approach comes the following limitation: If you rely on the loader to load your libraries, your libraries must be either in the same directory as the application file or somewhere in the system path.

From a usability standpoint, this means the only legitimate place to put your files is in the same directory as the application file, if you're going to rely on the automatic loading of the libraries. Why? Here's why:

> **RULE**   Don't mess with the user's system path.

As a user, I have two main reasons why I don't want applications messing with my system path:

- The system path is too easy for me, the user, to change, and that could cause your program to break.

- I don't want to see my system path getting longer, and longer, and longer.

Imagine if some user who was too smart for his own good decided to clean out the system path. (That's easy to do, remember!) Then, suddenly, your application doesn't run. Guess what comes next: support calls!

But modifying the system path has another problem: *If you modify the system path for the current user, then the path won't be modified for another user, and your program won't run for that other user.*

Of course, system restores and all kinds of other system-modifying tasks could alter the system path. Thus, as I just mentioned, if you're letting the system loader load your libraries for you, the only viable place to put them is in the same directory as the application. Then you don't need to touch the system path.

But with this comes two related issues that I want to bring to your attention; these issues apply more to the manual loading of dynamic libraries. First:

RULE   Don't hard-code any paths into your product!

And second:

RULE   Stay away from environment variables.

The first of these should go without saying. Don't hard-code the string `c:\Program Files\MeInc\` into your program. Users might decide to install your product elsewhere.

But what about environment variables? One good way to hard-code some paths might be to set an environment variable, say, `MeFiles`, to be the value `c:\Program Files\MeInc\`. And yes, this would work. But this has the same problems as modifying the system path. Personally, I, as a user, get upset when I discover that a whole bunch of programs all deemed it necessary to create a bunch of environment variables on my system. And second, when you switch to a different user, depending on how these variables are stored, they may go away. And third, some too-smart-for-his-own-good user might delete the variables, resulting in a support call.

Therefore, here are your primary options for deciding where to put your dynamic libraries:

- Put automatically loaded libraries in the same directory as the application's executable file.
- If you want to put the files elsewhere, load them manually.

Finally, if you feel the need for an environment variable storing, for example, the root directory of your products, here's a viable alternative: Store this directory in the Registry. From there, you can construct your directories by appending the subdirectory names to this root path. For example, if your root path is `c:\Program Files\MeInc\`, then you can append the string `Libraries\mecomm.dll\2.0` to locate version 2.0 of the `mecomm.dll` file. (But I'm still not totally pleased with this approach, because this again requires hard-coding certain information into your program.)

What is my favorite choice *as a user*? I prefer that you, as a programmer, write software that lands on my computer that uses the Registry approach that I describe in "Implementing Your Own Versioning System on Windows" in this chapter. That, of course, requires that you manually load your libraries. And if you refuse to manually load your libraries, then put the libraries in the same directory as the executable file.

Properly Using Resources in a Multitasking Environment (Think: Mutexes!)

If you write a library (either static or dynamic) that might be used by more than one application, and one that accesses resources of any kind (whether it's a file, a hardware device, or whatever), then you will want to make sure your library can survive being run in a multitasking environment.

For example, if your library writes to a single log file, what happens if two programs use the library simultaneously? If you aren't careful, you'll probably end up with intertwined text. And what if you have two programs using your library to simultaneously read from a port? Who knows what exactly will happen, but it will be messy.

RULE   Always expect that your library will be running in a multitasking environment. Code it as such.

The proper solution for sharing resources is to use mutexes. Remember, a *mutex* is a data structure that only one process or thread can own at any given time. Another process or thread can ask the operating system for ownership of the mutex, and that process or thread will freeze up until the other process or thread lets go of the mutex. Think of a mutex as a single key to access a device or other resource, and only one process can hold the key at any given time. Only when a process is finished with the key can another process take ownership of the key. Windows includes special functions for using mutexes, and the standard libraries on Unix (such as the Posix standard) contain various mutex functions.

Here's an example of a class that makes use of a mutex for writing to a log file. This class has a hard-coded log filename (generally a bad idea, but I wanted to keep this example simple). This class would go inside the library:

```
HANDLE hMutex;

class LogFile {
protected:
    HANDLE hMutex;
    ofstream *f;
public:
    void Open();
    void WriteLogLine(char *line);
    void Close();
};

void LogFile::Open() {
    hMutex = CreateMutex(NULL, FALSE, "MyIncLogFile");
    f = new ofstream("c:/temp/myfile.dat", ios_base::app);
}

void LogFile::WriteLogLine(char *line) {
    WaitForSingleObject(hMutex, INFINITE);
    *f << line << endl;
    ReleaseMutex(hMutex);
}

void LogFile::Close() {
    CloseHandle(hMutex);
}
```

As you can see, I'm using the Win32 mutex functions and data structures; if you want, you can instead use the Posix versions. Here's a sample main that uses this library:

```
int main(int argc, char* argv[])
{
    LogFile log;
    log.Open();
    char buf[200];
    for (int i=0; i<100000; i++) {
        sprintf (buf, "Hi there everybody, my number is %d", i);
        log.WriteLogLine(buf);
    }
    return 0;
}
```

This program writes out 100,000 lines to a log file. I compiled this program as console1.exe, and then I wrote a batch file that launches two instances of the program simultaneously. Here's the batch file:

```
start console1.exe
start console1.exe
```

When I ran this program without mutexes, I ended up with lines that were mixed together, as in

```
Hi there everybody, my number Hi there everybody my number is 10.
```

But when I used the mutexes, this intertwined output no longer occurred.

SUGGESTION

Remember to use mutexes when accessing resources. They are your friends.

Creating a Useable Library for Other Developers

If you are creating a third-party library that will be used by other developers, then those developers will be your users, and you want to give them a product that is highly useable. Many times I have been given a library by other developers (often within the same company I worked for at the time), and these libraries were practically unuseable. Therefore, here are some rules to help you create a highly useable library for other developers:

RULE   Allow for both static and dynamic linking.

Include two versions of your library: One is a dynamic library, and one is a static library. That way the other developer can choose whether to static-link your code right into an application or to ship your dynamic library with the application; let it be the developer's choice!

| RULE | Include the proper files with your library. |

This should go without saying. Always remember to ship all the necessary files with your library, including:

- The correct import libraries
- A prebuilt dynamic library
- A prebuilt static library
- The correct header files
- Possibly the source code

Of course, you might not want to ship the source code. But even if you do, please include prebuilt libraries so that the developers don't have to rebuild the libraries from scratch. (Besides, would you really want them rebuilding the dynamic library and then shipping their own custombuilt version of *your* dynamic library?)

| RULE | Remember to use that strange `declspec` stuff in your header files. |

A `declspec` line is a line in a Windows code file that specifies whether the function is exported by the library or imported into the application. Why include that line? Because you will typically use the same header file for both building the library and building the application using the library. But when building a dynamic library, you need to denote each function as being exported by the library. When building an application using the library, you need to denote each function as being imported from a dynamic library, if you're using a dynamic library. And if you're using static libraries, you neither import nor export the functions. And you specify this information all within a single header file.

The standard way to do this is by using some preprocessor definitions. People have different ways of defining the symbols, but here is one way I use that works:

- One symbol is set in the case of building the dynamic library.
- Another symbol is set in the case of building the application using the dynamic library.
- No symbols are set in the case of building the static library and the application using the static library.

Here's an example; this goes inside the header file:

```
#ifdef MYDLL_EXPORT
#define MYDLL_API __declspec(dllexport)
#elif defined(MYDLL_IMPORT)
#define MYDLL_API __declspec(dllimport)
#else
```

```
#define MYDLL_API
#endif

MYDLL_API int foo(void);
```

The preprocessor lines check whether the symbol `MYDLL_EXPORT` is defined, in which case the symbol `MYDLL_API` gets set to `__declspec(dllexport)`. Or, if the symbol `MYDLL_IMPORT` is defined, the symbol `MYDLL_API` gets set to `__declspec(dllimport)`. Or, if neither is defined, the symbol `MYDLL_API` gets set to *nothing*.

Now look at the function prototype; it begins with `MYDLL_API`. Thus, in the case of a dynamic library where `MYDLL_EXPORT` was defined, this function is preceded by the directive `__declspec(dllexport)`, telling the compiler to export the function.

In the case of an application using the dynamic library (where `MYDLL_IMPORT` was defined), the function will be preceded by the directive `__declspec(dllimport)`, which tells the compiler to import the function during link time.

And finally, in the case of either a static library being built or an application using the static library being built, the `MYDLL_API` symbol will be defined as nothing, putting no directive in front of the function, making the function neither imported nor exported.

This means that for your dynamic library project, you need to define the symbol `MYDLL_EXPORT` in your project settings. For an application using the dynamic library, you need to define the symbol `MYDLL_IMPORT` in your project settings. For a static library project, you do not define either symbol. And similarly, with a project for an application using the static library, again you do not define either symbol.

SUGGESTION

Don't require a gazillion other libraries in order to link.

Nothing is more frustrating than receiving a library, attempting to link the library into an application, and then receiving a bunch of *undefined symbol* errors. Don't require all sorts of other libraries, and if you do require these libraries, make it very clear when distributing your library that the other libraries are necessary.

RULE Don't require "dummy functions."

I'm serious. I've seen this happen: A developer creates a static library without realizing that the library requires certain functions that existed in the main test application and not the library itself. When another developer receives the library, she is distraught to learn that several functions are needed to make the library work, and the only way to get past this roadblock is to create dummy functions that do nothing but satisfy the linker. (Yes, I really *have* seen this happen!)

SUGGESTION

Document your library.

I shouldn't have to tell you the importance of documenting your library, but again, I've seen developers ship libraries without any documentation. Come on, folks, it doesn't take that long to write up a short synopsis of the functions and to include a sample or two. In fact, here are documentation items you should include with your library:

- Good documentation explaining what each function and class does. (In other words, this is a reference guide.)

- A general write-up explaining how to use the library. (Don't expect the developers to just read the entire reference guide and piece together the necessary functions!)

- Some samples that make use of the majority of the functions. (Yes, some of us prefer samples to abstract help documents.)

- Solid installation procedures for deploying the library with the application. Remember these developers will probably be shipping your library to end users' computers, and the developers will need solid instructions on how to install your library. This is especially true if you have implemented your own versioning system as I describe in "Implementing Your Own Versioning System on Windows," earlier in this chapter.

Moving Forward

The whole issue of dividing your software into chunks, pieces, globs, parts, and all-out guts spilled all over the hard drive can make for a usability nightmare. In this chapter I talked about the nightmares of DLLs, whether to use static libraries instead of DLLs, how to name your libraries, and how to work with versions. In the final section I showed you how to create a useable library for other developers. Can you believe how much usability transcends all aspects of programming, right into the development of libraries? Most people don't realize that, and that's why we, as users, get stuck with such a mess when we install other people's software on our computers.

In the next chapter I finally talk about a topic dear to many of our hearts: object-oriented programming, or OOP. Since I've already convinced you that library development has usability issues, you can probably imagine that I make a pretty good case for OOP also having usability issues. (I'm everywhere and I'm not going away!) See you there.

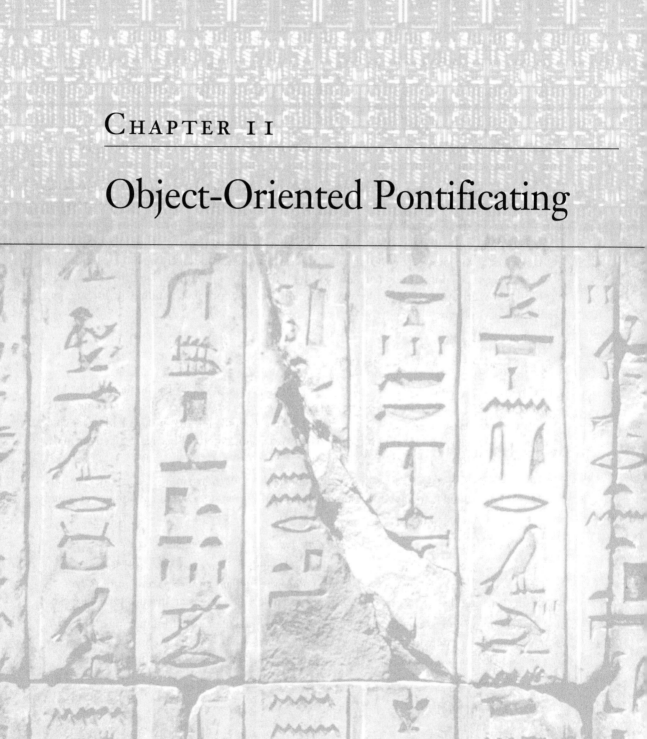

CHAPTER 11

Object-Oriented Pontificating

Talk about the buzzword of the twentieth century, object-oriented programming (OOP) sure left its mark in the advertisements. I remember reading an ad back in the early 1990s for a DOS-based GUI database-programming product that had no object-oriented features to speak of, and yet the ad claimed the product was object-oriented. Why? Because you could design forms using *objects* such as buttons and listboxes. Yuppers, those were objects and therefore the product was object-oriented.

But sadly, most people who would be using the product had no more clue what object-oriented meant than the marketing people who wrote the advertisement. Fortunately, however, today most people have a better idea of what so-called OOP is.

In this chapter I talk about what OOP is. But what does that have to do with usability? Well, for starters, if you know what OOP is, and you use it *properly*, you can create more useable software. Okay, that's not entirely true; not to sound negative, but more realistically, if you use OOP improperly, you can really destroy the usability of your product by filling it with bugs and all kinds of problems. Read on!

The Final Answer: What Is OOP?

How is that for a bold headline? Really, I'm being a bit sarcastic, because no matter how I (or you, or anybody else) define *object-oriented programming*, somebody will disagree. I once was having a conversation with somebody about Borland Delphi, and that person had never so much as even seen Delphi, and I referred to it as "object-oriented." This man looked me in the eyes and said with full authority, "No, it's not."

And by many regards, he was correct. If you expect OOP to live up to the original notions of Smalltalk (hailed by many as the standard on OOP), then no, Delphi isn't object-oriented.

Hogwash. Here's how I personally define OOP:

Object-oriented means you can encapsulate data and functions into classes.

Now most *better* OOP languages also allow inheritance: You can take one class and from it derive another class. And with inheritance comes the fundamental requirement of polymorphism, meaning that you can treat an instance of a derived class as an instance of a base class.

I'm assuming you've experienced enough OOP to understand what I'm talking about here, but this notion of polymorphism does sometimes cause some confusion. So let me just show you a quick example. Suppose you have two classes, `Base` and `Derived`, defined like so:

```
class Base {
public:
    string name;
};
```

```
class Derived : public Base {
public:
    int length;
};
```

You can see that `Derived` is derived from `Base`. Now suppose you have a function that takes an instance of `Base`:

```
void Objectorator(Base &obj) {
    cout << obj.name << endl;
}
```

Thanks to the principle of polymorphism, you can pass to this function an instance of `Base`, or an instance of any class *derived from* `Base`. Here's a complete gcc program demonstrating this:

```
#include <iostream>
#include <string>
using namespace std;

class Base {
public:
    string name;
};

class Derived : public Base {
public:
    int length;
};

void Objectorator(Base &obj) {
    cout << obj.name << endl;
}

int main() {
    Derived inst;
    inst.length = 10;
    inst.name = "me";
    Objectorator(inst);
}
```

Notice in the `main` that I'm creating an instance of `Derived`, setting its two members (`length`, which is its own, and `name`, which is derived from `Base`). And notice how I then call `Objectorator`, passing this instance of `Derived`, even though `Objectorator` is expecting an instance of `Base`.

Internally, the way most C++ compilers handle inheritance to accommodate polymorphism is that they group together the data members starting with the base class. For example, if a base class has three integer members A, B, and C, and from that base class you derive a class with three more integer members D, E, and F, then the internal structure of the derived class is six integers in this order: A, B, C, D, E, F. But if you look at this structure and are expecting to see an instance of the base class, then you will see an instance of the base class: You will see A, B, C and stop looking beyond that, not knowing (and not caring) that the data that follows is still a part of the structure. Thus, in the preceding code sample, the function Objectorator will receive a structure containing a single data member, name. When I pass an instance of Derived to this function, the function doesn't know that really Derived has additional data beyond its Base part. The function simply sees the first data element—a string—and accesses that string. Thus, the function thinks it has an instance of Base.

I like to envision polymorphism visually. In Figure 11.1, I demonstrate how I view polymorphism for a base class with members A, B, and C and a derived class with members A, B, C, D, E, and F. In this figure, you can see that the class Derived effectively contains an instance of the class Base. And that instance of Base is at the beginning, meaning the address of the instance of Base is the same as the address of the instance of Derived. And that means you can cast an instance of Derived to an instance of Base. (However, the C++ standard discourages us from doing a direct cast as in (Base)inst, even though that works. Instead, we're encouraged to use the dynamic_cast<Base&>(inst). But really, in general, you should have no reason to cast an instance of a derived class to a base class, because the compiler automatically casts in such cases, as I demonstrated by passing an instance of Derived to a function expecting an instance of Base.)

Figure 11.1 and my explanation of the figure show how C++ implements inheritance and polymorphism. Other languages use similar approaches.

Now back to our story. In the early 1990s, when C++ was new, people would argue over whether it was *truly* object-oriented. The self-proclaimed gurus would say it wasn't, and some people even came up with their own terms and definitions to work around suggesting that C++ and other languages were object-oriented. One such term was object-based. I remember being told, "Well, no, actually C++ and Delphi are both object-*based*." Once again I say: Hogwash. Both of these languages support encapsulation, inheritance, and polymorphism. Thus, they are object-oriented. End of story. Now leave me alone.

FIGURE 11.1
Polymorphism in C++ is possible due to the overlapping structures.

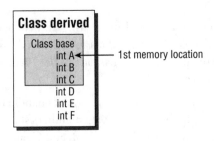

REAL WORLD SCENARIO

That Darn Remote! (And Why Does It Have an Eject Button?)

I'm sure you figured it was only a matter of time in this book before I talked about remotes. While *object-oriented* may have been the buzzword of the late twentieth century, the remote was probably the ubiquitous object of the twentieth century.

I remember sometime around maybe 1988 or 1989, a friend of mine bought a massive stereo system, which, of course, came with a remote. And my friend showed off this really "cool feature" of the stereo: When you used the remote to change the volume, the volume knob on the stereo itself would *turn*. Ooooh. I wonder how many engineers it took to design *that*. That knob was more than a basic potentiometer; it was motorized. I do have to wonder, however, what would happen if you used the remote to turn up the volume, while somebody stood by the stereo itself and manually forced the motorized knob in the opposite direction. Would the stereo explode? Or maybe you would discover some secret mode where the stereo could emit frequencies previously unheard by human ears?

While in college, I took several electrical engineering courses. I was talking about that once, and a friend of mine mentioned that her brother, who was in his early twenties, knew a lot about electronics. She then added, "I know he does because he bought this HUGE stereo system and managed to hook the whole thing up all by himself."

And how much you wanna bet that the stereo he hooked up (all by himself) has a Magical Rotating Volume Knob? Do you see what is happening here? We have stereos that are nearly impossible to use by most people, yet are filled with wow-cool factors. Consider the remote: How many buttons can you possibly squeeze into such a little remote, and how many colors of ink can you have on it? But do you know what each and every button does on each remote you have in your house? If I told you, "Quick, program the TV so when *The X Files* comes on tonight, the TV will start up and I can watch it, but the VCR will also be recording it," would you know what to do?

The stereo industry has been plagued by the problem of adding so many bells and whistles for the coolness factor without actually doing much in the way of usability studies. If we computer programmers aren't sure what all the buttons do without having to study the manual, imagine the mere mortals trying to figure them out. (Yes, we're not mortal; I admit it.)

But answer me this: Why does the VCR remote have an Eject button on it? The remote has come to symbolize the laziness of humans, but that one makes no sense: So you can eject the tape, but until we invent a robot that will go over and remove the tape and insert a different one, what's the point?

Don't let your designs get out of control. Focus on usability.

Avoid Letting Object-Oriented Programming Get out of Control

(Read this really fast.) Let's see, I'm writing a really cool program, so I need a class called Cool, and from that I'm going to derive a class called ReallyCool, but both of those are abstract, actually, so from ReallyCool I'm going to derive six classes, one called CoolA, one called CoolB, and so on through CoolF. But each of these needs to hold some members, and so I'm going to invent my own Integer class and call it JeffInteger (yeah!), and I'm not happy with the standard library's implementation of string, so I'm going to create a class with another great name, JeffString. But JeffInteger actually encapsulates several different types of integers, so from JeffInteger I'm going to derive JeffLongInteger, JeffShortInteger, JeffSuperShortInteger, JeffSuperLongInteger, and JeffSeriouslyIncrediblyLongInteger. The JeffString class, in turn, can hold both Unicode and multibyte strings, and so from JeffString I will derive JeffUnicodeString and JeffMultibyeString. And, of course, I'll overload the usual operators, including +=, -=, /=, *= for JeffInteger, and similar operators for JeffString as well as [].

Wait! Stop! This is getting just a *little* out of hand, wouldn't you say? But I have, in fact, witnessed this kind of thing going on. Let's backtrack just a little here. I'm not going to turn this into a course on OOP with a section on *discovering objects*, because you can find that in standard texts on object-oriented programming. But I will say this: Slow down, take a deep breath, and don't let your object discovery get out of hand. Why? Because if you have way too many classes, most likely you will lose control of the code and end up with bugs.

Also, besides going overboard on the class creation, another fundamental mistake here is in believing that the basic types and the standard classes are, in some way, inferior to your needs. Do you really need to reinvent the string class?

Now I won't suggest that you're not as good as the people who wrote the string class for the standard library. Instead, I'll suggest that you have more important things to worry about than rewriting the string class (don't you?). Your job is to create your application, and you probably have a deadline. Why spend the next two weeks perfecting a string class, when the current one works just fine?

What's going to happen when suddenly somebody using your string class needs to write out a string to stderr, and you suddenly realize you forgot to overload the insertion operator? (You know, the insertion operator is the << thing.) And what if somebody needs a function that will find the last instance of a character within a string? Are you going to spend a couple of days writing these two missing functions when your boss is looking over your shoulder to finish up the application? The standard string class has these functions in it already. Therefore, I encourage programmers to remember this:

RULE   Don't reinvent the wheel. Use the classes in the standard library and the built-in types.

I've said this many times throughout this book, but I'll say it again: Your goal is to create highly useable software, and that includes software that is bug-free. The classes in the standard library have been tested and tested *ad nauseam*, and the chances of them having bugs are next to nothing. If you spend a few days throwing together your own `string` class, do you really want to stand behind it? I consider myself an expert C++ programmer, and yet, I know better than to attempt such a thing, if for no other reason than a lot more people spent a lot more hours on the standard classes than I could spend on my own classes. I'm not saying that they're better than you or me; I'm saying that a lot more work has gone into them.

And with reinventing the wheel comes some other issues. For example:

RULE   Don't feel like you must use every last feature in OOP just because it's there. Don't template, virtualize, and polymorphize your code into a royal mess.

Some time back, I had a client who was developing a telecommunications library. They had previously brought in a self-proclaimed C++ guru, who told them that if they would rewrite their library using templates, they would be able to "snap out" the current communications protocol and "snap in" another protocol. And so the guru left, and they went to work, changing every last class in their library into a template class. By the time I got there, they had a royal mess on their hands. They had piles upon piles of templates, and they were forced to learn everything they could about template instantiation under different compilers, and they got to see firsthand just how *long* templates take to compile. And long after the self-proclaimed guru had moved on, the whole reason for creating this mess didn't even succeed: They were unable to "snap in" a new protocol. Instead, they were left with a bizarre set of templates that served no real purpose. I call this "templatizing, virtualizing, and polymorphizing your code into a royal mess."

RULE   Don't get carried away with creating a huge number of classes.

This idea has a very practical reason: While we'd all like to believe that this class must be bro-ken up into two classes, including an abstract base class so that the class can be used in many other applications over the next several decades, in fact, we know better. Unless you're actually building a class library and not an application, the reality is that your class probably won't find its way into other applications.

Yikes. I can see the Object-Oriented Purists getting ready to string me up with an object that is definitely *not* abstract for that statement I just made. But let's be serious: Your job is to create software that is on schedule and free of bugs. The more time you spend building abstract classes hoping and believing that these classes will find their way into other applications, the less time you can spend on more important issues such as *usability*. Who are you writing this code for? Your own personal glory or for the end users? As much as we like to think that our work is for our own personal glory (hey, I always enjoy seeing my name on the cover of a book or in the credits of a software application), the truth is that our software is for the *end users*. Yes, we work because we need the money, and that's usually the real reason we're grinding out those hours before the computer screen and keyboard. But like it or not, this software is not for *us*. It's for the users. So don't get carried away as you create the most amazing class library that the world has ever beheld. Skip it and write some good software instead.

> **NOTE**   But before I end this discussion and move on to the next section, I want to add a bit of a disclaimer. I'm *not* saying to forget all you know about sound OOP principles. Yes, please use OOP properly. What I am saying is that you don't need to go overboard and use every last feature OOP allows for, such as creating a million abstract classes.

Object-Oriented Usability

With the advent of object-oriented programming, I'd like to coin the term *object-oriented usability*. With a focus on usability, you can make object-oriented programming work for both you *and* your users.

Throughout this book I've raved about a command approach to software. At the beginning of the book with the code samples I didn't do much with classes and objects. But later on I needed a more sophisticated example, and so I immediately encapsulated the command system into classes. It was inevitable, and it was a good thing.

Now if you think about the various methodologies for designing object-oriented software, you'll see that one of the focuses is on discovering objects. Typically these involve figuring out who the users are, and from there you move on to designing use cases, and from there objects (or some variation thereof).

But those users aren't always humans. In fact, if you're designing some kind of middleware, the users definitely won't be humans; they'll be other software modules. And that's fine. However, users will still be present; such users will be the developers interfacing to your middleware and the system administrators running your middleware. In both cases, you will have a human interface.

Thus, from a usability perspective, I'd like to talk about these three levels of users:

- End users using your software
- System administrators using your software
- Developers writing software interfacing to your software

In the following sections, I talk about these three different types of users and how the choices you make in your designs affect these users.

Object-Oriented End Users

With the end users, you have a specific task ahead of you: You want to design your software with the best object-oriented approach possible, while abstracting the user from your designs. True, your designs might mimic what the users see and do; you might have a `MainWindow` class that encapsulates the main window, a `Toolbar` class that encapsulates the toolbar the user sees, and so on.

But you'll certainly have classes that don't have analogies in the user interface. And these classes present a bit of a problem to people just learning about object-oriented design. The reason is that a lot of object-oriented design methodologies focus on the notion of the user and the use cases. Clearly, then, if you're focusing on the user, how do you come up with classes that are "behind the scenes," so to speak? And further, how do you create such classes while keeping an eye on usability?

One approach I take is to make sure that even when I'm designing classes that go behind the scenes, I never let myself forget how these classes interact with the GUI. Now at first you might feel like this goes somewhat against what we're taught about encapsulation and OOP in general; we're told that each class should be a black box and an entire entity in its own right. But the truth of the matter is that people who design software under such assumptions quickly hit a lot of roadblocks when they have piles upon piles of classes and are trying to snap them all together like a giant jigsaw puzzle.

That's why in object-oriented design principles, we're also told to look at *modules*. Modules are groups of classes, and modules carefully fit together. And like the old division-of-labor concept, each person may have his or her job, but people can be more productive citizens if they keep in mind how their work fits into society as a whole. Similarly, a class can be far more useable if you remember how the class is a part of the whole application. Thus:

RULE   Never lose sight of the final application when you are working on a single class.

This is easier said than done, however, because you still want to make sure you maintain full encapsulation. You want your public interface into the class, and you don't want to open up all sorts of side doors into the class by making all your protected members public. Therefore, you also have to walk the fine line of remembering about good, solid encapsulation techniques. And this can be done.

But where does true usability fit into this picture? The true usability comes when you flip over to the other realm: You have some classes that are behind-the-scenes classes, and these classes do not have a direct analogy in the user interface. But on the other end you have the classes that do interact directly with the user interface, and these classes also interact with the behind-the-scenes classes. And that's where some usability problems can occur. Here's something to consider:

RULE   Keep your behind-the-scenes classes truly behind the scenes.

I don't mean that as something to be set in stone or to be taken too literally. Instead, what I mean is this: When presenting information to the user about the behind-the-scenes classes, don't bog the user down with technobabble regarding those other classes.

For example, suppose the user clicks a button that runs a command that in turn instantiates an instance of a TCP/IP class. But the TCP/IP instance is unable to allocate the proper resources, and so the instance returns an error code back to one of the GUI objects. The GUI object in turn displays the following message:

Error 37 while allocating resources.

Well, now, isn't that nice. But that is what happened, right? The object returned an error code of 37. But come on, now, you can do better than that. But please don't replace it with this message:

Unable to allocate resources while instantiating TCP/IP object.

Instead, include a proper error message such as, "Unable to connect to the Internet." In addition, please provide suggestions on how this can be fixed, as in, "No dial tone was present," or whatever.

This brings me to the final issue that I want to mention about the end users and object-oriented programming:

RULE   Don't require the end users to understand the underlying object structure just to use the software application.

The problem with the error messages I just described is that the programmer working on the GUI objects was well aware of the interaction between the objects. That programmer instantiated a TCP/IP object, and that object returned an error code. And so the programmer wrote code that would simply relay the message to the user. Remember, the users don't know about the object structure, and the users don't care and don't want to know about the object structure.

Finally, here's a rule to keep in mind to bring together OOP and usability:

RULE   When designing your individual classes, no matter how small or trivial, never lose sight of the goals of the end users.

Believe it or not, it is in fact possible to design some incredibly solid, well-architected software that does not meet the final goals of the users. Such software might be an amazing feat of engineering, but what good is it if it doesn't live up to the needs of the users?

Object-Oriented System Administrators

System administrators are a unique breed of people. While they are users by most regards, they are much more savvy than typical users, and many of them are, in fact, programmers as well. Therefore, you can expose more of your system to system administrators, and you probably want them to be aware of much of the underlying structure. That way, if a particular dynamic library, for example, is misbehaving, the system administrator can contact the vendor to see about a patch for that particular library.

Therefore, if you have several behind-the-scenes classes that do not interact with the GUI objects, you still might want to include ways to see the insides of these objects. Those can include, for example:

- Special public interfaces for a GUI for just the administrators
- Log files and interfaces for turning on and controlling the level of error output
- Error reports
- Interfaces for scripting languages

Most likely, the system administrators won't be writing code to instantiate your objects and interface to them. However, the administrators may write, for example, Perl scripts that interact with your library. Or they might want to be able to turn on an error-reporting feature.

However, one important thing to remember is this: You can't expect your system administrators to be experts in object-oriented programming. They have their job, and they don't want to get bogged down learning your job, too. Therefore, if you include a scripting language interface to your objects, think more on a functional level. Build yourself a single interface that includes a set of functions the administrators can use from their Perl scripts (or whatever language they prefer). But remember: Some languages, such as Python, are inherently more object-oriented than other languages, and for these languages you might want to build an object-oriented interface. Use your best judgment, and base this in part on what scripting languages the administrators will likely be using.

But what sort of things will administrators be doing with your product? I can't say for sure because I don't know what product you're building. But consider this example: Suppose you're building a document management system. The administrators will need a way to manage the system itself, such as adding users and whatnot. How will they do this? Well, they might want to write their own Perl scripts that interface to your libraries. Or they might want an entire GUI front end for managing the system. This chapter isn't about designing GUI front ends;

either way, when you design the library, you will want to be aware of the need for some interfaces into the objects that aren't a normal part of the end-user experience.

In addition, you will want your behind-the-scenes objects to support such features as logging and error reporting. Most administrators whom I've met prefer the error reporting and logging to go to a massive text file. Therefore, you might have a logging class that your other classes call into. And you might have an error-reporting class as well. And, because of encapsulation concepts, you know to keep the error-reporting and logging mechanisms inside their appropriate classes.

However, you will want to provide some way for the administrators to actually control the logging and error reporting. And this goes back to what I was saying about providing an interface into the objects. Here are some ways you can do this:

- Provide a programmable interface through a scripting language, whereby the administrator calls a function that turns on and off logging and error reporting.

- Let the administrator set an environment variable that controls logging and error reporting.

- Even though many admins want an interface through a scripting language, many will also want a GUI interface. Don't forget to build a strong, clean GUI for such people.

Finally, remember this:

RULE   All good usability principles apply to your system administration interface as they do to your regular user interface. However, with system administrators, you can assume a good bit more knowledge about computers and programming.

Object-Oriented Developers

If you're creating a class library for other developers to use, everything I describe in Chapter 10, "Modularity and Libraries," about creating good libraries for other developers applies. However, you also have the job of making a good object-oriented design in addition to creating a good library. Remember, in the case of a class library, the other developers are your users, and thus you want to create a highly useable class library.

What makes for a highly useable class library? Here are some points:

- Developers can derive new classes from your classes, thereby customizing the behavior.

- Your classes have a limited number of private members and instead you opt for protected members. This is a sticky issue, and a lot of programmers disagree with me on this. That's okay; we can agree to disagree. But my experience is that if I'm deriving a new class and the base class has too many private members, I'm usually unable to truly customize the class.

- You provide a solid class hierarchy that includes a good, strong set of classes.

REAL WORLD SCENARIO

Did You Know That Your Refrigerator Door Is Reversible? Really!

Like climbing Mount Everest, I came across something that I had to try out, simply *because it was there*. A few years ago I lived in an apartment, and the refrigerator door seemed to open on the wrong side. The refrigerator was near the edge of the kitchen, and to open the thing, I had to stand out in the hallway. Well, I was looking the thing over one time, and something struck me: The little screw holes and attachments looked completely symmetrical! I looked back and forth, and then I opened the door and looked on the inside, and sure enough: I'll be darned; the thing was reversible!

This was too good to be true. Being of a slightly mechanical bent, I found this to be more than I could resist! Even if I didn't need to reverse the door, just the mere thought of attempting such a project brought a twinge of excitement to my stomach.

I looked at the screws and figured out which tools I needed, grabbed my tool chest, and promptly went to work. This looked easy! I'd have this done in—oh, I don't know—10 minutes? Maybe less?

Along the way I encountered all sorts of difficulties. For one, after I managed to dislodge the door from its original position, I had to somehow hold it in place while putting in the screws on the other side. And you'd be surprised how heavy a refrigerator door is. This was definitely a job for two people. Unfortunately, I was all alone.

But finally, after maybe an hour, my efforts paid off. I got the door back on, and I could now open it on the other side! Amazing. As it happens, I found three or four screws on the floor and I had no idea what they went to, but that's okay; the door wasn't falling off and it opened, even if it was missing a few screws.

Now how about that for an engineering feat? A reversible door on a refrigerator. It's too bad most people don't know that you can switch your refrigerator door. And that makes me wonder, how many times do appliance stores get a call that a customer who just received a refrigerator wants to return it because the door opens on the wrong side? I do wonder.

- Your classes each serve a particular purpose, but you don't have them divided up so much that programmers are unsure about how to decide between two particular classes because the distinction between their uses isn't clear.

- Your class library isn't massive. This is a problem with a lot of the commercial class libraries; the developer is faced with an enormous pile of classes making up an enormous hierarchy. My experience is that libraries this huge are overwhelming and confusing.

- Your classes are more or less autonomous in that you don't need to first instantiate three other objects before using the object you want. Not to pick on Microsoft too much, but Microsoft Foundation Classes suffer from this problem. When you want to make a single window, you also need to make a frame and several other objects. Is that necessary? No. Borland's VCL has a single TForm class, which represents a window.

- Finally, remember your testers. They'll need ways to push your classes to the limits, and these ways might go beyond what the regular developers are going to do. For this topic, however, you will want to interact closely with your testers and make sure that they can interact with your classes in the ways they need. For example, you might have a protected member, but your testers might need direct access to the protected member as if it's a public member. How can you allow this? By making sure that the testers can derive a new class from your class, which can in turn directly access the protected member.

Moving Forward

This wraps up Part II of the book, which deals with programming-level issues within the realm of usability. Too many people think the term usability extends to just the GUI. But if you focus your usability on only the GUI aspects, your software will suffer.

In this chapter I looked at the usability issues pertaining specifically to object-oriented programming. OOP has a long history, with a lot of people misunderstanding it. In this chapter I gave you tips on how to solidify your own understanding of OOP and how to make it work for you while providing strong usability.

With the next chapter, I begin Part III, which is called "The Business of It All: It's 'Dollars and Sense.'" Whereas the present part demonstrates that usability extends to the programming realm, the following part shows you that usability has some business and financial aspects as well. Don't go away! Let's make some money.

PART III

The Business of It All: It's "Dollars and Sense"

CHAPTER 12

A Very Gross National Product: Business and Software Problems

Businesses spend a combined total of billions of dollars per year as a result of bugs in software. In fact, you want to know the real figure? According to The Sustainable Computing Consortium, U.S. companies alone spend a combined total of over $200 billion annually as a result of bugs in software. Can you imagine such a huge figure? (If you want to read more about this, visit `http://www.sustainablecomputing.org`.)

And just how much do the businesses spend as a result of bad interface design? How much time is spent in training; how much time is spent fiddling with software packages; how much time is spent jumping through hoops in the software? In other words, how much time is unnecessarily wasted on software?

In this chapter I talk about just how bad this problem really is and just what exactly you can do about it. This chapter is for everybody involved: the programmers, the bosses at corporations purchasing software, and the users working in offices using the software.

Building the "Killer App"—Forget It!

Back during the big dot-com boom of the late 1990s, a popular catch term (especially in the presence of venture capitalists) was "the killer app." Everybody claimed they had an idea for the ultimate application, the killer app. Now usually the people who thought up these killer apps were young men in their late teens and early twenties, people who were great at hacking out code but had zero business and marketing experience—and very little, if any, knowledge of usability. (Please don't be offended by that statement; it's just a simple fact of the background of the typical 20-year-old programmer. Very few have had experience working in marketing departments, for example, because their interests are usually strictly in programming.)

So everybody had an idea for the killer app. Let's see what applications are on this very computer I'm using.

- First, I have Microsoft Windows XP.
- Next, I have Outlook 2000.
- And I also have Netscape Navigator.
- Of course, I have Microsoft Word and Excel.
- Let's see, there's Internet Explorer.
- And WinZip.
- I have Microsoft Photo Editor.
- I have a trial version of Paint Shop Pro, which has expired and I can't use.
- I have a purchased version of Dreamweaver and Fireworks, both from Macromedia.
- I have purchased copies of older versions of Borland Delphi and Borland C++Builder.

- And yes, I admit, I have AOL 7.0 software on here.

- The computer came with McAfee virus-protection software.

Now look at this list carefully: Most of this software came from Microsoft. And then some came from AOL, which also owns Netscape. The programming tools—Borland Delphi and Borland C++Builder—came from Borland, which has been around since 1983. Macromedia, which makes Dreamweaver and Fireworks, has been around since the late 1980s. Paint Shop Pro came from Jasc Software, which started in 1991. And, of course, McAfee has been around forever, it seems. WinZip first appeared in the early 1990s.

In other words, how many software packages on my computer do I have that were the result of a dot-com that started right in the midst of the boom of the late 1990s? *None.* Zero! Not a single application. What happened to all those "killer apps"? They must have been more like "suicide apps" because they sure didn't kill any competition.

For that matter, did they even have any competition?

Let's look a little more closely and be a bit fairer. First, many of the dot-coms were creating software that runs out on the Internet, and today we do have a few of these software products out there. Google is a big one. And so are Yahoo!, eBay, Amazon, and Akamai. They're still going strong. But what about all those little dot-coms that had big ideas of how I was going to use my computer by the year 2000? They're all gone. And what was that I asked about competition? Well, remember, competition is a fundamental point in marketing. If you have competition, then you will have to work to beat the competition. If you have no competition and never did, then what does that say about your product if nobody else was willing to create something similar?

Here's an actual example: In the earlier Windows days (dare I say *daze*?), I came across a program, whose name I don't even remember, that was supposed to add a ton of functionality to Program Manager. (Remember, Program Manager was the precursor to today's Windows Explorer; it was the shell launcher.) Using various ugly hacking techniques (such as intercepting API calls), this program added menu items to Program Manager and had such silly features as new mouse pointers that looked like oversized hands. The marketing material claimed that this program added all the features that Microsoft *forgot*. Well, sorry, but Microsoft didn't *forget* these features. Instead, Microsoft chose not to include these features because they simply weren't needed. And indeed, nobody else seemed to want these features, and the product died a quick death.

Or here's another example: In the latter part of 1999 and early 2000, wireless technology was really starting to take off. People had all kinds of ideas for killer apps that would run on cell phones. For instance, one idea was that someday I could walk into a grocery store and immediately see a bunch of coupons appear on my cell phone. At that point, the story becomes vague and unclear, but I suppose I would show my cell phone to the nice person at the cash register, who would then type a coupon code into the register.

Well, I can think of several problems with this idea. First, what about people without cell phones? Do they just miss out? That's not fair. And second, why do you even need the cell phone? If the special is just for a little while in the store, why can't they just turn on a big flashing blue light and shout something into the PA system: "Helllllooo shoppers! We're having a special in hardware! Get over here in the next 10 minutes, and get your cans of white paint at 50 percent off!" And the really nice thing about this blinking blue light system is that it's much more robust and reliable, simply because it requires *no programming*.

No surprise, venture capitalists in their amazing insight flocked to the 20-something oracles with their ponytails and promises of killer apps and flooded them with money. And while the press releases made the technology sound like a given, today the companies are *gone* (along with the investment money).

In the dot-com boom, a lot of these killer apps were big ideas and big dreams about how I would use my computer today, and many of these applications really did have no competition. That's because the ideas were so incredibly far-fetched that only a zealot who could talk big to investors could get the product going.

A popular book during the late 1990s about the dot-com business (and still a good book) is *Crossing the Chasm*, rev. ed., by Geoffrey A. Moore (HarperBusiness, 2002). This book talks about the different stages of high-tech acceptance. The idea is that somebody would have a great idea, and initially the only people who would use the product were those called *early adopters*. Eventually, as the software company succeeded in moving past the early adopters to the general masses (a leap over the chasm), the company would make it into the big time.

It was over this chasm where most software companies died. A bunch of young programmers had a brilliant idea for the killer app, and they convinced the investors to fly with it. They got a basic version 1.0 finished, and a few early adopters started using it. (I'm very familiar with this because I was involved with at least two technologies that have since fizzled. My ego won't allow me to say what they were!) But beyond that, much to the dismay of the developers and investors, people just weren't interested.

But why did all this happen? Because the programmers were behaving like programmers, not users. They didn't step into the minds of the users and ask themselves, "What do users *really* want?" These programmers really wanted to believe that if they just built something awesome, the world would stand in amazement and start using the product.

Unfortunately, people just aren't that way. While some of us might be the first to jump at new technology, most people aren't. And this isn't because they're afraid of the technology; they simply don't see a *need* for it. Convince me that I must read my books on the computer in the form of an e-book. (Doesn't a regular paper book work fine?) Show me that I really need to carry a device into a retail store, and that device will display current specials and coupons. (Don't the big stores already have fliers printed on newsprint for us to grab when we go in, and doesn't that work fine?)

Back in the mid-1980s, I was sitting at an Apple II computer, and I had a program that would draw a 3D plot of a curve that looked basically like a peanut. It was just a vector graphic and quite boring. But I was impressed with it and I showed the screen to a young woman I knew. She looked at it and said, "But why?" That confused me. I said, "Isn't that cool?" And she again said, "Well, yes, but why do that? What's the point?"

I didn't have an answer. And you know what? I *still* don't. Just because the "cool technology" is there doesn't mean that the world is going to instantly embrace it.

So what makes a good software package survive? Two things:

- The world really does need it (or, at least the people believe they need it because it really does make their lives easier). Or the world really wants it for entertainment, as in exciting games.
- The software is highly useable.

I use the online banking feature of my bank. I go to the website, enter my username and password, and from there I can easily balance my checkbook. I rarely even look at the statements they send me in the mail anymore. The online banking application is easy to use, and it really does make my life easier. I don't have to wait every month for my statement. Instead, I can just go online anytime I want and see which checks have cleared.

And this application is incredibly easy to use; it's *simple*. It doesn't have a huge amount of complexity: It shows me a list of my accounts; I can click on an account and get the transactions so far for this month. And I can look at last month's transactions if I want, and the month before that.

Recently they added a nice feature where I can click on a check and see a scanned image of the check. That's a lot easier than ordering a check, and I can see to whom I made out the check.

I can also transfer funds between my accounts by clicking the Transfer Funds link, typing in the amount, and choosing the to and from accounts.

Does this qualify as a killer app? Not by any means! This program didn't require any programming wizardry (with all due respect to those who wrote the application), and it didn't require any work of sheer genius. It was simply a need; people wanted to be able to access their bank balances online, and so the banks started adding the capability as an extra feature included with your account.

In fact, the banks saw a need in this: Other banks had online services, so in order to compete, each bank needed to say that they too offered online banking services. And people have come to expect them.

And this online banking phenomenon has happened gradually; it evolved over time. Before online banking, we had phone banking. I don't know how far back phone banking goes, but I do know that I discovered it in the early 1990s. I could call an 800 number, find out my balance, see what checks and other transactions had cleared, transfer funds, and so on. In other words,

I could do almost everything I can with online banking today. Online banking was a natural "next step" from telephone banking. Again, this wasn't a sudden mark of genius where some 19-year-old guy with a ponytail woke up after a hard night of delivering pizzas and said, "Hey! I got it! Online banking! I'm gonna be a billionaire!" After which he ran to the investors, started a dot-com, and became a billionaire six times over.

Now what about something like the Yahoo! search engine? I would almost dare say this was a killer app. But was it? The idea was actually surprisingly simple: Let's get together and catalog the websites on the Internet. That's not too earth shattering. And if you recall the history of Yahoo!, the guys started it in their college dorm room, without any big plans to turn this into a megacorporation that would eventually go public, with a value in the billions. The Yahoo! company, however, has had a lot of ups and downs, and in recent times they've had to greatly rethink their direction. They're more than just a catalogue of the Internet now; they offer communities, e-mail, and loads of other services, some free and some for pay. (I myself sent in my $20 or whatever it was to increase my mailbox size.) And these features were all the result of careful, sound business decisions after bringing in loads of highly qualified individuals.

Let's face it: The killer app concept is a dead one that never even saw the light of day. And what does that mean for you? If you're a software developer, then I would suggest focusing on things that count. While you can certainly work on your secret projects (as Alan Cooper did when he invented Visual Basic and sold it to Microsoft), the truth is that if you want to eat and pay your bills, you must also focus on software that matters. (Alan Cooper was lucky that he managed to sell his product; a lot of other people never do. I wrote a WYSIWYG web editor back in the mid-to-late 1990s that would have given Dreamweaver a good run for its money, but I wasn't able to sell it, and so it now sits on my hard drive as an artifact of the software world.)

Therefore:

RULE   Base your software on what the world needs, not on what you think you can convince the world it needs.

And:

RULE   Don't worry about gee-whiz technology; instead, focus your time making your software good—that is, *useable*.

Finally, think of the concept car. Each year the major auto manufacturers make a concept car, something they hope we'll all be driving in years to come. But they know that these are just concepts and not totally serious. Certain parts of the technology will end up in our cars tomorrow (I would imagine cruise control was once part of a concept car). But the cars we continue to drive today look more like the cars from 10 years ago than the concept cars of recent years. Why? Because the existing concepts are proven, good, and solid. If you focus on making your software good and solid using proven technologies, you will be way ahead of the game. Leave the killer app for your evenings in the garage, and maybe you'll get lucky and sell it like Alan Cooper did.

How Software Affects Businesses

Just how much time do you waste with software? Suppose you're doing a report that you'll present at your next team meeting. You're using Microsoft Word. You need to number your headers so that all level-1 headers start with an automatically generated number. The level-2 headers are to be numbered in Roman numerals, and they start at I under each level-1 header. And finally, you want an appendix that starts with a level-1 header but doesn't have a number on it.

REAL WORLD SCENARIO

When I Pulled on the Paper Towel, the Roll Fell Off into the Puddle.

This isn't such a big deal. It really isn't. And so why should it bother me so much? For that matter, I suppose it's partly my own fault. Here's the scoop: I have a rather cheap paper towel holder attached to the door of the cabinet under the kitchen sink. And when I need a paper towel, I open the door, grab the end, pull a bit to reveal the entire square of paper towel, and then I yank—hard.

Well, the tension the holder puts on the tube inside the paper towel roll apparently isn't very strong, because the last few times I did this, instead of getting a single square of paper towel, the entire roll came loose from the holder, unwound, fell right to the floor, and landed in the very puddle of water I was about to clean up.

Now I suppose the irony here is that when the roll landed in the puddle, it soaked up the puddle and did the cleaning job it was supposed to do. Unfortunately, the water soaked through numerous layers and I had to forfeit half the roll to the trash can, which happily swallowed up all those wasted, wet paper towel squares. Such is life.

But the real question is this: Who would sell a product that works only half the time? And why should we, as users, put up with that?

Now you've heard me say this before, but I'll say it again: Imagine if somebody said that about *your* product. What I experienced was a hardware version of a software crash. (In fact, something soft did go crashing to the floor.)

Now quick: Make a Word document that does all this.

I just tried it. Because I use Word so much, I managed to do it in about three minutes. But I got lucky on one of the items (preventing numbers from appearing on the appendix). For the appendix, I wasn't sure how to keep the numbers from appearing, so I right-clicked on the appendix header, chose Bullets And Numbering, and in the dialog box clicked None. It worked.

But how quickly can most people do it if they never use the numbering schemes on Word? Well, consider what I had to do: I chose Format ➢ Style, and in the dialog box that appeared, I chose the Header 1 style and then clicked Modify to get the Modify Style dialog box. I then clicked the Format button, which produced a strange drop-down menu, in which I chose Numbering. This opened the Bullets And Numbering dialog box, and I clicked the Outline Numbered tab. I clicked on the first numbering sample and then chose Customize. (Oops, it looks like when I chose Customize, I actually modified the defaults in the dialog box. I'm not sure if my changes are permanent, though. The software could be a little clearer about this.) That opened the Customize Outline Numbered List dialog box. And that one is a seriously frightening dialog box to look at; I'm just lucky that I've used it many times and wasn't intimidated by it. But after messing with that dialog box, I managed to set my numbering scheme.

But hey, it looks like I messed up: While describing these steps to you, I realized that I took the long way around. I kept returning to the Modify Style dialog box; the first time I chose Heading 1 and went through the rigmarole of setting the numbering. Then I returned again to the Modify Style dialog box, this time choosing Heading 2 and then going through the same rigmarole. As I just now discovered, it turns out that in the final dialog box I cascaded to, the Customize Outline Numbered List dialog box (that's four cascading dialog boxes, mind you), I could have set the numbering for all the levels right then and there. I guess there was a faster way, and I didn't quite know what I was doing. That means I wasted some time.

And now imagine a new user who has never done all this before and the amount of time it would take to do this. Is it really necessary? Wouldn't some kind of wizard be easier? Besides, the final dialog box, the Customize Outline-whatever-it-was-called, seemed to operate rather independently of the previous dialog boxes. Why did I even have to go though those dialog boxes? I guess Microsoft wanted to sit back and laugh at me. I don't know.

Now think of the hours spent across the planet on that one task, which is a task that has tripped up many people. Imagine all the time spent, and the wages earned, and how much money could be saved worldwide by businesses if their employees didn't have to waste *any* such time on the computer.

Now look at your time spent at home on your own computer: How much time have you spent fiddling with a software installation or with setting up a network connection? And think how much more productive you could have been without having to go through that. (The days of messing with those mysterious things called IRQs in DOS and early versions of Windows come to mind for me. And, of course, I recall my adventures installing a DSL modem at home, which I talked about earlier in this book; see "Don't Reinvent the Wheel!" in Chapter 4, "Managing Your Software's Time.")

Imagine that if software was easier to use and much more straightforward, how many countless hours per month would be saved! Imagine the amount of time you could spend doing what you want to do on your home computer. Imagine how much time your company would save if the workers could get right to the task at hand and not have to fiddle with the software, trying to figure it all out! The prospect is, frankly, frightening. And further, when users are focusing on the software and not their actual work, they might even end up doing a sloppy job of their actual work.

But we, the programmers, have it within our power to change all this. Stop blaming the end users, and instead give the users what they *need*.

REAL WORLD SCENARIO

The DSL Modem Adventure, Part II

Back in Chapter 4, I lamented about the troubles I had getting the DSL modem set up on my laptop while visiting my sister. She already had the DSL modem and software all set up on her computer. To get it all on my computer, I had to go through a huge installation process.

Well, guess what: Just yesterday, I was at my sister's again, and she had a second computer that needed to be hooked up to DSL. This time I decided to be smart: I opted to not even use the installation CD the DSL provider had sent her. This was, after all, Windows XP, which was supposed to have all kinds of drivers and such already installed.

Here's what I did: I opened up the Network Control Panel and clicked Create A New Connection. The New Connection Wizard opened. I clicked Next (after reading a useless introductory screen), and then I chose Connect To The Internet. I clicked Next and then chose Set Up My Connection Manually. I clicked Next again and chose Connect Using A Broadband Connection That Requires A Username And Password. Then I clicked Next. I was asked for the ISP name, which, it turns out, is really just the name that will go below the icon in the Network Connections dialog box. I typed the name of the ISP and clicked Next. I was then asked for a username and password (as well as to confirm the password). I had to choose a few options; the first was whether to use this username and password for all users of the system; the next was whether to make this the default connection; and the last was whether to turn on the built-in firewall software.

I clicked Next, and a final screen came up asking me to verify everything. I clicked Finish. And lo and behold, the connection worked on the first try! I did it all by myself without the help of some silly installation program. Now I really have to wonder what in the world possessed the people at the ISP to write their own software!

Technology Has Improved, but Has the Usability?

This one is a no-brainer. Of course technology has improved. But if usability had improved as quickly as technology, we wouldn't have a need for this very book you're reading and the other books in the usability field.

But why is that? Why couldn't usability improve?

Well, first, usability *has* improved; don't get me wrong. The word processor I'm looking at right now is far better than some of the early word processors (anyone remember the original WordStar?). However, that's not to say that the usability has improved in the same leaps and bounds as the technology. The fact is, back around 1988 I had an Amiga 500 computer, which featured a graphical user interface very similar to the early Macintosh computers. And I had a word processor on that computer that looked, frankly, an awful lot like the current word processor I'm using right now, Microsoft Word. Yes, this new version of Word is light-years ahead of that early Amiga word processor in terms of power. But what about usability? I have to say, with all honesty, that that word processor was, in fact, easier to use than Word. But my answer is a bit weighted in that I'm comparing apples and oranges. In terms of setting the fonts and typing in the text, the two are about the same. But all those extra features that exist today in Word that didn't exist in that early Amiga word processor are actually a lot harder to use than anything I used on that old Amiga computer. And for that reason, I cannot say that the usability of Word is any better than the usability of the old Amiga word processor.

Let's face it; how much of Microsoft Word do you *really* use? Here's a list of some of the features of Word:

- If your office has a copy of Microsoft Office Server Extensions, you can be notified via e-mail of changes made to a document stored on the server.

- You can create a master document, which contains references to other documents. The master document is like a book, and the other documents are like individual chapters of the book stored in separate documents.

- You can create a form inside a document, populate the form with standard Windows controls, and then send the data over to Excel for analysis. (Try right-clicking on any toolbar, and in the drop-down menu choosing Forms to bring up the Forms toolbar. Then try playing with it.)

In addition, you can use some "fun" features such as these:

- Add a theme to a document that includes a custom background and custom font colors and sizes (just like in a web page).

- Use custom images for your bullets.

And then here are some really useful features that not everybody knows about:

- You can use AutoCorrect to simplify your typing. For example, if I had to type the word *Visual Studio .NET* over and over, I could choose Tools ➤ Auto Correct, and choose to replace *vsn* with *Visual Studio .NET*. Then every time I typed *vsn*, Word would automatically replace my text with *Visual Studio .NET*.

- If you have a word that you often spell wrong, you can right-click on the misspelled word, choose AutoCorrect in the pop-up menu, and then click the word that you want your common typo to be automatically replaced with in the future.

Okay, these are all features that most people probably don't use. And so why are they there? Well, some of them are, in fact, quite handy. But some of these aren't exactly the most useable; some of them are cumbersome to use.

This should be a wakeup call to us all as software developers. The technology is advancing forward, and we're sweeping ahead with it, but we're letting our usability lag. How can we do that? By realizing that we have only so many people-hours we can actually spend working on the software, and then figuring out what we have time for and what we don't have time for. That means opting for usability over feature bloat. And that's a topic I take up in the next section.

Choose Ease and Usability, Not a Gazillion Features

The purpose of this chapter is to talk about the business issues surrounding usability. I've spent a good bit of time talking about features throughout this book; now I'd like to focus on the issue of features from a business perspective.

When you develop software, you have a choice as to how to spend your time: by adding more and more features or by making sure the features you do have are absolutely correct in terms of usability. As you can guess, I'm going to say that you should focus on the usability issues, not on adding more and more features.

But is this practical from a business standpoint? While some users might get all excited over software that does everything from creating beautiful graphics to changing the oil filter in their car, most people don't want this kind of software. The reason is that software filled with features will, most likely, be filled with far more drop-down menus and toolbar buttons than the average user can comprehend. But from a business perspective, intimidation factors aside, the more features you have in your software, the more complex your software will be (or, at least, will *seem*). And with that comes more time spent finagling with the software. The users may have to spend time first just getting to the feature. And once they're at the magical dialog box that controls the feature, they may be confused and have to spend time figuring out how to use the feature.

The people who purchase software in large corporations know this. One of the first questions they ask of a software salesperson is about training: How much training is required? How much is the training going to cost? In other words, they're concerned about how difficult the software is to use.

Imagine these two scenarios:

- Your software package has 100 major features, and of those the majority are difficult to use.

- Your software package has eight major features, and each one is solid and easy to use and requires little training.

Look again at the first item. Not only is each feature difficult to use, but when you figure people are going to have to be trained on each of those 100 features, you can see that training will take a very long time. And more time spent in training is more time spent away from doing one's job.

But think about the second item: Let's say your salespeople waltzed into a client's office, set the client down at the laptop running the software, and in five minutes the client was up and running and using the software. That would be a pretty easy sell, wouldn't it?

The fact is, you have limited time to spend on your product. If you have a million years, yes, you could make an incredible product filled with every feature. But you don't. Therefore, you have to choose your tasks during those limited hours wisely. And one wise decision is to focus on making sure the few major features that you have are of top-notch quality. They're easy to use, they get the job done, and they're very clear in how they work.

REAL WORLD SCENARIO

Windows on Your Appliance? Time to Reboot the Fridge!

Some time back, Microsoft created an appliance version of Windows. As you can imagine, this opened up Microsoft for loads of jokes. After all, what happens if the refrigerator crashes? I guess you'll have to reboot it. And while it's in a crashed state, does your food spoil? Yeah, yeah, I'm sure Microsoft has heard them all.

But this is an example, perhaps, of technology gone just a bit too far. Do we really need Windows on our appliances? (Okay, so the refrigerator is a bit of an exaggeration, but they do have a form of Windows CE in car stereos.) How much technology do we really need, and how much is too much?

When you use a DVD player, you are interacting with some seriously sophisticated technology, which includes plenty of onboard software. Furthermore, these days all microwave ovens have computer chips inside them, and when you type on the keypad, you are interacting with the software. But does a microwave oven need software as feature-rich as what you find in a DVD player? I don't see any reason why it should.

Think about the features in your software, and ask yourself if the users are really going to use them. After all, nobody wants to have to reboot the refrigerator after the system software crashes, when the old twentieth-century refrigerators that were software-less worked just fine!

Being Aware of Industry Standards

As much as we developers may hate standards, they are a fact of life. Standards are not going away. And we can do ourselves a major service by adopting the standards.

From both a usability and business perspective, adopting standards is a wise choice. For example, I worked for a bit in the e-book business. A few years ago this was supposed to take the world by storm. It didn't. It was another early adopter technology that never went past the early adopters.

Yet, one form of e-book lives on: PDF files. Yes, most people have a love/hate relationship with PDF files. But like them or not, PDF files are here to stay. And the reason they survived the e-book fallout is twofold:

- The PDF format existed before the e-book craze.
- The PDF format is a standard.

Not very often is a private company able to create a proprietary format, open the format up for all to adopt, and successfully declare the format a standard. Yet, that's exactly what Adobe managed to do with PDF. Part of the reason for their enormous success in PDF is that they give away a read-only version of their Acrobat product for free. With Acrobat Reader, you can open PDF files right inside your web browser. People have, in turn, put PDF files on websites left and right. PDF is a fact of life and it's here to stay.

But what happened to the rest of the people in the e-book business? Many of the companies decided to go with their own proprietary format. Instead of using a standard format, they created their own. And that meant e-books created for their format could be viewed only with their readers. And so if you, as an e-book user, were to look at a catalog of e-books, you would have to first see if you have the viewer for the particular e-book. And that could mean having five or six separate viewers. Or if you looked at the catalog for a particular viewer, you would be missing out on all the e-books for the other viewers.

People saw right through this, and the whole thing was a flop. Almost none of the companies that were proudly displaying their products at the e-book conventions back in 1999 are in existence anymore. Nearly all of them folded.

The moral here is this: If you have a product that reads or displays documents, at least *support* the various standards. Occasionally I'll see shareware graphics programs that maintain their own proprietary format and don't support the standard formats such as JPG and PNG. What good is such a program? Imagine how many people will turn away from the software package simply because of the lack of standards. From a business perspective, ignoring standards can be a very bad idea.

This doesn't mean you have to make one of the standards your native format. A lot of the better graphics programs have their own format, for example, and then you can import from and export to the standard formats.

When a Standard Isn't Always the Best Standard

Back in 1999 when I spent a little bit of time in the e-book business, many of us were well aware of the Great PDF Monster lurking on the horizon. We knew that PDF was frankly not the best solution for reading a book online, whereas a format such as HTML was far better. The reason is that PDF is a fixed-page layout, whereas with HTML a browser reflows the text to fit the screen. You can see where PDF has a problem when you have text arranged in columns on a single page, such as in a typical book index. If you've ever looked at an index page in Acrobat Viewer, you know what I'm talking about: The text in both columns might scroll down past the bottom of the screen. If you're scanning the left column, you will scroll down to the bottom, and then when you get to the bottom, you'll have to scroll back up to the top to get to the column on the right side.

Furthermore, if you have a page that's printed with an extremely tiny font, and you zoom in to make the font big enough to read, the margins of the page may now extend off the sides of your screen. You must then scroll horizontally. And if you've ever tried to read a document that's too wide for the screen and requires horizontal scrolling, you know what a nightmare it is.

Yet, those of us in the e-book business were well aware that PDF was a standard and was *not* going away. Further, we knew that it would behoove us to adopt PDF into our e-book software programs. But alas, many companies chose not to, and they paid the price—they vanished.

Today PDF lives on and it is definitely one of the most popular online formats, and certainly one of the most successful, even though it's far from perfect. Yet, you could say that about almost any product that has been successful. People who used OS/2 extensively knew that OS/2 was far superior in many ways to its competitor at the time, Windows 95. But it didn't matter; Windows 95 quickly took off as the operating system of choice, and OS/2 withered away. And programmers who embraced OS/2 as the platform for their software were quickly disappointed in their lack of sales.

Therefore, remember: Embrace the standards and the leading technologies, even if you know they're not perfect. Your job, after all, is to sell products, right?

Even the well-known software applications that have a proprietary format often support importing from and exporting to competitors' formats. For example, the copy of Microsoft Word I'm using right now can read and write WordPerfect 5.0 files.

Ways You Can Defend Your Business against Problems

I'm going to assume that only software developers will be reading this book. As much as I'd like to see people from other areas reading this book, most of you are software developers. Therefore, I'm going to focus on what you can do within your software development organization to help defend against problems.

The problems you might encounter can fall into these two main categories:

- Your organization might purchase software for the employees, and this software might have usability problems.

- Your organization might be creating software that has usability problems.

If your organization is purchasing software, here's the single biggest thing you can do to help in the cause to make software better:

RULE   Demand only the best.

No longer should you settle for *pretty good* or *fair*. Surely you have software that you use on a daily basis that you have gripes about, right? If you've read the previous 11 chapters you can see that I sure have plenty of gripes. It's time to take a stand and demand better software *now*.

If you're analyzing software for a potential purpose and you find problems, let the developers know. In fact, if these problems have convinced you to not purchase the software, let them know as well! If you've already purchased the software, tell them you're thinking about ditching their product and going with the competition, and make a list of things that you don't like about their software. Don't worry about being kind. Give it all you've got, and let them know exactly how you feel. They need to hear it!

I can't tell you how many companies I've worked for where two or three major software applications were in use, and my coworkers all griped endlessly about the software. And yet the companies continued to use the software packages. But in hindsight, did any of us bother to contact the people who made the software and let them know that we were upset? No. So did the company even know about these problems? Maybe. But even if they did, if they've received very few complaints, then maybe they pushed them off to a severity-4 bug, meaning the problem will *never* get fixed!

But don't complain only about bugs. Complain about general usability issues as well. Does the software package contain cascading dialog boxes that are cumbersome to use? Let them know about it. Are there features that would be better suited on the toolbar, but you can't customize the toolbar? Complain! Be vocal about it. They need to know if you know of a way for them to improve their software package. (And if you're feeling particularly mischievous, you might send them an e-mail with your gripes and CC their competition. That might be a good wakeup call for them!)

But now walk over to the other side of the fence. Suppose you are the software developer. Then this should be your motto:

RULE   Build only the best.

How do you know what's best? By following all the guidelines I've put forward in this book and by following the guidelines in all the other great books on usability. Resources are everywhere; study them. But don't put usability at a low priority, as if it's just one more issue you need to look into. Usability should be the *top* priority. You want your software to be the *best*, even if it has fewer features than the competition. After all, what good are those extra features in the competitor's software if they're impossible to use?

Here are ways you can guard your business and ensure that you will release only the finest, highest-quality software:

- Include full usability studies when you are designing the software.
- Get feedback from your testers on usability.
- Focus on usability during beta testing; don't just look for bugs.
- Listen to customer complaints and gripes and take them seriously.
- Be open-minded and ask yourself how you can improve the usability of your software.

The final item should take place throughout the development process, not just when you're thinking about the next version. Be open-minded, and don't be afraid to be self-critical. When you and the others on your team are designing the software, put yourself in the shoes of the end users. Pretend you are not very computer literate. Allow yourself to be your own worst user nightmare.

Only when you can be open-minded and truly see your software the way that your users do can you improve it. And finally, remember this:

| RULE | Respect your users. You need them more than they need you! |

Moving Forward

As you can see, the whole idea of usability has far-reaching consequences right into the financial aspects of your business. Simply put, if you create junk, your business will suffer. And even if you're the only one making a type of software, it's only a matter of time before somebody else comes along with a superior product.

As I said in this chapter, the way you can ensure that you will create good software is by focusing on the users and their needs. If you wake up in the night with an amazing idea that came to you through a dream, don't just run to the computer and start coding. Instead, first find out if the users really need your new killer app. And if not, move on!

And speaking of moving on, in the next chapter I talk about the next step of software development: After you've decided that you really do have a viable product, and you've actually built the thing, you still need to *test it*. And for that reason, you need a devoted team of *quality assurance* people. But such people need to be trained on how to catch not just run-of-the-mill bugs but usability bugs as well. I'll meet you in the next chapter.

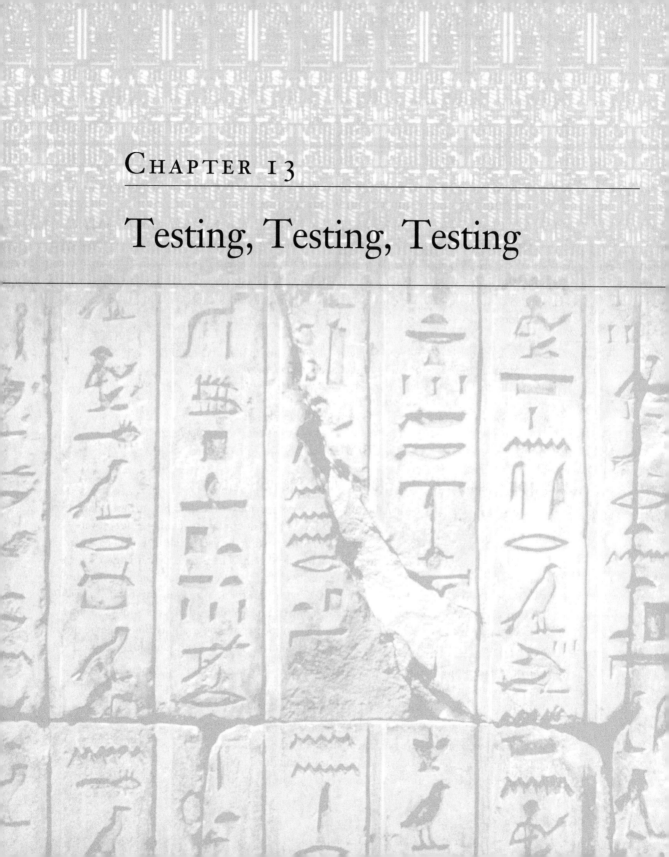

CHAPTER 13

Testing, Testing, Testing

Before I get into the meat of this chapter, I want to point out something: The second word in the title *test engineer* is *engineer*. Why am I mentioning this? Because a lot of programmers tend to forget this point. I'm not lying. Some people actually pursue the field of test engineering, or as some of them call it, quality assurance (QA). (That's what I'm going to call them in this chapter: QA engineers, or just QA people. And occasionally I'll say *tester*.) And such people are not simply "hoping to move up into programming."

True, some companies start younger, entry-level people out in the QA department, and such people eventually get promoted into actual programming. But if this is the way you do business, then you are making a big mistake. I explain why in this chapter.

But the primary focus of this chapter is usability. Yeah, yeah, I've been tooting that horn since I came into your previously perfect world. But testing really does have a role in usability. And *that's* the focus of this chapter.

> **NOTE**   The more common use of the term *software testing* refers to the process of finding bugs in code that cause the code to break. This is a laborious task with very few good tools on the market. For that type of testing, you might want to take a look at the new book, *Software Test Automation: Developing an Automated Software Testing Tool* by Kanglin Li and Mengqi Wu (Sybex, 2004), which teaches testing procedures and takes the reader through the steps to develop an automated testing tool. All of the code for the tool is provided with the book.

Why You Need a QA Team (and What They Should Do)

The QA team has a big job on their shoulders. They need to make sure that the software does not get out the door without any bugs. (Yikes.) But having bugs doesn't just mean that the software explodes the monitor and wipes out the hard drive while posting the user's Yahoo! e-mail password on the Web. (Sakes, if your software does all that by mistake, maybe it's time to find a new career.) In addition to catching what we traditionally think of as bugs, the QA team must catch any usability bugs. What are usability bugs? Exactly what you're trying to prevent by reading this book. A *usability bug* is any problem in usability. If you create highly useable software, then your software is free of usability bugs. What are usability bugs? In the section "Searching for Usability Bugs" later in this chapter, I list some examples; here are a few more concrete examples of usability bugs:

- The macro recording shortcut system functions as it is expected, but it's cumbersome to use: The icons on the buttons on the macro recording toolbar are not clear. Also, when the user clicks the Stop button, the Stop button doesn't become disabled, and the toolbar gives the appearance that the macro is still being recorded.

- When the user is highlighting text by holding down the Shift key and pressing the arrow keys, and she backs up, the text doesn't become un-highlighted in the usual way. Instead, the highlighting expands in the other direction, which is not standard. This will confuse users.

These are bugs in the software! Even though the features may function as the designers expected, they do not function as the users might expect.

Of course, you don't want your software to reach the point of QA only to find out that the software is free of regular bugs but totally unuseable. That's why the programmers need to read this book, not just the QA people. (Usability engineering takes place throughout the development cycle!) If a QA team spends hours upon hours making sure that the software functions as expected and without bugs but does not test for usability problems, and the software is *filled* with usability problems, then what's the point in even bothering with QA? Just because software is bug-free doesn't mean the software isn't a piece of junk.

The QA team, therefore, needs to be mindful of usability. While testing for the usual kinds of bugs such as memory leaks and general protection faults, they need to also watch for usability bugs.

But these usability bugs they're going to find are not big things like the presence of cascading dialog boxes. (Those types of usability problems should not even have existed because the developers did their homework and knew better than to put them in in the first place. Right?) Instead, the kinds of bugs the QA team is looking for are the smaller, less-obvious usability bugs. (I talk about the different kinds of usability bugs and ways of tracking them down in the section "Searching for Usability Bugs" later in this chapter.)

Typically, the QA team will probably want to work usability into their schedule of tests. And the managers will want to make sure that the whole QA team is constantly on the lookout for usability problems even when testing for regular bugs.

Why Your QA Department Should *Not* Be a Stepping-stone to Development

Want to make a new hire angry? Advertise for a software engineer position and interview candidates, pick the best, and when the new hire arrives for the first day of work, tell her, "You will be working in system testing for six months while you learn how our product works."

If you do that, you will find that you have huge employee turnover. But besides the obvious part of making somebody angry, you're completely undermining the whole notion of system testing. Why fill such an important team with disgruntled, frustrated people?

Too many companies, especially dot-coms, have made the QA department a stepping-stone to programming. In addition to making programmers angry and creating a QA team that might not live up to its charter, you are also attaching a dangerous stigma to the QA team, resulting in a dangerous caste system within your organization. As a few of the brighter people get "promoted out" of QA, those who remain will start to feel like they have *QA* written on their shirts in huge scarlet letters. Morale will drop. And bad morale in one team will bleed over into other teams. (Think about it: How many times have you worked for a company that has a terrible morale problem, and if you look more closely you can trace the problem to one small group of people?)

QA is a vital part of an organization. Treat the QA engineers as equals to the people with the title *software engineer*: Pay both sides the same, and make it clear that they are on the same level. Invite people to make a lateral move from development to QA, with the same pay rate, which is an opposite move from what most people expect.

Who Should Work in QA?

If you read the first paragraph of this chapter, you heard me point out that the QA people are, indeed, engineers. These are not just partially skilled people who know a bit about computers. Instead, you should staff your QA department with highly skilled people who know how to program.

Imagine a bug report like this:

```
Test Engineer: Nikki Ward
Assigned to: Jeff Cogswell
Short Description: Illegal Instruction Error
Long Description: When I opened a file, the program
gave me an illegal instruction error. I can reproduce
it by opening the attached file. However, the problem
occurs only on my computer, not Sue's computer.
```

Okay, if you're the developer who gets assigned this report, you'll have to open the attached file. And when the bug doesn't occur, what do you do? Well, you'll probably have to walk down the hallway to the tester's computer, try it out, and see the bug occur. Then what? Does the QA computer have development tools on it? Maybe, if the tester is so inclined to install them. But what if it does not? Then what do you do? You could spend the better part of the day trying to reproduce the problem on your own computer. Then when your manager is coming down on you, you may eventually just flag the bug as "cannot reproduce" and move on, leaving it in place.

But suppose instead you receive the following report:

```
Test Engineer: Nikki Ward
Assigned to: Jeff Cogswell
Short Description: Illegal Instruction Error
Long Description: When I opened a file, the program
gave me an illegal instruction error. I can reproduce
it by opening the attached file. However, the problem
occurs only on my computer, not Sue's computer. I ran
the product inside the debugger and discovered that the
problem is a memory overwrite in somefile.cpp, inside
the function somefunction. It seems that the index
of the array is larger than the array itself.
```

Well, that's a lot better information! Memory problems are, after all, some of the hardest bugs to catch, because the results can be so sporadic. If you accidentally write to some memory outside of an array, your program might be fine. Or it might not be, depending on how that memory outside the array is used. And now, thanks to Nikki's fine bug work (and well-written bug report), you can go into the actual function and figure out why the index is out of bounds. You can then start backtracking, figure out where the real bug is causing the index to get messed up, and so on.

Now because the tester had the development tools on her computer, as soon as the problem occurred she was able to immediately launch the debugger and go from there. Maybe 15 minutes later, she had the problem isolated and then sent in an excellent bug report. You, in turn, spent another half-hour tracking down the rest of the memory problem and fixing it.

What am I saying here, then? I'm saying:

RULE   Your testers should be reasonably proficient in programming.

They don't need to be experts in software development. (Instead, they should be experts in test engineering or at least spending their time becoming experts.) But they should be reasonably proficient in programming. They might not need to know how to derive a template class from a non-template class, but they should know how to use a debugger to trace into a template class function (and not be intimidated by the fact that it's a template), set breakpoints, inspect the variables, and the like.

They are not, after all, writing code. But they are reading code. If you have studied a foreign language, you know that most foreign language departments at universities have a watered-down version of the studies with an emphasis on *reading*. For example, a German department might offer a track of classes for learning to speak German. And separately, they might offer Reading German, which doesn't focus on memorizing all the genders of the nouns and such. Instead, it focuses on being able to read and understand German.

Likewise, the QA team's knowledge of programming need only be analogous to the Reading German class. The QA team members are, of course, free to learn as much as they can about programming, and indeed, the more they know, the better.

But requiring less programming knowledge does not imply that the testers know less than the programmers. A QA position is not a step below programming. The QA team doesn't write code, so how can it be on the same advancement ladder as programming? The QA team is a separate career path with its own skill set. Being reasonably proficient in programming is only one job requirement out of many. A test engineer must also be able to do several things programmers don't do on a regular basis, such as devise an entire testing plan that puts the program through the wringer, testing as many combinations as possible. Thus:

SUGGESTION

A tester's expected knowledge should not be a subset of a programmer's expected knowledge. That is, a programmer isn't a tester who simply "knows more" and has therefore "moved up."

From my own experience, I think every QA team should have at least one person who either has made a lateral move from development or has been promoted from development. This person isn't somebody who just couldn't hold his weight in the development team and out of management frustration got pushed over, kicking and screaming, into testing. This person should instead be a skilled programmer who can easily go into the code and track down problems quickly and efficiently. This person also needs to have engineering skills to be able to create and execute an entire testing plan. But also, lest we lose sight of the focus of this book, the test engineer must be able to test the software from a usability perspective. This often requires being able to stand in the shoes of the average user. Can a typical programmer do that? Usually not. Most programmers are so advanced in computer usage that they have lost sight of what it's like to be a beginner.

RULE	A good test engineer should be able to stand in the shoes of the end user.

QA and Showstoppers

Do you remember the TV commercial from several years ago by the Hanes company where the woman who was supposedly a QA inspector said, "They don't say Hanes until *I* say they say Hanes!"? Well, that's the way you should run your software organization. Your QA people should be allowed to stop the show when they find a bug that they deem too severe.

A lot of people in the software world simply accept that some bugs will go out in their software. (I have heard lots of mixed opinions about this idea, but the fact is, it's a common practice.) But some bugs should not be allowed to get out the door.

Certainly, if the latest build causes the software to crash when it first starts up, the software can't go out the door. That's a showstopper. But what about usability bugs? If the software functions as is but has some problems with usability, should the QA team be allowed to call a showstopper and demand that the bug be fixed?

To be honest, I just can't imagine this happening, as much as I'd like it to. I have been in the software business long enough that I imagine most software managers and VPs simply won't do it. They have a serious deadline that's already been pushed back three times, and the last thing they want is a tester calling a showstopper because the GUI might confuse some poor sap who doesn't know how to use computers anyway.

First, let me say that that's not the only kind of bug I'm talking about here. Usability extends far beyond catering to the neophytes. Second, as much as managers and VPs might resist, it is my hope that they will get their hands on this book and see the light: You simply must treat usability bugs as legitimate bugs.

Of course, testers typically assign a severity level to a bug. A "sev-1" bug (as most shops call it) is a showstopper. A "sev-4" bug is one they plan to never fix, even when that one guy in

Upper Zambobia who happens to be a SQL guru and is using your software for pure enjoyment during his snowbound winter runs into the bug.

The question is, then, what usability bugs qualify as sev-1 bugs, or showstoppers? As much as I'd like to suggest that they all should be sev-1 bugs, the reality is they aren't. Some are worse than others.

I can't simply list all the types of bugs here and assign severity levels for you. Instead, the QA staff needs to be so accustomed to usability issues that they can gauge just how bad the different bugs are. Here are some examples:

- Did a programmer fail to follow the designs and create a cascading dialog box somewhere deep in the program? I'd say this is a sev-2, maybe sev-3, depending on how often people are likely to use the particular dialog box. It's not a showstopper. But it should be looked at by a programmer and considered for repair.

- Did the programmer open a system-modal dialog box that freezes up the whole computer? I'd call that a sev-1, or at least a sev-2. Nah, make it a sev-1. A system modal dialog box is something no program should ever do.

- Did a programmer include a task that waits for a long timeout under certain conditions (such as waiting for a dial tone on the modem when no phone cable is connected) but with no way to cancel the operation? A bug like this isn't going to be the end of the world, but it will definitely be an annoyance to a lot of users. Choose either sev-1 or sev-2, depending on how much you care about annoying your users. (Personally, I'd make it a sev-1, but I'm obsessed with usability, if that's not obvious.)

Are you getting the idea here? Showstoppers are problems that are simply unacceptable, usability errors that no software should ever commit. These are bugs that seriously hamper the users' ability to achieve their goals. Sev-2 bugs are those that really should be fixed, but you don't have to call in the programmers at midnight. They're bugs that may hinder the usability of your software and might cause the users to employ time-consuming workarounds. Sev-3 bugs and sev-4 bugs are those that would be really nice to fix; they're typically cosmetic bugs or minor performance bugs.

Now if you're hoping that I'm going to come up with an example of a sev-4 usability bug, forget it. I can't think of any, because I personally feel all usability bugs are at least a sev-2. Others may disagree. But it's your choice: Do you want to have customers get frustrated and choose the competing software?

Here's a very good example: A friend of mine does a lot of image editing for her eBay auctions, which she does full time. She was looking for a new image-editing software package. She found a trial version of one that was quite good, except it didn't allow a multiple-level undo, and the undo it did offer was extremely limited. (It would undo an entire batch of commands if the commands were all the same kind, such as floodfill.) But she needed a better undo. Sometimes she made multiple changes to an image and wanted to backtrack through several to compare and then redo the changes to compare again.

REAL WORLD SCENARIO

Help, I've Fallen into Development and I Can't Get Out!

On a personal note, tracking down problems in code and fixing them was always one of my strengths. Yet, because I was also a skilled developer, the one time back in the mid '90s when I told my boss I wanted to move to testing, he wouldn't allow me to. "We need you in development," he told me. That was a big mistake on his part. If you're a manager and you have a programmer who wants to move to QA, let him go over!

Now you might be worried about two things: First, if the grass looks greener over in QA and the pay scale is the same, you could end up with a brain drain where you lose all your good programmers. Second, what if your star programmer wants to go over to testing?

As for the brain drain problem, trust me, you won't have that happen. Most people who know how to program prefer to program. But if they really don't want to program, then why force them to stay? You need sharp minds in all your groups, not just development. So don't worry about brain drain; it's a moot point.

But what if your star programmer wants to leave the group? My advice is to move him over to testing. If that will make him happy, then let it be! The reason is that if all your programming talent is confined to a single person, then you have a serious problem on your hands that's much bigger than simply whether this one person wants to leave. What if the star programmer gets a job offer across town and resigns? Or, heaven forbid, what if the star programmer dies? (It can and does happen, after all.) Then what? Do you close up shop, congratulate everybody on the fun time you've had, and retire? Certainly not! You simply cannot allow one member of your development team to be the sole brain while everybody else is simply an appendage to the operation, controlled by the star programmer. Because when (not if, but *when*) that programmer gets a job offer across town, you're going to have a serious problem on your hands.

Train your programmers well. Work with them, find mentors, and turn everybody into star programmers. (Start by having them read this book. I'm serious!) Teach them how to design good software, and that way you won't be relying on a single person who might up and leave.

And when that person does want to leave the development group but stay in the company, count your blessings that this person is still on the payroll, and happily send him over to QA. (Besides, realistically, people will be coming to him on a regular basis for help, and you'll still have that brain you were afraid of losing.)

Now some people might rank a limited undo as a sev-3 bug or a sev-4 bug and move it out of the bugs and into the "features for next release" category. Well, I hate to break the news to the people who made this particular image editor, but my friend didn't buy your $100 package and instead went with the competitor. You lost a sale because of this usability bug.

So what level would you assign to this usability bug? I'd make it a sev-1 or sev-2. The software shouldn't go out with it. But it's your software and your sales. And maybe you're competing with my product, and I'll make sure to include the feature in *mine*.

Usability Testing Strategies

People have written entire books on testing. My goal here isn't to teach you how to test software. Instead, my goal is to teach you how to test for usability bugs. Of course, before you can test for usability bugs, you have to know what usability bugs *are*. And to figure out what usability bugs are, read this book, and read as many other books and articles on usability as you can. But don't just take our word for it; talk to the customers using your previous software versions; listen to the beta testers; listen to the tech writers when they have a gripe; listen to everybody. In other words, get the thoughts of the *people*.

In addition to listening to others, however, you (or your testers) can search for usability bugs yourself. In the following sections, I talk about ways to do testing that is relevant to usability.

Searching for Usability Bugs

How exactly do you search for usability bugs? Here are three separate areas the QA team needs to explore:

- Bugs that the original design never covered
- Bugs that violate the original design
- Bugs in the original design

For example, sometimes programmers (or an entire team of programmers) might end up going off on a tangent, adding some new feature that wasn't mentioned in the original design documents. They might, for example, add some fancy export feature, allowing the program to export data to Microsoft Excel. While this might be a good feature, the fact is, it wasn't in the final design documents and therefore shouldn't be in the program. What should the testers do? They should not test out the feature, making sure it creates valid Excel files. Instead, they should write up a bug report stating that an extraneous feature is present and must be removed.

As another example, the design documents might clearly state a set of menu items under the View menu, but the programmer didn't include them all, and the programmer added a few extras or perhaps simply renamed them. The testers should catch this problem. Instead of testing the new menu items, the testers need to file a bug report stating that *the menu is not laid out as expected.*

In other words, if the software engineers and architects and all those nice people did their job, they planned for usability early on. They designed the software to be highly useable. But the programmers who wrote the code might have diverged from the original designs.

Such divergences from the original design would be no surprise. Software development houses all too often give too much freedom to a programmer's whim of the day. As I mentioned earlier in the book, a programmer might arbitrarily declare that the product can open only 10 documents at once, simply because 10 seemed like a nice number. Similarly, a programmer might be given the chore of designing a dialog box. The engineering documents might have simply said, "We will create an Options dialog box," and left the details up to the programmer. (This happens all too often!) These bugs would fall into the first category, bugs that the original design never covered.

But on the other hand, a programmer might ignore the design document. The design document might have presented a very nice dialog box that is highly useable. But the programmer might decide that it is flawed and then go on her own way, designing it completely differently. While the people who designed the dialog box on paper or in a design document had the best of intentions, the programmer is the one who ultimately builds the thing.

In both cases, this is where the QA team comes in. *Somebody* must catch these problems. The architects and team leaders and all those people who should know better might not catch the problems, because their job isn't to go through and test every last feature of the product. They probably don't have time. But the test engineers do have time, because testing every feature is indeed their job responsibility. (And I mean *every* feature. That's what I talk about in the next section, "Doing a 'Full Pass' Test on Your Software.")

The third category, bugs in the original design, might create the biggest political problems in the whole development process, because declaring a bug in the original design might not exactly make the designers happy. The original designers might yell things like, "Oh, come on, if the users can't figure this out, they must be stupid!" And that's why the QA team needs to have a certain amount of showstopping authority. The QA team must be given the authority to say no to such problems and to demand that they be fixed. And that probably means one of the top people in the organization must give the QA team such authority.

So how exactly do the people in the QA team find the usability bugs? They do a full pass on the software, which I discuss in the next section.

REAL WORLD SCENARIO

The Microwave That Reminds You (and Reminds You, and Reminds You...)

"Okay! I get the point! Now leave me alone!"

That's how I feel when I'm dealing with my microwave oven. Over the past few years, I have moved a lot for various reasons. Because of my mobile tendencies, a couple years ago when it came time to buy a new microwave oven, I based my decision on one factor: I bought the *lightest* one that was within the size range I wanted. And fortunately, the lightest one was also a pretty good one: it had a rotating platter and that ever-so-important *popcorn* button, among other features.

But the microwave oven also has a "feature" that is, to be honest, seriously annoying. When I cook something in the oven and walk away, I listen for the beep to tell me when the cooking is done. But if I don't return to the oven and open the door, the microwave will beep again in 30 seconds. Okay, that's fine; my mother used to forget about the coffee mug full of water she was warming in the microwave to make instant coffee, and other family members would find it six hours later. (I can say this because she doesn't read my books. She just puts them on the bookshelf and brags to her friends about them!) Because some people forget about the stuff they just heated in the microwave, I can understand the need for the 30-second reminder.

But this isn't just a 30-second reminder. It's a 30-, 60-, 90-, 120-, 150-, 180-, 210-second reminder, and probably more. (But I wouldn't know. By the sixth or seventh beep, my blood pressure is so high that you can be *sure* I have removed the food from the oven!)

Maybe some microwave oven designers are reading this book. If so:

Dear Mr./Ms. Microwave Designer:

   How do you turn off that darn reminder beep???? I'm considering donating your microwave oven to charity and buying a different brand of oven, except that I care about the poor people and don't want to curse them with this abomination that you call a microwave oven. Help!

Irritably yours,

Jeff Cogswell

As best as I can figure, the microwave has no way to turn off this warning. I think next time I'll buy a different brand of microwave oven. The *other* brands don't have this problem. And I don't care if the one I get does weigh a bit more!

Doing a "Full Pass" Test on Your Software

Test engineers sometimes speak of a "full pass" in their test. A full pass is where they use an automation program, and they test every single feature of the software, pushing in as many combinations and permutations as possible. If they are testing a program that allows the user to type an e-mail address into an edit control, they write a test script that will grind through all sorts of possible entries for the edit control, including several examples of text that is not a valid e-mail address, as well as text that is a valid e-mail address. And with the help of automation, they can grind through thousands of possibilities in minutes. They can then test the response of the software to determine whether the software responded correctly. Did the entry of each invalid e-mail address cause the software to issue a friendly message or did some get through? That's what the test engineers must determine. But such a test is not a test of usability.

Where does the usability test come in? The usability test is determining whether the software's response to an invalid e-mail address was, in fact, polite and easy for the users to handle. That, of course, requires a lot more subjectivity and less automation. The automation software can't parse the error message and determine whether some people will be offended by it.

But the automation software can (or at least should be able to) test for some items. For example, the automation software should be able to detect a system modal box. The automation software should be able to spot cascading dialog boxes. The automation software should be able to spot misspellings in the window text. And if not, then either the QA engineers need to write better scripts or they need to find better automation software. (Ahhh, you have to appreciate the irony of test software that itself isn't highly useable because its QA team didn't do a usability test on it!)

As for the usability tests that can't be automated, the only real way is for a real, live human being to sit down and go through *every single feature* of the software, keeping an eye out for usability problems. Doing so is a *full pass of usability*.

But how can the test engineer realistically do a full pass? He needs a game plan, a written document guiding him through it. Further, he needs to enlist the help of his trusty automation utility to help him make sure he goes through all the features, one by one. And creating this game plan will typically require the help of multiple people, just to ensure that every feature is covered. The test engineer could then check off each feature, noting any problems with usability. And if he encounters any problems, he can then submit a bug report, assigning a severity level.

And all this, of course, requires that the test engineer and the team that helped create the test are all familiar with usability standards. In other words, test engineers need to read all the same usability books (such as the one in your hands) that the designers read! (If you're in charge of a software company, that means you need to order an extra hundred copies of this book you're holding. Everybody needs a copy, and I wouldn't mind having a bestseller on my hands!) Also, remember that a usability test doesn't just surround the GUI. I group other issues in with usability, as I mentioned in Part II of this book. For example, if some function in the software runs in a tight loop and causes the CPU usage to fly up to 100 percent, the QA team should catch this.

Performing a Consumer Usability Test on Your Software

Try as you might, the only real way to find out how consumers will respond to your software is to let the consumers try it. Test engineers have a Catch-22 on their hands. They want to put themselves in the shoes of the consumers, yet at the same time, the company needs them to be engineers with a strong computer background. And unless you're designing tools for computer people, that is a contradiction, or a Catch-22.

Some people like to use the term *beta test* when they issue an early release for people to try out. I prefer the term *consumer usability test*. The reason is, they hope that the beta testers won't encounter any traditional bugs. Or, if they do, they hope that the QA team already knows about them. Yet, traditional bugs are all too often what software shops are hoping that the beta testers will find. Instead, you want your consumer testers to spot and report usability problems in addition to the few traditional bugs that might slip past QA.

You don't want the consumer testers to be readers of this book. (Of course, if they want to buy this book, please don't stop them. Instead, find different testers. I would never tell somebody not to buy one of my books or any of my software!) Remember, you want your consumer testers to be a good cross-section of your consumer base. You want the testers to consist of typical people who will be using your product.

One good way for them to test is to give them a simple job: Tell them to determine how easy the product is to use. Ask them to be on the lookout for any part of the software that's difficult to use, confusing, or downright annoying. And have them determine whether the software is a *good neighbor*. That is, does the computer still run well when your software is running alongside other software packages? Does your software get in the way of the other programs?

NOTE However, I do offer such advice with a slight reservation: Some software that, for example, models a complex business process might be a bit complex to use at first, but after somebody uses the software a couple dozen times or more, it might become easy to use.

All these are basic questions and *not technical*. If you find yourself asking them to run a profiler on the software and by some miracle they actually do it, then you have picked the wrong consumer testers and are asking for the wrong tests. These technical tests are the ones the QA team should be doing. Instead:

RULE Think *nontechnical* when assigning consumer usability tests! Don't require the consumers to have any technical knowledge. In fact, the best case is that they don't.

And Finally, Remaining Open-Minded to the Test Results

Nobody likes criticism, especially when the criticism is not constructive. Yet, when you send out your software for a consumer test, criticism is exactly what you're likely to receive, and some of it might be worded in an angry way. But take it seriously! These are the people who really are going to be using your software. Remember:

> **RULE**   One meaning of *highly useable* is that the software doesn't anger people!

The QA team, of course, shouldn't be getting angry. But similarly, you, as a software developer, shouldn't get angry when you hear back from either the QA team or the consumer testers. (Okay, I'll allow you to get a little angry at the QA team on occasion. That's to be expected sometimes, because they're your coworkers.)

Therefore:

> **RULE**   Remain open-minded about whatever comments the consumer testers have. If they hate a certain part of your program, take their concerns seriously!

You want the best possible software on the planet, right? And you don't want the consumers to get angry, toss your software in the trash, buy the competition, and then tell all their friends to avoid your software, do you?

Now realistically, you're going to get some complaints that are not well founded. You're going to hear from users who are actually having a problem with the operating system but think your software is at fault. You're going to encounter users who need to learn what a mouse is and how to click the button. That's to be expected, and you can handle such complaints however you feel is best. But if you get a call such as this:

When I opened the document a second time by mistake, and then made changes, I lost all my previous changes!

Don't respond with, "Well, don't do that, you moron." Instead, consider whether your software needs some kind of safeguard to prevent two openings of the same document from clashing. Sit back, relax, and put yourself in their shoes. They have their job to do, and they're using your software to help them do that job. Your software isn't their job; it's *your* job. They have some other job where the software plays just a minor role. I'm writing a book right now, for example, and that's my work. My work isn't Microsoft Word. But I spend an awful lot of time staring at Microsoft Word, and the last thing I want is for the software to mess up. And if it does mess up, I expect Microsoft to be understanding of my concerns when I call them. (And you can be sure that I *will* contact them!) And will they be open-minded to my concerns? Let's hope so.

Didn't Work? Try It Again! And Again! And Again!

The other day I witnessed something strange, and this certainly wasn't the first time that I'd seen this happen. I was next in line at the checkout of a grocery store. The register ran out of tape when the cashier tried to print the receipt for the customer ahead of me. The cashier walked away, and she returned with a new roll of tape, which she quickly fed into the register. She then typed a three-key sequence into the register. The register responded with an error beep. Frustrated, she typed the same three keys again. Same error beep. So she typed the same three keys yet again. And again, the same error beep happened. She did this several times, the same three keys each time, followed by the same error beep. Now, as a programmer, I was a bit astounded that the woman somehow believed that by her typing the same key sequence over and over, the computer inside the register would somehow finally get it right and do what it was supposed to do. Of course, computers don't work that way. I watched her try to type in the same sequence no less than 10 times, each time yielding the same error beep.

I then switched to a different checkout lane, and I never got to see how the story was resolved. But on the drive home, I was thinking about what happened. We computer people know that if you feed a computer the exact same data over and over, the computer will usually respond with the same output each time. If you type the wrong password over and over, the computer won't finally figure that you're serious and let you in *anyway*. So why did this woman somehow think the register would sooner or later accept the keystrokes? Did she not understand computers?

And that's when it hit me: Think about a car. Suppose you go out and try to start your car, and it just won't go. The engine cranks, but it doesn't want to start up. What do you do? You try again and again, until you finally get the thing started (as long as you don't drain the battery). Most objects work this way. If you turn on a fluorescent light, and you see a faint glow but it doesn't start, you flick the switch off and turn it on again until the light comes on. If you're using a lighter to start your gas grill, and the lighter doesn't start, you flick it a few more times until it finally starts.

Computers, however, don't work this way. Clearly, this woman was typing the wrong keystrokes. But that didn't occur to her (until the manager probably came over to help her, I imagine). Instead, she simply thought that the computer just wasn't taking the seemingly correct data, and sooner or later the computer would accept it. In other words, she was basing her understanding of computers on everyday devices that are very different from computers.

Remember this story when programming computers. They aren't like other devices. What was the solution? Whoever wrote the program for this computerized cash register could have done this poor woman a big favor by displaying an error message such as, "I don't recognize the numbers 5 7 9" (or whatever keys she typed in). Now the computer, of course, didn't know what she was trying to do (or it could have done what she wanted, not what she said!), so it couldn't say, "That's not the correct keystroke to reset the roll of paper." But it could have displayed some message that was more descriptive than an insulting beep. Don't just have your software beep, please.

Continued on next page

And remember, if for some reason you insist on having your software beep, allow the user to *turn it off*. I was taking some grad courses at a university recently, and I was using one of the well-known mathematical software packages. I had my laptop with me in the library, and just to be safe, I had the Windows volume controls set to *mute*. I was in a library, after all. But you know what? When I did something wrong, this crazy program made the computer beep! This beep came through some internal speaker separate from the stereo speakers and it was *loud*. Everybody turned and glared at me. I apologized and went into the math program's configuration to turn off all sounds. Well, those sounds in the configuration turned off the wave files but not the beep! I thought all was fine and five minutes later…*BEEP!* One young woman turned and glared at me, closed her book, gathered her stuff, and walked to the other end of the room and sat down, resuming her studies. Thanks, software. How embarrassing.

Remember, then: Don't make your software just beep in error. Give a message that's a bit more descriptive. But if you feel some inner need to provide a beep, allow me to disable it, please.

Moving Forward

Testing is a vital part of software development. What's sad is how many software shops don't include usability testing when they test. Imagine how much better software could be if developers knocked out the usability bugs before releasing the software. Never underestimate the value of a good test engineer.

Now if you've been reading this book all the way through, you'll be happy to know that you have only two more chapters to go. Chapter 14, "Installing, Training, and Helping," covers three final topics for you programmer types out there: training, installers, and online help. (And by *training* I mean on both ends: training people to use your software as well as seeking training for you and your coworkers.) Installers and online help are two fundamental issues to software as well.

And then Chapter 15, "Book in a Book: A Guide for Programming Bosses," everybody can read, but it's primarily for managers. It talks about some issues (some of which are human resource–related) that managers need to especially be aware of when they are overseeing a team of programmers trying to design highly useable software. Have fun!

CHAPTER 14

Installing, Training, and Helping

Two of the major obstacles in putting out a highly useable software package are getting the software easily installed on the user's computer and helping the user learn the software. For installing software, many software companies use a third-party installation program (such as Wise for Windows Installer and InstallShield). And some companies write their own installation programs.

For helping people learn the software, companies can offer training courses and online help. In this chapter, I talk about these three issues: installing your software, providing online help, and creating a training course. And as usual, all are under the realm of highly useable software.

Installing Your Software

Here's a quick quiz in the form of an essay question:

Describe the software package your company is creating.

Unless you work for a company that creates one of the commercial installers (such as InstallShield), you probably didn't say anything about an installer. You talked about what the software does, not how it gets installed on the user's computer.

So why, then, do so many companies devote so much time to an installer? I know of a great many companies that refuse to use one of the commercial installers and instead write their own installer. A lot of these companies spend a lot more time on the software product itself than the installer (rightly so). But the installer is itself a software package that has its own usability issues and can be filled with bugs. Imagine if you have the best program out there, but your installer stinks and half the people encounter bugs and can't even get your software installed! Or what if the people have to jump through major hoops and can't get your software installed? If they do successfully get your software installed, a junky installer will not leave a good first impression in their minds.

What an Installer Does

At heart, what does an installer do? It copies files to the hard drive. If you're old enough to remember the early personal and home computers that actually had hard drives, you'll probably remember having to run various batch files that would simply copy the files to the hard drive, hopefully in their own directory. (However, I do remember doing some consulting for people who had no directories besides a root and kept all the files for all their programs in that main directory!)

But even if you don't remember the simple install procedures from back then, you're probably keenly aware that an installer simply puts the files on the hard drive. And that's part of the problem: Installing software is actually much more complex and sophisticated than just copying files. If installation were simply a matter of copying files, companies that make installers probably wouldn't need to exist. And further, how would you like to be told that the product you've been working on is trivial and something anybody could build? Certainly the people who work for the installer companies wouldn't appreciate being told that, because they know just how complex their products really are.

Other than the fact that the installer packages are typically complex with sophisticated scripting languages, the final installer that you ship with your product does a great deal more than just copy files. Here are some things *good* installers do:

- Check for a previous version of the software and possibly uninstall the previous version, or ask the user for permission to uninstall the previous version. And if they're asking for permission, carefully explain to the user the ramifications of the user's decision.

- Create a directory tree to hold the new files, or in the case of a previously existing version, they might use the existing directory tree.

- Copy files into the directory tree and occasionally into the system directory. (Although I've made clear throughout this book my feelings about the system directory: Keep out!)

- Compare versions when attempting to copy a file but the file already exists.

- Update the Registry (on Windows).

- Register OLE and COM components (on Windows), again carefully tracking versions.

- Set up file extension associations (and ask the users whether to modify associations that already exist). And, as usual, carefully explain to the users why they might want the file associations and how they'll be able to then double-click filenames in Windows Explorer to start up your program.

- Possibly create property sheet components that run when a user right-clicks a certain file in Windows Explorer.

- Optionally install icons on the desktop and add groups to the Start menu.

- Accomplish all this in a highly useable manner, following all the design rules that I've given throughout this book! (The installer is, after all, software in its own right.)

This list shows that creating a good installer is a *lot* of work. Are you really up for all this? To create a good installer, you really need to implement a complete software engineering cycle, using a sound methodology, just as you would do to create any good software. The installation program cannot be an afterthought. This means that where you were creating the most awesome application on the planet, you're now creating *two* software packages, each being the most awesome application in its particular class. Do you have the time? Do you have the people? And if you have three more programmers, do you really want to devote them full time to your installer?

I think you're getting my point here. Before writing your own installation program, please give serious consideration to purchasing one of the prepackaged installers such as InstallShield or Wise. If nothing more, consider the cost: You could have three people spending months on an installer, fixing the bugs and such, or you could purchase the installer program and have one person spend maybe two weeks on it, give or take some time depending on the complexity of your own needs. And remember, the installer is a part of your software package, and you will have to support it in the same way that you support the main program you're selling. If you wrote your own installer and it crashes, your support team has to deal with it.

True, a third-party installer *could* crash. I think I once saw InstallShield crash. *Once*. And I went to their website and found that I had an outdated file on my computer. I got the new file and all was fine. But you know what? InstallShield took care of me. When I was installing your program and encountered this crash, I didn't bother contacting you; instead I went to InstallShield for help.

But besides the support issue, the bigger issue is that word *once* that I threw into the preceding paragraph. I've seen InstallShield crash only *once*. Now I'm not being paid by the folks at InstallShield to say these great things about them (I've never even met them), so this isn't some kind of commercial advertisement. I'm just pointing out that they have a pretty solid program, so why should you waste your time trying to top it? Remember, they have one up on you: They've been around for years. I first encountered them back in something like 1993, a decade ago. That's a lot of time to work out the bugs. And InstallShield isn't the only company that makes installers. Wise for Windows Installer is another fine program. Microsoft also ships a pretty decent one with its Visual Studio products.

In the following sections, I talk about usability and installation. I've already talked in previous chapters about installing libraries, dealing with version issues, and my own hot button about putting files into *my* computer's system directory. So I won't harp on those again. But I will say a few more words about other usability issues.

But I hesitate to talk about another issue, and that's the *if you insist* issue. If you insist on writing your own installer, you will have some similar usability issues to work through. I've already made my opinion known about writing your own installer, but probably a few of you believe that your needs are somehow unique and that the commercial installers just can't cut it. (I find that hard to believe, but again... *if you insist*.) For you cowboys out there, I will say this: The following sections apply to you as well. Whether you're writing your own installer or not, you'll still have to deal with dialog box issues that require good design and so on.

The Standard Choices

You've seen the three choices when installing software:

Typical   The most commonly used components in the package will be installed. (Note that sometimes installers instead have an option called Complete, where the entire package is installed.)

Custom   The user can choose which components to install.

Minimal   Only the components absolutely necessary will be installed.

For the first choice, if you're going to use Complete rather than Typical, please really do make it complete. Install *everything*. Many times I've chosen Complete, only to discover later that a few esoteric libraries and help files were left off, and I was informed that I needed to insert the original CD when I tried to use those features. Because I had chosen Complete, I was a bit irritated.

Remember who probably uses Custom. That would be the power users. Beginners rarely use the Custom install. So the real question is, What do you use for the defaults under Custom? My personal preference is that when I choose Custom, and then get to select which options I want to install, I prefer to have everything selected initially. From there, I can go through and remove the options I don't care to install. Remember, I'm a power user, and this isn't a problem. Where I do get frustrated is when the Custom installation opens up with some options checked and some not. If this is Custom, why did somebody already choose some defaults for me? How do they know what I want to install and not install?

The Minimal installation is a bit tricky. Originally, I think developers included this goal for use on laptops and other computers with limited resources. But today, most medium-priced laptops are nearly as powerful as medium-priced desktops, and the laptops certainly have plenty of disk space. Instead, then, today some people expect the Minimal option to be for the beginners and novices who might not need all the extra bells and whistles. They might want just the basic features. They might not want all the additional templates or whatever you might offer along with your product.

But be careful with the Minimal install. If you are targeting beginners with Minimal, then the beginners probably want online help. Do you include online help in the Minimal install? Typically, install programs treat the Minimal install as only the minimal components necessary to get the application to run. If you're shipping a word processor, this would mean no extra templates and clip art and translators and all that jazz. But what about online help? If Minimal is for beginners, then they'll need the online help.

Personally, when I'm teaching courses to beginners, I tell them to go with the Typical option. The reality is that rarely will the Minimal option be good for the beginners. Beginners need online help, and they usually need components to help them get going, such as wizards and templates. Because power users tend to fill their hard drives a lot more quickly than beginners, most likely disk space won't be a problem with beginners. Therefore, here's what I recommend:

SUGGESTION

Consider not even offering a Minimal install option. Instead, offer a Typical option for most people and a Custom option for advanced and power users.

In your dialog box where the user chooses Typical or Custom, consider including some text explaining that the Custom option is for advanced users. (That's probably a bit safer than the reverse, stating that the Typical option is for beginners. A lot of power users will opt for Typical, and you don't want to insult them. Software insults people too much as it is.)

Some people offer another option, Run From CD. These days, with 80-Gig hard drives the norm, running off the CD isn't particularly important. But some people might want it in case they've filled up their hard drive.

And in some cases, you might have another CD-oriented option. Take a look at Microsoft Streets and Trips, which is Microsoft's very nice mapping software. That software came with a laptop computer I recently bought, and I noticed during installation that I had the option of keeping all the data on the CD, which would require that I insert the data CD whenever I ran the program, or of installing all the data to the hard drive. Now interestingly, the default was to not copy all the data to the hard drive. But if I have my laptop in the front seat of my car (no, I don't use the computer while driving...really...trust me), the last thing I want to do is have to fiddle with inserting a CD into the computer every time I want to use the mapping software.

> **RULE**   If your software includes a large data CD, give the users the option of installing all the data to the hard drive. With huge hard drives these days, that shouldn't be a problem.

For what it's worth, I just checked how much disk space my full Microsoft Streets and Trips installation takes up, including the data. The total is 872,004,297 bytes. That's a bit less than a Gig, which is not a problem at all. (And also, the program runs faster off a hard drive compared to a CD!)

In the past, another Microsoft product, the MSDN developer CD, didn't give you the option of copying the data to the hard drive. A company I once worked for ordered a copy for me, and I got tired of inserting the CD every time I wanted to use it. So I copied the whole database to the hard drive, but then I had to tweak the Registry. That was a bit messy, and I would have been happier if they had just given me the option to install the data right to the hard drive.

Reinstalling, Repairing, and Removing

Some installers give the user a repair option. When the user starts up the installer, and the installer detects that they've already installed the software, the installer offers to repair a current installation. The repair makes sure that all the installed files are present and makes sure that the Registry entries are all present and correct. If anything is missing or corrupt, the installer fixes the problem by either copying the missing or corrupt files or by adding or fixing the Registry entries.

Those Touchy COM Components

If your program installs various COM components (such as ActiveX controls), the notion of staying out of the system directory isn't as clean as I might hope. When you install a COM component, you register it with the system. If some other program registered the COM component that you're about to install, and then you save the component to your own directory, you could end up wiping out the previous registration and pointing the registration to your own copy of the component. Then when you uninstall, the other program will no longer function properly.

Further, if the other program runs, it doesn't make a whole lot of sense to have the other program run a library that's in your directory. (As a power user, I tend to get a bit suspicious if I check up on the libraries that, for example, program A is using and I see it's using a library in another program's directory, say program B. My suspicion is that program B somehow hijacked program A and is doing something it's not supposed to be doing.)

For this reason, I'm probably willing to give a bit and allow you to put the COM component in the system directory under the specific conditions that you did not create the COM component or, if you did, you are using the COM component for several different programs that you wrote.

The repair option is important. Anything can go wrong; a user might accidentally delete a file, or the user might go mucking around inside the Registry and make a mess. And so you can save the users from themselves by offering a repair option.

However, I do recommend that you also offer a complete reinstall option. Sometimes I have found that repairs don't always work. Typically, a repair option doesn't go through and compare byte by byte every file with the original on the CD, and so the repair could potentially miss a few things. And for that reason, a reinstall option would be nice.

And, of course, you definitely need a remove (or "uninstall") option. But always be extremely careful when uninstalling. The last thing you want to do is uninstall a system library that you thought was used only by your program.

Of course, this system library idea gets back to my assertion that you should stay out of the system directory. If all your DLLs are in the program's own directory, you'll have no problems with uninstalls. Simply remove all the files in the directory and don't touch the system directory. Remember also to clean out the Registry entries during the uninstall.

Gathering Custom Options

The standard way to gather user options is by presenting a treeview control (or some variation thereof), whereby the user can choose exactly which options or components to install. Figure 14.1 shows an example of a Microsoft installation. This treeview divides the installation into various components, each containing smaller components. The user can choose entire sets of components to install or only individual subcomponents.

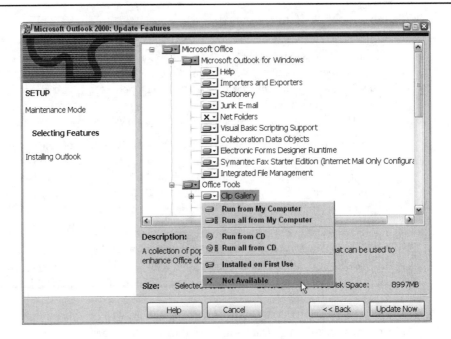

FIGURE 14.1
The options are available in a treeview-like component.

The options that Microsoft uses are, however, not very clear to beginners. The options allow the user to install the component to the hard drive, not install it at all, or keep the component on the CD and prompt the user to install the CD when the feature is needed.

The problem I have is that the beginner will probably be greatly confused over the difference between not installing the feature at all and keeping the option on the CD, installing the option only when it is needed. In fact, come to think of it, I'm not sure that I understand the difference. By not installing a feature, does that mean the feature's menu item will simply not be present, making it impossible for me to attempt to use the feature? Or will the menu item be present? And what happens if I choose the menu item? (But this, of course, assumes that the feature is linked to a menu item.) Therefore:

RULE   If you decide to implement both "not install" and "install from CD when needed," make sure you explain in detail to the user what exactly you mean by these options. Remember: Think *clarity*.

Different installation programs use different means to specify the options that will be available to your users. Go ahead and use whatever is available to you in your chosen installation program. The major installers are so common that these days you can't really go wrong, provided you don't start building your own dialog boxes.

Gathering User Information

In order to gather information from the user, your installer might have custom dialog boxes that you wrote. These are dialog boxes that extend beyond the standard dialog boxes the third-party installer software offers. If you're going to be building your own dialog boxes, then, remember to follow all the usability rules for dialog boxes and controls.

In fact, I would almost daresay that the rules are even stricter with these dialog boxes than with the ones in application software. The reason is that you're doing some pretty severe things here: You're installing files and possibly overwriting files that might cause another program to break.

Therefore, when communicating with the user, you have to be extremely clear about your intentions, and you have to make sure the user's intentions are extremely clear. Here are some examples of some *unclear* messages you might have in a dialog box or message box:

- *File mystuff.dll already exists. Overwrite?* This message would have a Yes button and a No button. This situation is clearly bad because the user has no idea what the implications are either way. If I say no, will the software that I'm installing work? And if I say yes, will some other program break? And what is `mystuff.dll` anyway?

- *Overwrite myfile.dll (date January 1, 2002) with file myfile.dll (date January 1, 2000)?* This variation of the preceding message would also have Yes and No buttons. And also like the preceding message, my response is, *How should I know?* I don't know if your software can function with the newer version that's already on my drive. The solution? Write your own version in your own directory, not the system directory.

- *Cannot write file. Aborting.* Come on now. If your installer can't write the file, don't just yell at me about it. Find a way to write it. I have plenty of disk space. Maybe you encountered a bad sector when trying to write the file. Well, figure it out and work around it. Don't just give up, leaving me stuck.

- Any type of double-negative situation, even if the grammar is fine. Examples are, *Are you sure you don't want to install the coolfun library?* followed by Yes and No buttons and, *Would you like to skip the installation of the coolfun library?* Both of these are unclear and better served by the replacement, *Would you like to install the coolfun library?* But see the following, because this isn't perfect either.

- *Would you like to install the coolfun library?* Okay, fine. I have a choice. But what are the implications either way? Do I need the coolfun library? What features does it add? And what happens if I don't install it?

| RULE | Never leave the user wondering what to do: Clearly tell the user the implications of all installation choices. |

And, of course, we have the issue of bad grammar and just plain confusing sentences. *Are you sure you don't want to not uninstall the library before exiting?* is very similar to one I've *actually seen* (I'm not lying). If you struggle with grammar (which may be the case if you're writing in a language that's not your first), then please have a native speaker do a good copy edit on your dialog boxes and other text. (And this advice extends to your entire software package, not just the installer.)

And regarding the final option in the preceding list, if you get to the point where you are asking the user specifically whether to install a particular library, then you made a mistake. You shouldn't be opening dialog boxes asking about specific options during the actual copying of files. Instead, you should have a general dialog box before the copying begins, whereby you gather all the user's choices for what to install and what not to install. See the previous section, "Gathering Custom Options."

Offering Online Help

The area of online help is a huge topic, and therefore in this section I'd like to focus on the usability issues of your software interacting with the online help system. First and foremost, remember to include an online help system. Don't take the easy way out and simply have an About item on the Help menu. That's not good enough. Users need a way to get help when using your software.

However, and this might seem like a contradiction, if you design your software properly in terms of usability, then ideally you shouldn't need an online help. Yet, please *do* include a complete, extensive online help system. The logic is that you want to go at the usability from two directions: Make your software easy to use, *and* provide an excellent online help system. The two aspects will then complement each other nicely. Don't skip the online help just because you think your software is incredibly easy to use, and certainly don't make your software hard to use...well, I don't even need to say that.

Windows includes two primary help engines:

WinHelp   This is the old, original help system. However, Windows actually has two versions of this, a really old original one and a slightly old one. The really old one is `c:\windows\winhelp.exe`, which is a 16-bit application intended for (eek!) Windows 3.1 and earlier. The slightly old one is `c:\windows\winhlp32.exe`, which appeared with NT and 95. Both versions of WinHelp read files that have an `.hlp` extension.

HTMLHelp   This is a newer online help system from Microsoft, and it reads files with the extension `.chm`. The help system uses HTML files under the hood, which are much more versatile than the older hypertext help files with WinHelp. The executable for HTMLHelp is `hh.exe`, which is basically a wrapper around Internet Explorer. (You can see this by running `hh.exe` *myfile.html*, where *myfile.html* is some HTML file.)

In addition, the Java system includes its own online help engine, called JavaHelp. These days, skip WinHelp and go right to HTMLHelp. A lot of programs still use WinHelp, but they seem antiquated. The last thing you want is for your users to open up the online help and think your program must be old simply because the program uses an older online help system!

When you start building your online help, here's a pretty good rule to keep in mind:

RULE   Online help is a reference guide. Therefore, structure your online help as such, and don't expect (or require) the users to read it from start to finish.

And with a good online reference guide, of course, comes a good index. Take time to build a thorough index, using as many keywords as possible. Don't just make the index and alphabetized table of contents. I know I get frustrated when I open up the index to an online help and see only 10 entries. I want to see a lot of entries in the index. And if the index doesn't have what I need, then I expect to find my item in question by using the search engine. Fortunately, however, with most help systems you don't have to implement a search facility; the help engine will perform the searches for you on the user's computer.

In addition to a reference guide, you might also consider a pretty-darn-good tutorial. Unlike a reference guide, a tutorial usually needs to be read from start to finish, and the user really can't just dive into the middle. That's fine, but make sure you set up the tutorial to be easily navigated. The help engine provides the necessary navigation tools for you, provided you build your online help using the appropriate help-building tools.

If you decide to include a tutorial, however, I recommend two important points:

- *Make sure the tutorial is easily accessible.* Some people like to put a menu item right on the Help menu for the tutorial. I also like to include my tutorial right in the table of contents of the main help, usually right at the beginning.

- *You might consider including a tutorial directory in your product installation, where you include the sample files for the tutorial.* You could have several subdirectories, one for each tutorial lesson, showing the sample files in various stages of completion.

However, if you choose to include sample files, I recommend also including a backup directory under each subdirectory containing copies of the tutorial files. The reason is that if the user is working through the tutorial, then he might accidentally modify the sample files, forever changing them. You should probably also include in your tutorial instructions for copying the tutorial files to the user's own directory, leaving the backups present *just in case* the user modifies the original tutorial files.

In addition, you might consider a functional section in your online help. This is a section organized by task. For example, in the functional section of the online help for a word processor, you might include information about how to do higher-level tasks such as mail merges or creating templates. Such tasks are usually more than just toolbar button clicks; they require sequences of primitive actions. However, they are common uses for your software, and you want your users to be able to quickly learn how to perform these actions.

The Pitfalls of Converting the Manual to Online Help

Several years ago, I reviewed a bunch of online help programs for a magazine. A couple of the programs prided themselves in the way they could convert a manual to online help. Now I don't want to badmouth any software programs, and the reality is that this review was circa 1994, and since then the surviving programs have evolved greatly into software that's pretty darn good. But as with any software package, you get out of it what you put into it. When designing online help, a lot of people think the easiest way is to simply convert their manuals into some kind of online hypertext document.

This is a bad idea. Researchers (and laypeople, for that matter) have found that people use books very differently from the way they use online help. Online help is, by nature, hypertext-oriented, and regardless of the intentions of the help designers, people simply don't read them cover to cover, start to finish. People might use a tutorial to get up and running, and from there they will use the online help as a reference guide.

The hypertext issue is particularly problematic. Some people, when converting their manuals to online help, will have the help generator automatically turn every indexed word into a hyperlink. The problem is that the users won't know if they *must* click every link or not in order to understand the topic. For example, suppose I'm reading the entry on the Discombobulator, and in the middle of a sentence the word *create* is underlined as a hyperlink. Am I required to click the link and first read the entry called *Creating a Discombobulator* before I understand the topic I was previously reading? See, a hyperlink creates a disjoint in the reading. (Instead, a better choice is to include a section of related topics somewhere in the page, probably at the end.)

Further, I've seen occasional online help entries that say, "See the next chapter for more information." But what's a chapter in the online help world? This particular online help offered no table of contents, and so I was completely lost. I had no idea where the "next chapter" was. And on a similar note, the same online help said, "As you learned in the previous chapter," which implied that they expected me to read the whole thing cover to cover, which I wasn't trying to do.

Therefore, simply converting a manual to online help is nothing more than a lazy attempt at getting something out the door as soon as possible. Take some time to make a good online help.

And finally, remember that going in the other direction is at least as bad, if not worse: Don't just print up every page in the online help to create your manual and then bind and ship the manual with the product. (At least one major software vender does this.) That's a major waste of paper and a serious disappointment; I feel cheated.

Finally, remember to integrate your online help into your application. Don't just include a Help menu. Also include context-sensitive help. If the user is performing a certain action or displaying a dialog box, allow the user to press F1 to open up help specific to the topic. And in your dialog boxes, also include the famous little question mark icon in the upper-right corner, allowing the user to click the button and then click an item in question on the dialog box. This will open up a small window providing help for the user. (The way to implement this depends on your programming tools. Most SDKs these days include a class or some easy way to implement the feature.)

What about PDF?

It all started years ago. Somebody decided that they could take the easy way out and ship a single set of PDF files that would suffice as both the manuals and the online help. A lot of usability experts have criticized PDF files, and now I'd like to chime in.

First, I think PDF is a great standard and has its place. The problem is, people don't seem to understand where PDFs belong. Please do not—I repeat, *do not*—simply offer up your online manuals and help as PDF files. Here's the problem: PDF files are a fixed layout (unlike HTML, which is far more suited to the computer screen). For the most part, reading PDF files is more or less painless, unless you are forced to read multicolumn pages.

Multicolumn pages are a nightmare on the computer screen, because you are forced to continually scroll down, then back, then down, then back. Figure 14.2 shows a multicolumn page in Acrobat Reader of a PDF file that I created. You can see that when you're reading the first column, you have to scroll down to get to the rest of the column and then scroll back up to the start of the second column.

Figure 14.3 shows another problematic text. This is an index from another Sybex book. When you print this (as Sybex intended), you'll be fine. But reading it on the screen is difficult. In this case, you're not just trying to read from start to finish. Instead, you're trying to scan the columns with your eyes, noting the alphabetical order, as you search for the entry you want. One of the entries is *Array class*. You can see that that entry will come after the text that's visible in the first column but before the text in the second column. So do you scroll up to find it or down to find it? Who knows; it depends on which column the text is in. Because the first main entry in the second column is *ArrayTypeMismatchException*, my first inclination would be to scroll up, expecting to see *Array class* toward the top of the second column. But, in fact, the entry is at the bottom of the first column. Try again.

FIGURE 14.2

The text is divided into columns, making scrolling a pain.

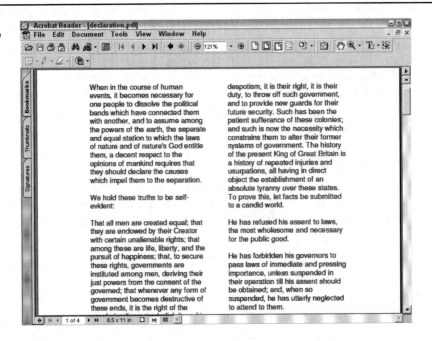

FIGURE 14.3

This PDF has an index divided into columns, which is a nightmare on the screen.

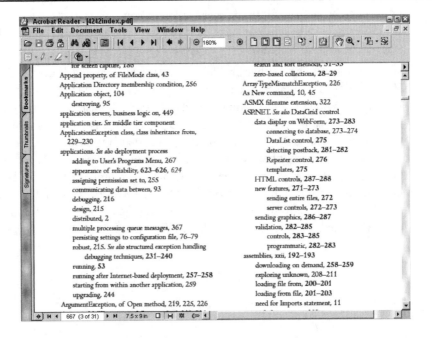

FIGURE 14.4
This text is too wide for the screen. But if you shrink the page so that the text fits, the font will be too small.

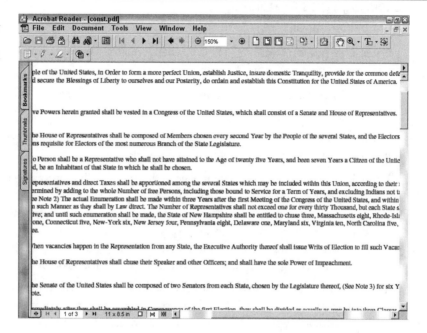

Wide columns are an even bigger problem. Remember, PDF is intended for printing. And some people might want to print their pages in Landscape orientation. But with wide columns on the screen, you have to either continually scroll left and right as you read the text or shrink the page down so that the column fits, possibly making the text too small to read! Figure 14.4 shows an example of this problem.

Training with Ease

As with online help, in theory, if you create a software package that is incredibly easy to use, you shouldn't *need* training. But you should have it anyway. For one thing, regardless of how easy your product is to use, large corporations love to send their people off to training sessions. I'm not sure why this is, but every large corporation that I've dealt with has had some kind of strange fixation on training. I think the VPs in charge of the divisions find it important to make sure that their workers have a certificate claiming competency in a certain topic or software application.

Now my own experience in attending training sessions is that some sessions are great; some are, frankly, horrible. The weeklong sessions tend to be far better than the daylong sessions, because many topics simply can't be taught in a day or an afternoon. In this section, I talk about training programs and how you can have a great training program, as well as what you should consider in building your training program.

Choosing Types of Training

Here are three possibilities in the training that you might offer:

Onsite, in-person training   This is where you send somebody to the customer's site to train users how to use your software.

Offsite, in-person training   This is where the customer comes to you (or some facilities you have rented) to get training on how to use your software

Online training   This is a new form of training that not many companies offer yet, where you offer online courses in how to use your software.

You might also consider sending in a consultant who will mentor the users. However, be careful suggesting something like this, because companies tend to be a bit suspicious of such a notion. A lot of companies figure that if a consultant comes in to help teach how to use the software, that person might not be working very hard for the money being paid out (that is, they see it as a money-making scam) or the software might be too complex. So be careful even suggesting such an arrangement unless a customer specifically asks for it.

Typically, the customer will want to choose whether to have your teacher come to them or to send their students to you. Therefore, you will often want to offer both types of training. Different customers will see different values in both. Some might see bringing in a trainer to their own place as a cheaper alternative than sending out a group of employees to another city, which requires plane tickets, hotel rooms, and a rental car or two.

But on the other hand, some customers might not have any place to hold a training session, and even if they do have the space, they might not have a dozen or so extra computers to put in the training room. These customers might be more inclined to send the employees to your place for training. (Plus, some employees like to go on business trips and explore other cities and the local nightlife, and they see such training sessions as perks.)

As an alternative to both onsite and offsite training, you might consider a newer option, online training. Online training is useful because nobody has to go anywhere, and students can complete the courses in their own time. You can even offer certificates after students complete the online training course.

Typically, you will want an online training course to be self-guided, without real-time instructor interaction. In other words, no text or voice chat would be available. But you could have an instructor answering questions in an online message forum. Of course, you're free to offer live text or voice chat, but that would require a more fixed schedule.

TIP   If you offer in-person training, you must decide how long to have the training. Weeklong sessions are common, but so are single-day or half-day sessions. Normally, if students are going to fly to your city and attend training at your site, they will expect something more than a day, perhaps even an entire week.

Building a Highly Useable Training Course

Remember, the more professional your course is, the more respect students will give to you, your organization, and, in turn, your software. And that's the goal: To make millions of dollars by having the most useable software on the market. How do you make your course professional? By making it highly useable, of course. This includes two aspects:

- A professional presentation

- A great course that teaches the students what they need to know

Please don't underestimate the importance of a professional presentation. Indeed, the course has to be good as well, but you want the students to be impressed with the overall look, so they take the course seriously. This includes:

- Binders with nicely printed notes that the students can take home with them.

- Possibly a free manual or instruction book (professionally printed) that they can read on their own time.

- Quizzes, perhaps where the students score them themselves without turning them in, or possibly turning them in for scoring by your organization. These quizzes could be printed or on the computer.

- A projection system showing professional-looking graphics in full color. (Here's a hint: Make use of nice colors and clip art, which is available free with programs such as Microsoft PowerPoint.)

Remember, and this might seem trivial, but please make sure that all the paperwork you give to the students, including the binders with the notes and the written quizzes, is printed as professional quality, either on your own laser printers or at the local printer's or copy shop. Please don't pass out cheap-looking photocopies. You want to *impress* the students.

TIP	You can be most successful in building a highly useable course if you recognize this important fact: Your students cannot possibly learn everything there is to know about your software during one session, even a weeklong session.

Okay, that's enough about the presentation aspect of the course. I could fill pages and pages with tips, but you get the basic idea: Make it *look good*. Now on to the course itself.

Suppose you're teaching a course on installing and maintaining a network for a 2000-employee organization. Can you really take students from square one all the way through advanced template programming in a single week and expect the students to retain the material after the week is over? Speaking as a professional teacher with a great deal of experience, my answer is, *Of course not*. Now you certainly could cover all that material during a week; that's not the problem. The problem is that if you do, the students will become so overwhelmed that their heads will probably explode somewhere around Thursday morning, with a few die-hards making it to Thursday afternoon.

Instead, you need to offer a course that will get the students up and running with your software so they are comfortable using it and know where to go when they need more help. Therefore:

During your training session, keep showing the students how to refer to the online help and other online reference guides.

Doing so will help them get accustomed to finding out the answers for themselves once they are alone, back at their offices, and are using your software for real, not just for practice.

For a weeklong course, I recommend that you spend Monday through Wednesday getting the students up and running. Focus on the essentials, and be thorough. For example, in a course on using Microsoft Word, you might spend the first three days showing how to manipulate files (open, save, save as, close, new, create from a template, and the various wizards), set fonts, create styles, create templates, print, edit, use AutoCorrect and AutoFormat, create tables, and so on. In other words, the basics. Three days is plenty of time to go through the basics. Then, on Thursday and Friday, you can venture into more advanced topics. Here, you won't be thorough. Instead, you'll introduce the students to as many advanced topics as possible. You'll show the students what the advanced features are, how to get to them, and maybe a couple of examples of using the advanced features.

Of course, if your software isn't terribly complex, you might be able to go through the entire package in great detail in a single week. However, remember not to overwhelm the students. If you go through a million features in complete detail, by the time the student returns to her office the following week, her boss might come to her and say, "Show me how to use the software." She might stare at the computer and say, "Uhhhhhhhhh…" because in getting so overwhelmed, she forgot the basics.

And when that happens, the boss isn't going to blame the employee for not paying attention or perhaps for skipping class. Instead, the boss will blame *you and your organization* for charging a ton of money and doing a poor job of training the employee. So much for a highly useable course!

Now if you're offering only a daylong or half-day course, then you have to really tighten everything up. Instead, focus only on the basics. Spend the whole time getting the students up to speed on the basics, and then spend maybe a half-hour or an hour briefly demonstrating some of the advanced features. As with a weeklong course, focus on how the students can get help when they're back at work. And your goal should be to teach the students how to get up and running with your software and how to perform the basic, most common functions that focus on their own goals and needs. Then, when the students return to work, they'll understand the basics of how to use your software.

Setting Up (and Being Ready for) a Training Session

Let's say you bring in two dozen people from all over the planet for your first training session. These people are eager to get started learning to use your software. (Or, more realistically, their bosses are eager for them to learn how to use it. They're probably there just for the free trip and pastries.)

Now let's say everybody sits down and you're ready to start the training session, but wouldn't you know, the projector won't work, and two of the computers can't seem to get on the network. You have to call in the MIS guy, and he fiddles for an hour, while you (or whoever is teaching) mingle embarrassingly. How will this look to the students? Believe it or not, most likely the students won't be concerned about the money they're spending because they're likely not the ones spending the money. They don't care. But they will become impatient, and they'll become a bit distrustful of your software. And then when you finally get the class going, they won't be in a very good mood (nor will you). So make sure all your equipment is running. Test everything out in advance. If it's Monday morning, come in at 7:00 (or Sunday evening) to make sure everything is in order.

How should you set up your training room? Most training rooms have a separate computer for each student to use. That way, they can get hands-on training rather than just sit and listen to the teacher lecture. In general, if you have computers for the students, make sure each student has his own computer. There's a practical reason for this: Some of your students might work for competing companies. As crazy as that sounds, their bosses might be a bit distraught if they find out they were sharing a computer at a training session with a competitor.

Now if you do have a computer set up for each student, you might wonder if you should allow Internet access. And should you allow other programs such as chat programs? Of course, only you can decide whether you want such programs, but I would suggest yes to the Internet access (or at least partial access where the students can get to the Yahoo! mail and Hotmail sites so they can check their e-mail). And as for chat, maybe or maybe not. Some students like to be able to talk to one another during the training session. If you think the students might be having important, valuable discussions about the course, then chat might be a good thing. If you think they might just be wasting time and ignoring the class, then chat probably isn't a good thing. It's up to you, really, but weigh the options.

Some students might bring their own laptop computers. Use your best judgment on this issue, especially relating to the copying of your software. You might want to put the software on the students' laptops and then network the laptops into your own network. The obvious problem here, however, is that you just put your software on their computers, and they might not have paid for a license for these particular computers. The licenses their organizations purchased might be for desktops back at the office. A good solution is this:

SUGGESTION

Tell the students they can use their own laptops provided they bring the laptops with licensed copies of the software already installed.

But you will probably want to add that you're not going to spend time installing the software on their laptops. Your job is to train the students, and your sales engineers would be happy to help them install the software at a different time.

Finally, what if the training is to be held at the customer's site? In this case, you will probably want to ask them to have a room with computers set up, each with the software installed. But you might have a problem, because the customer might not have purchased licenses for the computers in the training room they're providing. Further, you might get to the customer site and find that they have a disaster: The computers are there, some have the software installed, some computers are not functioning, none of them seem to be able to get on the network, and their MIS guy is running around at 9:30 on Monday morning, frantically trying to get everything up and running.

Be prepared for the worst if you're teaching the course at the customer site. Plan to have your laptop, your projector, your binders, and notes, and be ready to teach from just those, without the help of the customer's computers. Consider the computers perks that might or might not be present. That means building and planning your course without requiring the students to do any hands-on work.

Finally, I'd like to say a note about your projector slides. Most people use Microsoft Power-Point for such notes. And remember, PowerPoint is great for just that: *notes*. Don't expect to fill in all the details on your slides. If you've seen a lot of PowerPoint presentations, you know that you can put a handful of bullet points on each slide. This leaves little room for detailed instructions.

But having only bullet points on the slides means you don't want to offer up just these slides to the students as their own notes. Suppose you have the following notes on a single slide for a course on Microsoft Word:

Setting styles includes:

- Choosing a name for the style
- Selecting font information
- Applying the new style

This is hardly a detailed description of working with styles in Microsoft Word. If you've ever gone online to find information about a topic that you know nothing about and found a Power-Point presentation, you've probably seen how worthless such notes are without a teacher explaining each point.

I recommend that you include printouts of the PowerPoint presentations at the back of the binder but also include considerably more detailed notes in the binder. This means, of course, spending some time on the notes, having you (or the tech writers) creating the notes. But the time will be well spent when the student is finished with the course, back at work, gets stuck, and has something to refer to. A bulleted list won't help the student much, but detailed notes will.

Running a Training Session

If you've done all your work in advance, actually running your training session will be a snap. Of course, you're going to run into problems along the way. But if you play the game right, the students will be patient, and you'll quickly recover from such problems.

For example, what if you're the teacher, and a student stumps you with a question that you can't answer? What do you do? Lie? Take 45 minutes to fiddle with the software to come up with the answer?

How about none of the above? You certainly don't want to lie. And if you spend 45 minutes fiddling, the other students will become impatient and will, frankly, start to think you're stupid. Instead, be honest. Say something like, "Wow, that's a new one. I haven't come across that one. Let me check with the engineers during the next break and find the answer for you." And then move on. (Oh, and if you are an engineer who got stuck teaching the class, this is a time to simply swallow your pride and still say you're going to check with the engineers. These people don't know you, and why do you care if they think you're "just a teacher"?)

Here are some additional tips to help keep the session going smoothly:

- Give them free food! Bring pastries and other junk to make them happy.

- Give them plenty of breaks, *at least one an hour*. I know most people think two or three hours is fine before a break, but some of us have trouble sitting for such a long time. Let us get up and walk around at least once an hour. Please?

- Keep it interesting! Don't be boring. Don't talk in a monotone voice. Tell jokes, make them laugh, tell interesting stories of how other customers have used the product, tell anecdotes of funny things happening to customers, whatever it takes. But keep it lively and interesting. If you have to, use goofy, funny names in your examples.

- Offer a specific question-and-answer time, and make sure everyone gets their say.

Regarding the final point, a question-and-answer time can be touchy. First, don't allow some unruly student to keep interrupting you, taking you down tangents, away from what the other students want to learn. If a student tries, encourage him to save the questions for question-and-answer time.

Of course, you want the students to feel free to ask questions if anything you explain isn't clear. Just don't spend more than a few minutes answering each question. Remember, you want to maintain the order and direction of the class.

And finally, when the time comes for the class to adjourn, don't continue taking questions from the students, letting the course run 20 or 30 minutes late. At two minutes before 5:00, say, "I have time for only one more question. After that, we'll end class and I'll be here for another hour to answer individual questions." Then live up to your word: one more question, a quick answer, and dismiss everybody. They're eager to go out and have dinner with the new people they've met (that's true especially for the singles in the room). Don't make them sit through somebody else's questions.

REAL WORLD SCENARIO

A Note to Teachers: Relax!

I recently attended a training session and the teacher seemed like she was about to have a nervous breakdown. Her voice was shaking through the whole thing and she was quite obviously *terrified*.

If you've been given the honors of teaching a training course…relax! These people aren't sitting out there as your final judges awaiting just the smallest mistake from you, ready to cast you into Hades. Instead, they look at you as a peer. As one of them. The more you can convey the image of being one of them, the more comfortable they'll be with you, and the more comfortable *you'll be with them*.

Here are some tips to help you relax. (Speaking as somebody with stage-fright issues, trust me, these work!) The best tip I have found is that when students are first coming in, move around the room and introduce yourself. Learn their names and a bit about them, so they become friendly, human beings, not just robots with eagle eyes staring at you.

Next, use the projector to your advantage. Allow that to be the focus of attention so people aren't staring you down.

Have a chair for yourself at the front of the room with a desk or folding table in front of it. If you get nervous, feel free to sit down and feel like you're hiding behind the desk until you're relaxed. I've found that having something in between the students and me gives me the feeling of having a shield, which helps me relax.

When you're standing up, hold a notebook in front of your chest. You will feel like you're hiding behind the notebook, thereby providing a safe, comfortable feeling. (But please don't fiddle with a pen, or you'll appear nervous. Just hide behind the notebook. And don't put the notebook in front of your face, obviously.)

Keep a glass of water handy and drink up if your mouth gets dry. If you're jittery, then if necessary, turn your back to the students when drinking.

Next, this might seem like a strange way to fight the jitters, but trust me, it really works: Look the students in the eyes! Don't stare at the back of the room as those silly public speaking teachers tell us. If you look the students in the eyes, you will see friendly human beings, not just robots. And then it just becomes a room of regular people where you happen to be the one talking, which is a much more relaxing atmosphere than a public-speaking situation.

Finally, remember that people are patient! If you make a mistake or fumble over your words, laugh, let them laugh, and move on. They don't care. They know you're only human.

Moving Forward

If you've been reading this book from the start, then congratulations! You've almost finished. Only one more chapter follows, which is a special chapter devoted to managers.

In the present chapter, I talked about the usability issues in installation programs, online help, and training. Who would have thought that even training has usability issues? But anybody who has sat through a bad training session knows that such sessions certainly lack usability.

Finally, remember the way that the parts all fit together: A great software program is so easy to use that the user won't need much online help or training. But a great software package includes great online help and great training, just in case. They all fit together!

CHAPTER 15

Book in a Book: A Guide for Programming Bosses

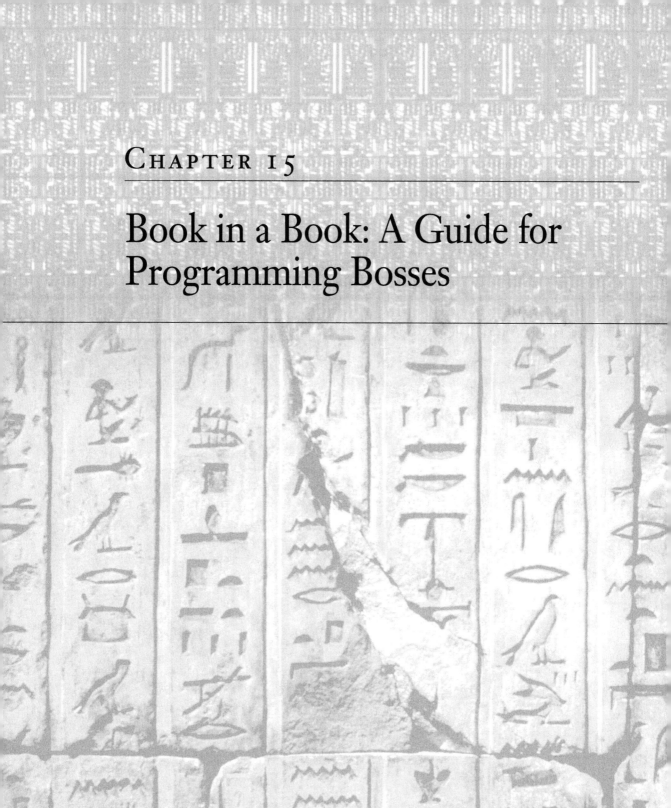

In this chapter, I'm talking especially to you bosses and managers. (However, I don't mind if you're a programmer and want to read this chapter too!) I understand that bosses and managers have unique needs when it comes to developing highly useable software. For example, the managers have to oversee the programmers and try to keep them on course and working together as a team, in an effort to build great software.

Before moving forward, however, I want to point out that if you're a manager or boss and are starting out the book by reading this chapter, I do encourage you to read the entire book. If some of the areas are too technical for you (with apologies to the managers who are technically adept), you can skip those sections. But the idea behind this entire book is to help you build the absolute best software you can build so that your company can be as profitable as possible. But who is building the software? The programmers are.

REAL WORLD SCENARIO

The Most Important People in the Company?

Back in the mid-1990s, I was good friends with a woman who worked for the marketing department of the company where I was working. I was a programmer. She told me that the people in the marketing department knew that they were the "most important people in the company." She was very proud to have such a label.

Why were they the most important people? Because they were selling the products. Without them, no money would come in and the company would not profit. I, of course, pointed out that if it weren't for me and the other programmers, she wouldn't have a product to sell. (I didn't add that I was more important; I let her draw her own conclusions.)

For many years up until perhaps the 1980s, my grandmother worked for a power company. She said the president of the company had a huge office and fancied himself the most important person in the company. Yet he could take as many vacations as he wanted, and all would be fine. But the day the "mail boy" (as the fellow was called) called in sick, the whole company was in chaos. My grandmother talked about how, in fact, the mail boy demonstrated himself to be far more important than the president.

But in a modern software company (or in a big company that includes a software team), who is the most important person?

The answer is everybody. Don't let yourself be fooled into thinking somebody is more important than somebody else. Even if you, as a manager, have a programmer who seems to be the best you've ever seen, you still can't build the product without everybody involved, including the programmers and the testers. Value all the positions in your teams. And let them know how important they are.

And so in this chapter, I talk about how to recognize different types of programmers and work with them accordingly to help them build the most useable software possible. I also talk about other nonpersonnel issues such as when (and when not) to use the latest technology.

Programmers, Decision Makers, and Egos

Let's be realistic. Our field is not exactly known for its humbleness. But that's to be expected when you work in a field that most of the world not only doesn't understand but, frankly, fears. Think how many people for so long wanted nothing to do with computers, thinking they were some kind of super-beings that could outsmart them. (I'll stop here before I get myself worked up into an egotistical frenzy.)

So we know we're good, and we're proud of our work. But you, as a manager or boss, aren't interested in egos. You just want the job done, egos or not. And now I'm here to warn you that egos are the very thing that could hurt your software, making it less useable. Therefore, you need to know how to manage egos in addition to managing software projects. In this section I talk about this very issue of egos.

The Kinds of Programmers

In order to understand how to manage programmers (and their egos!), you need to understand the main types of programmers. The types I'm about to describe here are not drawn from a psychology textbook or from a human resources journal. These are the types that I've personally observed in my years as a programmer:

- The ideal, confident, knowledgeable programmer
- The cowboy programmer
- The stuntman programmer
- The unsure, nervous programmer
- The helpful programmer
- The overconfident programmer

Not all programmers fall into these groups. But most do. And some programmers fall into more than one group. (For example, a programmer might be both an ideal programmer as well as a helpful programmer—a good mix indeed!)

The Ideal Programmer

The ideal programmer comes to work almost everyday, occasionally gets sick and stays home (I say that for a reason; read on), is understanding of the tasks, and knows her shortcomings and limitations. But in spite of her shortcomings, she knows her resources and how to get help online. She knows where to find answers to her problems. She admits that she doesn't know everything and that she's not perfect. She creates good, solid code. She writes to the established coding standards. She finishes the code on time. And she creates highly useable software.

> **RULE**   Every programmer should strive toward being an ideal programmer. But few make it.

The Cowboy Programmer

Next on the list is the cowboy programmer. This is the programmer who locks himself in his office, won't let anybody talk to him, and just goes and goes. But the problem is he doesn't always write good code. He might not adhere to the best standards, and his code might have some really hard-to-find bugs. The problem with the cowboy programmer is that he does everything his own way. He's not a team player, and he doesn't trust other programmers. He'd just as soon write the whole program himself.

But the real problem with the cowboy programmer is that he usually has the boss (that is, *you*) fooled. You think he's the most amazing programmer on the planet. You love him because he works 70 hours per week. He creates an amazing amount of code. But you need to recognize this rule:

> **RULE**   Just because a programmer grinds out piles of code that seems to work doesn't mean the code is 100 percent correct.

Dealing with a cowboy programmer is a touchy issue. You don't want to discourage him! He's working, and he's working hard and, frankly, doing a pretty darn good job.

Further, he's probably a serious introvert and really doesn't want to be forced to play with the other kids. Instead, let him be. But, for your own protection, you need to do the following:

- *Keep tabs on him and make sure he's staying on task.* While they aren't likely to spend hours playing Tetris, some cowboy programmers might spend hours adding a cool new feature they think is necessary but is not part of the plan. Of course, staying on task includes making sure he's staying on track with the design documents, as well.

- *Make sure he stays healthy and gets some food on occasion.* Seriously! These people sometimes starve themselves quite by accident. (I don't personally have that problem. I like food too much, as my scale would attest.)

- *Perform regular reviews on his code.* (Don't wait until the end! This guy's cranking out lots of code!)

- *Make sure the code is to the company standards.* This is a problem, because a lot of cowboy programmers don't particularly like coding standards.

The code review is vital here. You need to watch this guy's code because it may be great, but, more likely, it'll have a few errors here and there. (Not many, but a few.) If you have some ideal programmers, make sure they go through the code very carefully during the review.

Now with the coding standards, the problem with the cowboy programmer is that he tends to scoff at various standards. Therefore, one thing that can help you is to do a special code review very early on. Make sure the cowboy is creating the expected classes and member functions and sticking to them. Cowboy programmers have a tendency to write a lot of hack functions to work around (rather than *through*) a problem. By this regard, a lot of cowboy programmers tend not to be the best *engineers*.

For example, left to their own devices, they might write a gazillion lines of code swarming through a million functions. But toward the end, they realize that three of the functions don't work correctly. While the problem really occurred during the initial phases of the coding, it's now too late to go back and fix it. So they'll write 10 other special-purpose functions to aid the faulty functions.

They'll do this quickly and get it out the door, and it will work. For the most part. But every once in awhile, the code might break, showing some bizarre protection fault that nobody can seem to reproduce. The bug is probably a needle of code in a giant, moon-sized haystack. But the real problem is in the whole layout and design of the code, the bigger picture. The design is wrong. And that's what you need to catch. And worse, most managers and bosses are often unaware of this kind of problem.

Most managers and bosses simply see tons of code that, frankly, *works*. How could it be wrong? But it is wrong:

RULE   Creating software is more than just grinding out code that works most of the time. Creating software is about engineering a product from start to finish using sound design principles.

But as I said, don't discourage the cowboy programmer! He really is doing a good job. You just need to keep tabs on him. And the cool thing about the cowboy programmer is he's usually quite humble. Therefore, if you go through his code and find some problems, he probably won't mind at all. He'll be happy to go through and fix them. Cowboy programmers are easy to work with. They wrote the majority of the code during the dot-com revolution of the 1990s, and they aren't necessarily a bad thing.

The Stuntman Programmer

The stuntman programmer is the one who writes obfuscated code that is impossible to read and impossible to maintain. Such programmers often work very quickly and are exceedingly confident of their work.

While their code may be good (it's very hard to tell), you really can't have this kind of work in your project. Why would you want code that other programmers are unable to read and maintain? And if the code has a bug in it, tracing through the code can be a nightmare.

But the fundamental problem with such code is the question of who can decide whether such code is legitimate code or stuntman code. The code, of course, will be perfectly readable to the programmer who created it, and perhaps most of the other programmers just aren't "good enough" to understand it. But suggesting that other programmers aren't good enough to understand it is itself a clue to trouble:

RULE   Code should be so well written, well commented, and clear that most programmers can understand and follow it. If not, the code must be rewritten.

Stuntman programmers can be difficult because you may have no choice but to deal with them directly. Code reviews are a start: If the other programmers find the code overly complex, then the issue must be addressed ASAP. But the problem is now you're dealing with an ego. This is one instance where you'll simply have to be firm. Your organization simply cannot afford to have stuntman code in its software. I'm not about to offer advice on personality and human resources issues, but you do need to stop stuntman programming.

The Unsure, Nervous Programmer

Most people who don't work in the programming group will agree that these programmers—the unsure, nervous programmers—are some of the nicest people in the whole bunch. They don't have inflated egos, and they tend to be chatty and personable.

Such people also usually aren't very good programmers, and they know it. They're constantly asking for the help of the other programmers, which makes them a bit of a thorn in the sides of the other programmers. (The overconfident programmers tend to despise the unsure, nervous programmers.)

And these programmers, unfortunately, can also be a thorn in the side of the software itself. Bosses usually like these programmers and want to help them succeed and do well. The bosses will then give the programmers some pretty hefty duties that might be a bit out of their reach. But the unsure programmers usually work very hard and are willing to spend a lot of hours on their work. That's a good thing.

I have three suggestions for dealing with unsure, nervous programmers:

- Keep sending them to training courses.

- Assign them a mentor.

- Find somebody who can teach them how to use online help and other online resources for quickly finding answers.

One of the real differences between the unsure programmer and the ideal programmer is that the ideal programmer has discovered how to quickly find answers to her questions without automatically asking somebody else for help. The unsure programmer isn't necessarily less intelligent or less capable; rather, it's an issue of confidence. Teach the unsure programmer how to find answers for herself, and she will gain confidence and likely do very well.

However, as with any other programmer, you need to do code reviews and watch the unsure programmers. The fact is, they tend to not be very good programmers (at least not *yet*; they're still learning). And so you need to watch their code closely. Otherwise, other programmers will end up fixing the unsure programmers' bugs, resulting in frustration and other personality issues.

The Helpful Programmer

The helpful programmer is the one the unsure programmer runs to when she needs help. The helpful programmer is friendly and easy to get along with (just like the unsure programmer) and is usually willing to help the unsure programmer.

But helpful programmers have their own set of problems, relating more to human interaction and less to coding. The helpful programmers can easily get bogged down spending so much time helping everybody that they aren't able to get to their own work.

I tend to carry the role of the helpful programmer, and I know firsthand that it can be frustrating at times to have everybody running to me for help. I enjoy helping people (that's why I teach and write as well as program), but at the same time I occasionally need to put up the *Do not disturb* sign.

One possibility for handling helpful programmers is to divide up their time and officially make them a mentor, giving them a reduced programming load. Most development groups can stand for a mentor or two, and the helpful programmers are ideal for this role.

But be careful with helpful programmers: Just because they can explain things well and are friendly doesn't necessarily mean they're always right. They need code reviews just as much as anybody else, and so do the people they are helping.

The Overconfident Programmer

Of all the programmers in the list, this programmer is the most difficult to deal with. This is the programmer who tends to be extremely arrogant and unwilling to work with other people. This is, in essence, the stereotypical computer guy whom laypeople don't like dealing with.

Since I'm not writing a psychology book here, I won't even begin to try to understand what kinds of issues cause people to become this way. But the overconfident programmer can be detrimental to the entire project. The reason is the overconfident programmer will tend to take on more work than he can handle, will grind out an enormous amount of code, and will bully people around into thinking he's always right, that his code is perfect, and that he knows best. Yet, he's not perfect, and he will have bugs but will probably refuse to allow others to help fix them. (He may even resist a code review.)

Some other programmers even reach the point where they are afraid of the overconfident programmer. And worse, this programmer might actually drive away some of the ideal programmers, and they will seek work elsewhere.

Now I'm probably stereotyping a bit here, but the truth is, every single place I've worked has had at least a couple of people who fit this description. And worse, the overconfident programmer's work rarely is that much better than the other programmers. Some are good, and some are very good programmers. (But those really good ones still need code reviews, because nobody is perfect.) Others aren't good, and the ideal programmers know it but have trouble convincing *you*, the boss, of the truth.

How do you deal with an overconfident programmer? One good way is by resisting your urges to give him too much authority. You, as the boss, may easily start to feel like he really is the superhuman he wants you to think he is, and you will seriously consider promoting him and putting him in charge of huge amounts of work. He's demonstrated to you that he is *good*, after all, right?

But promoting him has an inherent problem: If you promote him and put him in charge of a team, why is he still spending all his time grinding out code? Because at heart, he really doesn't want to be in charge of a team. He wants to write code.

Let him be a coder. And if he really wants to move up the ladder, send him to some manager training programs, and then let him decide what he wants to do. If he still wants to be promoted, let him know that a promotion will mean spending less time coding. Is he okay with that? If so, go for it, provided he's had the appropriate managerial training.

I don't want to be too hard on these people, but I want you, as a boss, to fully understand what is happening. So here goes:

SUGGESTION

> My personal experience is that the overconfident programmers are responsible for the majority of the kinds of bugs that result in software crashes. Therefore, be aware of who the overconfident programmers are and have plenty of reviews of their code.

Finally, try to get the input of the ideal programmers. You know who the ideal programmers are. You can recognize them because they do a great job, and they don't bully people around. Let the ideal programmers watch over the overconfident programmers. You will probably be surprised to learn that the overconfident programmers aren't always the superhumans you thought they were.

Avoiding Letting One Great Programmer Rule the Ship

I don't know if this really happened, but sometime back I heard a story from a coworker about a guy who was the top programmer at a company. (However, he was also the overconfident programmer who bullied everybody around.) The company had a tight deadline, and one day the programmer walked into the boss's office and said, "You know I'm the only one who can do this work. And if I quit, your product will never make it out the door. So double my salary or I'll quit." The company felt stuck, so they doubled the guy's salary. Then the moment the project was over, they fired him.

Never, ever, *ever* let your company get into this situation. This company made a major mistake in letting the organization get to the point where only one guy knew how to complete the project. Because the fact is, *nobody* is irreplaceable. What if the programmer quit anyway? Then what would the company do?

If you have only one programmer who knows the majority of the system, then you must invest some time in bringing other programmers up to speed. Most programming shops have one person who seems to be the head programmer who all the other programmers look up to. Try to dispel this situation. Involve the other programmers in high-level meetings. Assign important work to the other programmers. And try to spread out the knowledge more evenly among the programmers.

The fact is, the one programmer may be smarter or more experienced than the others. But that doesn't mean the others are incapable. And further, that doesn't mean you can't hire more programmers who are as sharp as the main programmer. Because if you have one programmer ruling the ship, then you have an extremely volatile situation that could mean the end of your organization.

If I were the boss who had the guy come up to me and demand a double salary, I would have told him to forget it and get back to work and to remember that he has bills to pay and had best not risk being fired.

Remember, you are trying to build a successful business by selling highly useable software. If you're going to allow the overconfident programmers to have too much authority because you mistakenly thought they were better than they are, you will greatly risk releasing software that isn't nearly as good as it could be.

Checks and Balances

A large software product is a highly complex machine. Think about this: A rotary car engine (found in, for example, Mazda RX-7 and the recent RX-8 cars) has only a few moving parts. With only a few moving parts, not many states are possible. This means less complexity and fewer breakdowns. (In case you're curious, even though many people have shown that the rotary engine is superior in many ways to the traditional piston engine, the reason why it isn't used in many cars is that the rotary engine is extremely difficult to build to various emissions standards.)

In general, the more states a machine has, the more complex it is, and the harder it is to maintain. Now look at how many states your program has: *a whole lot*. Your software is incredibly complex. But not only is the software complex, so is the code.

For this complexity reason, you absolutely *must* perform code reviews. You cannot risk letting problems slip through that would have otherwise been caught by a code review. And even the best programmers can make mistakes. As the old saying goes, two eyes are better than one. (Or, in the case of bespectacled programmers like me, eight eyes are better than four.)

Good code reviews serve as a system of checks and balances. Most governments have recognized that no matter how good people are, mistakes can be made. And therefore such governments have implemented a system of checks and balances. And you can benefit from also recognizing that nobody is perfect by implementing a code review.

But you can implement other checks and balances. In addition to the obvious one of having a quality assurance groups, you can ask that all your programmers constantly be on the lookout for problems in the software, even when it's not related to their own part. (Remind them that they are, after all, a team.) And teach them how to post bug reports. (I'm serious—a lot of programmers honestly don't know how to post bug reports, because they don't think it's their job to do so! If you start watching the behavior of your programmers, you might be surprised!)

Another way of performing checks and balances is to periodically rotate the programmers, working in different areas of the code. Now, in theory, I suppose swapping programmers around when they're in the middle of writing their code might be an interesting experiment, but frankly, I wouldn't try it. You could end up with a mess. Instead, swap programmers as they finish up sections of code.

Also, if you have ideal programmers, I would suggest letting them do code maintenance and bug fixing on somebody else's code. I've had exceptionally good luck in such areas, because they are usually good at tracking down other problems. (The overconfident programmers are sometimes good at this too, although they might get angry at the mistakes they see.)

Placing New Hires

Be careful with new hires. A lot of programmers for some reason have the impression that they're being brought into a complete disaster and they are the last hope to valiantly save the ship. Yet, you, as the manager, know this just isn't true.

Such an ego trip can have a detrimental effect on the usability of your software. The problem is that the new hires will likely have a lot of ambition and will grind out an enormous amount of code. However, this new code:

- Might not interface well with the other code in the project.
- Might not be up to the company's coding standards.
- Might display a user interface that is not consistent with the rest of the product or is simply difficult to use.

None of these are necessarily the result of a bad programmer. So please don't just assume the person lied about his qualifications. Rather, it's a simple matter of a good programmer working in a new company. This is where providing a mentor is a good thing:

SUGGESTION

Team up the new hire with a programmer who has been around awhile. Make sure both people realize that neither is the boss over the other.

But what do you do if the new hire immediately begins criticizing everything left and right, saying what a mess everything is and how she clearly knows of a better way to do all this? (I've seen this happen more times than I would prefer, and you probably have, too).

Such a situation is a touchy one at best. You don't want to knock the person down and criticize her, making her hate the new job. But you also don't want her to run rampant, convincing everybody else how bad everything is. What you want is for the new programmer to write some good, solid code and to be happy with her job.

I'm not a human resources expert, and the purpose of this book is usability. However, the impact such HR problems can have on usability is extremely high. As a manager, one thing that I've found that works is to sit down with the new programmer and take her through the architectural documents. Give her copies of them, and let her read them in their entirety. This will give her a better idea of the decisions you made before she came around. And it should help her respect your decisions. And besides helping her fit in and not criticize your work, you'll have the added benefit that now she'll have a much better understanding of the entire project.

But what about the code the new programmer writes? You don't want to watch over the programmer's shoulders. That would likely irritate her. Instead, go back to the tried-and-tested code review concept:

RULE

Code reviews are especially important for new hires, since they don't yet fully understand the full architecture of your system.

I can't tell you how many times I've seen a new programmer dive in and start writing a lot of code (which surely impresses the bosses!) yet is developing code that doesn't necessarily work correctly. The code may appear to work from the GUI perspective, but underneath there may be numerous errors.

Of course, code reviews are important for more than just the code written by the new hire. Everybody needs code reviews. Another problem I've seen a great deal is where the senior-most programmer cranks out some code that everybody assumes is perfect but is far from it.

He Said, She Said

Sooner or later you're going to be faced with the issue of two programmers telling you conflicting things. One wants to design the code one way; the other wants a different way. What do you do?

This is an extremely difficult situation to be in. They can't both be right. So look more closely at the situation. When you look deeply into the problem, you will likely see that it's not just a matter of he said/she said. Instead, you'll see that one programmer is a more senior-level programmer, and the other is slightly less senior and may well have a valid concern. The senior one may be a star programmer in the company, or a team leader, and has a lot of respect from the company. If so, *don't automatically assume the star, senior programmer is right.*

I can't speak for all situations, but the situation I've encountered the most often is that the star programmer wants to do something one way, and somebody else who is not the star programmer sees something wrong with the star programmer's solution. In effect, the star programmer is really the overconfident programmer and is now defending his decisions.

RULE   Listen to what the other programmer says. The other programmer may well have a valid point, so don't automatically discount it. The usability of your software may be at stake!

Regardless of whether somebody is more senior than the other, you might consider having each programmer write up some quick test code to demonstrate his or her respective assertion. Then you might have some other programmers review the test code and come to a decision about which is best. You, after all, are the boss. As much as you might not want to admit it, you might not have the technical knowledge to make a sound decision in this matter. And that's why you don't want to just automatically assume one person is right.

Remember:

RULE   Your job may be partly to help out during personnel disputes, but your ultimate job is to build highly useable software.

Making a Decision, and Staying Up-To-Date

As a manager, you need to be aware of something your programmers are doing: *They are making arbitrary decisions.* For example, your programmer who is writing the part of the software that opens the files may well have put in an arbitrary limit on how many files your software can have open. Is that a good thing? No! And don't let your programmers tell you it's the only way possible. Remind them of this topic: *dynamic memory allocation*. Or this one: *container classes*.

Too often programmers make arbitrary decisions as they are coding. They might arbitrarily decide how much memory something should have or hold, or how big a data structure should be, or how many times a function should be called, and so on. These decisions may then make their way into the general feature set of the product without anybody realizing it. And will the decisions be mentioned in the product documentation? Will the users be aware of them? Most likely *not*.

What do you do about arbitrary decisions? For starters, you can have your programmers *read this book*. If they do, they will then understand how such arbitrary decisions impact the usability of the product. Further, you can instruct all of the people attending code reviews to be on the lookout for arbitrary decisions. And the best way to handle such decisions during the code review is for the reviewers to ask, "Why did you do this?" Perhaps the programmer had a good reason. But perhaps not. It's best to ask. And if the decision was arbitrary, have the programmer go back and look at the design documents and make sure the decision was what was expected. And if not, *change it*. (And, of course, this means you must have design documents!)

Keeping Up with the Technological Joneses

If you have a competition to your software that, as much as you hate to admit it, is selling better than your software, you might suspect that you need to add more features to your product to keep up. But it might not be the sheer number of features that's holding back your product! Perhaps the other product is more solidly built or is easier to use. (In other words, the other product might be more *useable*.) But even if you don't have a competitor that sells better, you still might feel like the only way to stay ahead is to add as many features as possible. And that's a topic I discuss in the following sections.

Running Rampant: Managing Feature Creep

Remember back to a year before Windows 95 came out? People were constantly getting into arguments that bordered on the religious over whether Windows 95 or the new IBM OS/2 was better.

Well, news flash: In terms of technology and features, OS/2 pretty much won without a question. But look who the survivor was. It turns out the feature comparison didn't determine the winner. It was all about the marketing. Microsoft has always been a serious marketing machine. I've had very little experience with OS/2, so I wouldn't be honest if I tried to compare the usability of Windows 95 to OS/2. However, I would daresay that Microsoft did spend a good amount of time on the usability of Windows 95. And they didn't worry about out-featuring the competition.

Too many companies have this notion that they need to keep adding feature after feature to their products. I don't need to explain to you that going overboard on features will simply delay the release of your product. But going overboard on the features can also impact the usability of your product.

The more features you have, the more menu items you'll probably have, the more windows and controls you might have, and the more confusing your product may be. Of course, I'm not trying to say you shouldn't have a feature-rich product. What I am saying is that if you want a lot of features, make sure you do the following:

- Create features that are well defined.
- Make sure the features are clear to the user.
- Make sure the features you include are actually needed by the user.
- Create a product that doesn't overwhelm the user with all its features.
- Don't continue adding features once the coding stages of development begin.
- Draw a line during the various planning stages at which point you agree that the feature set is complete and you won't be defining new features.

If you continue to think up new features after the project begins, or if you just keep defining more and more features and delay the actual coding of the project, you are falling victim to feature bloat. The way to avoid feature bloat is to recognize that having more and more features does not necessarily make a better product. Instead, pick your set of features, stick to them, and make those features as highly useable as possible by following the guidelines throughout this book.

Then, while the competition is busy going overboard on their features and none of them work well, you'll have a clear set of features that are powerful and easy to use. Add to that the wizardry of your marketing department (something I'm not qualified to teach you about!), and your product will *easily* outdo the competition.

But just how do you draw a line on your features? How do you know when to stop? If you take time to test the usability of your designs, you will get a clear idea of which features are vital to the product, which features are nice to have, which features are added fluff, and which features are totally unnecessary.

However:

RULE   The development group won't be the ones choosing the features. By nature, programmers aren't necessarily involved with the end users and may not know what the end users need and want.

Instead, the marketing people and the sales engineers and other people will be gathering information on what should and should not go into the product. Of course, the engineers can also have a say by suggesting some new features, as can the testers and anybody else. But after you have a solid set of features, describe them in detail in a feature document, and then have the head of marketing sign off on the document. This will indicate that the marketing people agreed to the features.

Of course, after the signing off, people are going to still be suggesting features. What do you do with these suggestions? You save them for the next release. You have to. Otherwise, you'll start down the feature creep path.

Similar to feature creep is a problem that Fred Brooks describes in his book *The Mythical Man-Month*. This problem is called *second-system effect*, and it refers to what happens when you have a decent version 1.0 product, and then you get excited and decide to create for version 2.0 the absolutely most amazing, stunning, awesome product on the planet. But instead you end up with something that's so bloated with needless bells and whistles that the product nearly implodes from its own weight like a black hole. But more concretely, such feature overload usually simply results in software that is too big and bulky and difficult to use.

The way to manage the second-system effect is by not getting carried away with version 2.0. Become extremely conscientious of the second-system effect. Don't just pile on all the features you didn't have time to add in version 1.0.

Here's an example: The team is working on version 1.0, and in the middle of a meeting, somebody suggests a new feature. You, as the manager, do the right thing by saying, "Too late, we've already frozen the features on version 1.0." But then, you add, "Let's get that in for version 2.0." You make a note of it, and the decision is made.

Did you go through the usual process of adding a feature? No. Instead of interviewing end users and working with the marketing department, you slipped in a new feature much like a rider secretly snuck into a bill before Congress: It's perfectly legal but not always ethical. And in your case, ethics aside, it's rarely beneficial.

RULE   Follow the correct path for adding features, and don't just plan on version 2.0 being the ultimate killer app.

Running Rampant 2.0: Avoiding the Latest Whiz-Bang Technologies

If you've read this whole book up to now, what I'm going to say in this section will be no surprise to you:

RULE   Don't choose exciting new technologies for your product simply because they're there; instead, choose them only when you need them.

As computer people, we're always quick to embrace new technologies. And as people looking to make a lot of money, we especially want to jump onto new technologies, being the first to write software for the technology. And that's perfectly fine, provided you move forward *carefully*.

If Palm, for example, is going to release a brand-new handheld product with several new features and a fully revised operating system, you just might want to be the first to write software for the device. But before diving in, ask yourself, do you want to also support older Palm models? And if so, do you want to create separate products, one for the newer Palm devices and one for the older?

I can't answer these questions for you; your answers will certainly depend on the particular needs of your organization. But remember, if you say you don't care to support the older models, do you really want to risk everything on something that might not catch on? In the case of Palm, these days if they release a new product, it's almost guaranteed to be a hit, of course. But if you're writing for some brand-new technology (whether hardware such as a PDA device or software such as a new operating system), consider all the risks.

Some time back, Apple released their Newton product, which was a pretty powerful PDA. Unfortunately, for reasons I'm not aware of, the product didn't catch on, and they discontinued it. What if you had invested all your money into software for the Newton? Similarly, around the time Windows 3.1 came out in the early 1990s, a company called Quarterdeck came out with a product called Desqview/X. This was, in essence, a complete competitor to Windows 3.1. It was a GUI system based on the popular X Windows system found on Unix systems, and it provided an advanced multitasking system. Now what if you had invested all your time and energy into writing software that would run on Desqview/X before you had a chance to see if it would last in the marketplace? (Hint: It didn't, unfortunately. Quarterdeck did have several other popular products, and the company got sold to Symantec.)

Of course, these are extreme examples, talking about devices and operating systems. What about new technologies that run on Windows? For example, you might be writing a system that's going to communicate with other computers, and you might discover a brand-new communications protocol that you're sure will take off. Within no time, you can see every device on the planet supporting this protocol.

But, soon after you finish your product, you discover that a competing protocol (one that is clearly inferior) is the one that everybody embraces, rendering your product useless.

NOTE   If you work in the telecom field, you may have seen this happen between the protocols called SNMP and TL1. The TL1 protocol is far more powerful than SNMP. Yet, SNMP was the one that took off. Thus, companies that embraced TL1 instead of SNMP quickly found themselves with a problem on their hands: Go out of business or add SNMP capabilities to their products.

Remember that *standardization* is more powerful than *better features*. Suppose someone came up with a better electrical outlet that required rewiring buildings and was incompatible with the current electrical plugs. Would you care? No. It would be more trouble than it's worth.

Someday, such technologies as Windows, TCP-IP, and XML will be replaced with better tools, but not because someone came up with a substitute that worked a little better or had a few more features. Replacing a standard is like moving a mountain: It can be done, but there has to be a darn good reason for it.

The big question is, then, how do you know if a technology is worth pursuing? That's more of a business question, and I would hesitate to give you solid business advice beyond engineering advice. However, here are some questions you can ask yourself:

- If you do a web search on a new technology, will you find other companies embracing it?

- Who is creating the new technology and how much marketing effort are they putting into it. (For example, is Microsoft creating it?)

- Does the technology seem like something users are really going to need? (Remember, needs and wants are two different things, and technologies survive based on needs more often than wants!)

- Does the new technology utilize current platforms? This might not always be important, but it's something to consider.

SUGGESTION

Be careful with new technology. In this computer world, technology comes and goes so quickly that you usually can't risk embracing new whiz-bang technology unless you are absolutely sure it will be a hit.

Moving Forward

If you've made it through the whole book, congratulations! You are well on your way to designing highly useable software. As you venture forward, please keep this book handy as a reference guide and review it when you can. You should be able to easily find the information pertaining to your current task. If you're working on designing your windows, for example, you can refer to Chapter 3 of this book, "Laying Out Your Windows and Dialog Boxes." If you're concerned about some of your code, you can refer to Chapter 8, "Under the Hood."

But please don't stop with this book. I don't claim to have all the answers, and I'm not going to let an inflated ego make that claim either. My goal is to see the world filled with only software that is highly useable. It is a mission of mine, and I am going to make this goal, even if it has to be one programmer at a time, starting with *you*. We are all in this together.

For your next step, see the Appendix, "Software Design Resources." It lists groups, organizations, newsletters, magazines, websites, and books—all devoted to designing software for usability. Keep studying on your own, keep an eye out for usability as you are building your software, and make the best software you possibly can. (And lots of money, too.)

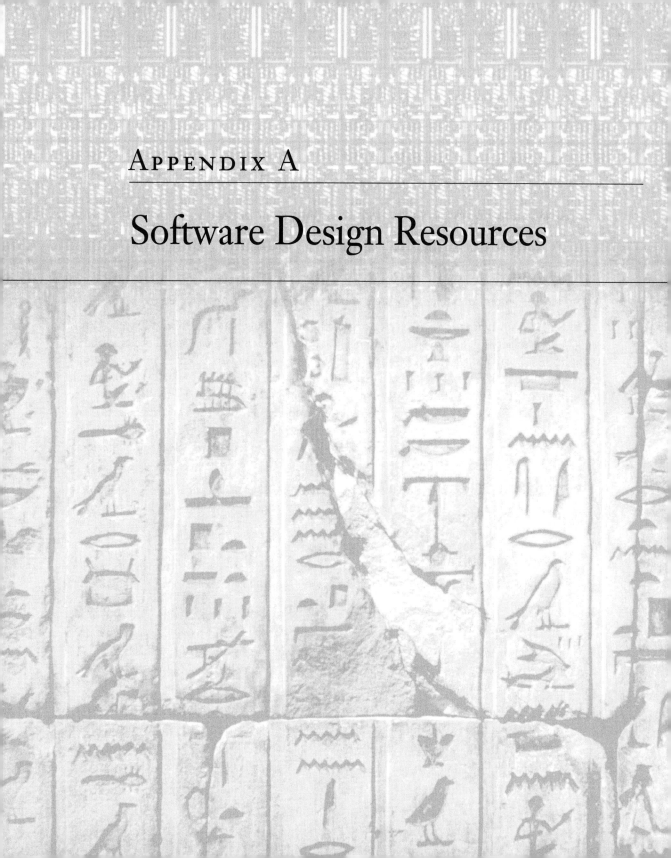

Appendix A

Software Design Resources

This appendix provides several good resources for designing software.

Groups and Organizations

Below are a few groups and organizations you might find helpful:

Usability Professionals' Association (http://www.upassoc.org/)   One of the larger associations dealing with usability, this organization holds annual conferences, provides a network of people interested in usability, and includes two publications. The first is an online-only magazine called *UPA Voice*, and the other is a printed magazine called *User Experience*. (See *UPA Voice* and *User Experience* in "Newsletters and Magazines" in this appendix.) They also have several local chapters, which you can explore on their website.

STC Usabilty (http://www.stcsig.org/usability/)   This is a special interest group (SIG) of the Society for Technical Communication (STC), which is a professional organization of technical writers. This SIG includes a sprinkling of local chapters. While it might seem odd that technical writers would have a usability chapter, the reality in organizations is often that the technical writers are the ones who end up being the GUI experts, providing critiques to the usability of the software. Further, the STC has more than just technical writers as its members these days. Today, many engineers belong to the organization as well. The STC's main site is `http://www.stc.org`. (See also *Usability Interface*, under "Newsletters and Magazines" in this Appendix.)

ACM SIGCHI (http://www.acm.org/sigchi/)   ACM SIGCHI is the Computer-Human Interaction special interest group for the ACM (Association of Computing Machinery).

Newsletters and Magazines

The following newsletters and magazines are good resources:

UPA Voice **(http://www.upassoc.org/voice/index.html)**   The Usability Professionals' Association created this online newsletter.

User Experience **(http://www.upassoc.org/outreach/ux_index.html)**   This is the printed magazine created by the Usability Professionals' Association. (The articles are *not* available online.)

Usability Interface **(http://www.stcsig.org/usability/newsletter/index.html)**   This quarterly magazine is put out by the STC Usability group, which is a special interest group within the Society for Technical Communication. It is a printed magazine but has many online articles.

Interactions and *Interactions Online* (http://www.acm.org/interactions/)   The Computer-Human Interaction special interest group of the ACM puts out this printed magazine (and its online version).

Websites

Below are some excellent websites:

HCI Index (http://degraaff.org/hci/)   This site is essentially a portal to many websites dealing with usability. (HCI stands for Human-Computer Interaction, although this site is not a part of the HCI special interest group of the ACM.) *If you're going to bookmark only one website, make it this one.*

useit.com (http://www.useit.com/)   The official site of Jakob Nielsen, one of the great gurus in the usability world, this site is simple, almost entirely text, and absolutely filled with useful information. In addition, the site includes Dr. Nielsen's famous "Alertbox" column.

Don Norman's jnd website (http://www.jnd.org/)   Don Norman, another great guru in the usability world (and business partner with Jakob Nielsen and Tog), wrote one of the great classic books in usability called *The Design of Everyday Things*, as well as several other books. His official website includes his own reviews of other books, recommended readings, and a huge list of his own essays that you can read online.

AskTog (http://www.asktog.com/tog.html)   The official site of Bruce Tognazzini, aka "Tog," includes tons of his columns. He's also a business partner of Jakob Nielsen and Don Norman, and he enjoys a good bit of fame within the usability circles. Oh yes, you can write to him through his site and ask him a question (although he recently quit answering questions, he says he may start back up any time).

The Nielsen Norman Group (http://www.nngroup.com/)   I suppose if I'm going to mention Jakob Nielsen, Don Norman, and Tog individually, it would be wrong to leave out their consulting firm, the Nielsen Norman Group.

Usability.gov (http://usability.gov/)   Yes, even the U.S. government has a usability group. (Interestingly, it's under the National Cancer Institute, but it's about usability.) This site is *packed* with information, and I won't even begin to try to describe it all. Just go check it out.

> **Usability.gov U-Group Listserv (http://usability.gov/pubs/u_group_ listserv.html)**   This is the discussion group that accompanies the usability.gov site

Microsoft Usability (http://www.microsoft.com/usability/)   Microsoft includes its own usability group, which has its own website.

Usability First (http://www.usabilityfirst.com)   This is the usability website for a private company called diamondbullet.com, which is a consulting firm for usability. The website includes many good links and a list of good books in the usability field.

European Union Usability Net (http://www.usabilitynet.org)   The site for Usability Net, which is funded by the European Union, includes many links to other sites.

Books

Here is a list of some helpful books:

About Face 2.0: The Essentials of Interaction Design by Alan Cooper and Robert Reimann (Wiley, 2003)

One of the most popular books about usability, written by Alan Cooper (he's the guy who invented Visual Basic), this book has recently been completely rewritten. The original edition came out in 1995. The second edition is now available.

The Inmates Are Running the Asylum: Why High Tech Products Drive Us Crazy and How to Restore the Sanity by Alan Cooper (Sams, 1999)

This is a classic book that doesn't include many screenshots because it simply talks about issues and problems in software. It includes some rather shocking stories, such as how a computer caused a plane to crash when the pilot typed something wrong into it. Scary stuff, and it definitely makes you think about how computers impact our lives.

Emotional Design: Why We Love (or Hate) Everyday Things by Donald A. Norman (Basic Books, 2004)

This book is a rewrite of a true classic (originally called *The Design of Everyday Things*), and all engineers should buy it, regardless of whether they are mechanical engineers, electrical engineers, software engineers, train engineers, domestic engineers, or whatever.

The Invisible Computer: Why Good Products Can Fail, the Personal Computer Is So Complex, and Information Appliances Are the Solution, reprint edition, by Donald A. Norman (MIT Press, 1999)

Another book by the same author as the classic *The Design of Everyday Things*, it focuses on the complexity issues behind computer-operated devices.

The Humane Interface: New Directions for Designing Interactive Systems by Jef Raskin (Addison-Wesley, 2000)

Jef Raskin is one of the original designers of the Macintosh GUI, and so he's certainly been working in GUIs for a long time. In this book he covers ergonomics, navigation, and many other issues. Some people have accused him of being a bit extreme, but like most of us, he has his ideas and they are worth listening to.

Don't Make Me Think: A Common Sense Approach to Web Usability by Steve Krug and Roger Black (Que, 2000)

This is a fantastic book that has done quite well; it provides specific guides to creating web pages and websites that are highly usable. Although the information focuses on the Web, much of it carries over to software in general.

Designing Web Usability: The Practice of Simplicity by Jakob Nielsen (New Riders, 2000)

Jakob Nielsen is one of the gurus in the field of usability, and anything he has written would be an excellent choice to read. This book focuses on the Web. However, be forewarned that some graphic artists tend to disagree completely with some of his fundamental arguments, primarily because he focuses on the Web as a medium for conveying information, not a medium for pretty graphics.

GUI Bloopers by Jeff Johnson (Morgan Kaufmann, 2000)

This excellent book (and a big seller) focuses primarily on what people are doing wrong in their software. At times it gets a bit too specific on the do's and don'ts, in my opinion, but I find that it makes a great reference guide to have on your desk.

Index

Note to the Reader: Throughout this index boldfaced page numbers indicate primary discussions of a topic. Italicized page numbers indicate illustrations.

TELL US WHAT YOU THINK!

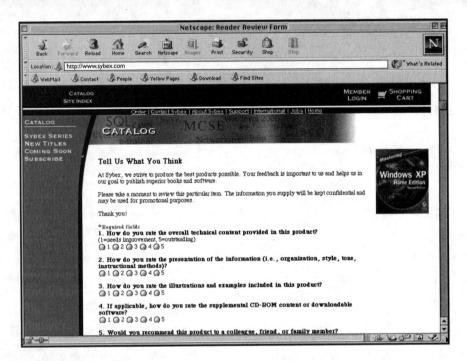

Your feedback is critical to our efforts to provide you with the best books and software on the market. Tell us what you think about the products you've purchased. It's simple:

1. Go to the Sybex website.
2. Find your book by typing the ISBN or title into the Search field.
3. Click on the book title when it appears.
4. Click **Submit a Review.**
5. Fill out the questionnaire and comments.
6. Click **Submit.**

With your feedback, we can continue to publish the highest quality computer books and software products that today's busy IT professionals deserve.

www.sybex.com

SYBEX Inc. • 1151 Marina Village Parkway, Alameda, CA 94501 • 510-523-8233